A CONCISE GLOSSARY OF
Contemporary
Literary Theory
JEREMY HAWTHORN

A CONCISE GLOSSARY OF
Contemporary Literary Theory

JEREMY HAWTHORN

Professor of Modern British Literature,
University of Trondheim, Norway

Edward Arnold
A division of Hodder & Stoughton
LONDON NEW YORK MELBOURNE AUCKLAND

© 1992 Jeremy Hawthorn

First published in Great Britain 1992

Distributed in the USA by Routledge, Chapman and Hall, Inc.
29 West 35th Street, New York, NY 10001

British Library Cataloguing in Publication Data

Hawthorn, Jeremy
  A concise glossary of contemporary literary theory.
  I. Title
  801.03

  ISBN 0–340–53911–9

Library of Congress Cataloging-in-Publication Data

Hawthorn, Jeremy.
    A concise glossary of contemporary literary theory / Jeremy
  Hawthorn.
      p. cm.
    Includes bibliographical references.
    ISBN 0–340–53911–9 : $15.95
      1. Criticism—Terminology.   2. Literature—Terminology.
    3. English language—Terms and phrases.   I. Title.
  PN44.5.H365   1992
  801′.95′014—dc20   91–33911
                                                            CIP

Typeset by the author.
Printed and bound in Great Britain for Edward Arnold,
a division of Hodder and Stoughton Limited,
Mill Road, Dunton Green, Sevenoaks, Kent TN13 2YA
by Biddles Limited, Guildford and King's Lynn

9-20-93

This book is for Richard, Joanna, Dinah and Nancy,
who have put us up (and up with us) so many times
we have lost count, and especially for Nancy, who
decided to ignore her mother's advice and
study English literature at university.

Using the Glossary

I have attempted to group related terms in common entries so as to avoid repetition and so as to permit entries that have a certain completeness. Thus rather than having separate entries for *plot*, *story*, *fabula* and *sjužet*, I have a single entry entitled STORY AND PLOT. The negative result of such a policy, inevitably, is that those searching for the meaning of terms must frequently tolerate having to find their way to the substantive entry via cross-entries. I hope that the gains of this procedure will be deemed to outweigh the losses.

The use of small capitals (e.g. DECONSTRUCTION) betokens the existence of an entry on the term so presented. Sometimes the actual entry may be under a cognate term; thus DECONSTRUCT refers the reader to the entry for the term DECONSTRUCTION. I have normally limited this use of small capitals to the *first* mention only of the term in question within each entry. To avoid confusion the use of small capitals generally directs the reader to substantive (rather than cross-reference) entries, although I have made exceptions to this rule in the case of particularly important terms.

Bracketed references with page numbers refer the reader to the bibliography at the end of the book, which provides full publication details of works quoted from. Books which are referred to but not quoted from are not generally included in the bibliography, and dates given for such books indicate the year of initial publication.

Many of the terms with which I deal are of foreign origin, and often it has had to be a matter of personal judgement as to whether they are sufficiently assimilated to be written without the use of the italics that indicate a loan word. I have based my decision here upon the extent to which the words in question can be said to be in frequent use amongst theorists: thus I give *épistème* and *méconnaissance* italics, but not écriture or jouissance. In transliterating Russian names and terms I have adopted the more traditional versions (e.g. Eichenbaum rather than Èjxenbaum), unless I am referring to a published source. Thus both of these variants appear in the bibliography and in textual references.

This glossary is also available in hardback in a longer, reference edition, which contains some entries not available in the paperback edition, as well as a more extended discussion of some of the terms in the paperback edition.

Introduction

1 Is this glossary really necessary?

When I studied English literature at university in Britain in the early 1960s, I felt no need for a book such as the one you now hold in your hand. Critics did, of course, make use of specialist terms, but if they did not themselves explain what they meant by them, and if a standard dictionary could not provide a definition, then a general dictionary of literary terms would supply the needed explanation. Indeed, I think that if my undergraduate self had been asked what was meant by the term 'literary theory' I might have been puzzled, although along with many of my fellow students I felt the need for more systematic study and discussion of literary criticism.

But during the 1970s, as the separate study of literary criticism became a more and more normal part of undergraduate literary-studies courses, this study spawned its own meta-study: literary-critical *theory*, a word that was increasingly likely to be used independent of any association with the word *criticism*. And alongside this growth a new need was born: the need for help in mastering a far more abstract and philosophical enterprise with a far more abstract and philosophical vocabulary.

I should put my cards on the table and declare here and now that for all that there are many negative aspects to this development, in general I feel that it was both positive and necessary. If I find the loss of a more general commitment to accessibility and comprehensibility to be regretted, I welcome the fact that students of literature are now no longer expected just to 'do' literature – to learn a craft or a set of skills – but to contemplate exactly what it is that they are doing and to reflect upon the nature of the discipline and its practices. If I regret the self-indulgence that sometimes lies behind the coining of new terms, and if I deplore the formalism that, not content with cutting literature off from life proceeds then to cut criticism off from literature and theory off from criticism, I nonetheless welcome the opening of Literary Studies to ideas, influences, and (inevitably) terminologies from other disciplines. And other cultures: in the early 1960s I read almost no books written by those whose native language was not English, and those that I did read were not normally 'on the syllabus'. Literary Studies in Britain and the USA is a good deal less insular today, and that I welcome.

At least part of the impulse behind the compilation of this glossary is a desire to demystify. Students who read important works of literary theory should be able to find out what the specialist terms used by various theorists mean without wasting too much time. It is a form of academic snobbery to assume that students need no help in tracing such meanings.

Should the reader try to adopt as many of the terms in this glossary as he or she can? I certainly do not intend the glossary to be treated as the Literary Studies equivalent of those 'How to increase your word-power' pages that the *Reader's Digest* used to offer to its would-be upwardly mobile subscribers (perhaps it still does). But if a term isolates an important concept or distinction, one which it is hard or impossible to capture without the term, then clearly that term has a right to be admitted into more general use. On the other hand, if a term only offers a less familiar way of saying something for which a familiar term already exists, or if it offers an unfamiliar way of saying something unnecessary, then it should be encouraged to accept early retirement. You the reader have to make such decisions, although you will notice that I frequently hint at what my own opinion is.

2 Criteria for selection of terms

My aim in the pages that follow has been to provide the reader with sufficient information to enable him or her to make sense of those of the more common specialist terms used by recent literary critics or theorists which cannot be found in more general dictionaries or glossaries of literary terms. By 'recent' I mean, generally, from about 1970, although I have tried not to apply this criterion too rigidly. Terms that have entered Anglo-American theoretical discussion via recent English translations of older works (by Bakhtin and Ingarden, for example) are also included. Older terms which are now used in different ways are also included; thus, for example, AUTHOR is included. *Trope*, on the other hand, although its use has become more fashionable of late, is not included, because its meaning seems to me to be unchanged.

3 Schools and approaches

As an additional aid to those using this glossary I append here a list of most of the terms included in it, grouped according to their intellectual associations or origins. It will be seen that the groups belong to very different categories: academic disciplines such as Linguistics, critical schools such as the 'Bakhtin group', ideological and political groupings such as Marxism and Feminism, groups categorized according to a methodology or a focus of concern such as reader-response criticism, and so on.

My groupings are crude, and should be treated only as a convenient indication of which glossed terms have something of interest for, for example, those interested in Deconstruction, or Feminism. Where terms are asterisked this is to suggest either that they represent concepts central to the grouping in question, or that the entry thus indicated contains information about the school or approach. Those wanting a fuller account of such groupings should consult Ann Jefferson and David Robey (eds), *Modern Literary Theory* (2nd edn., Batsford, 1986).

Anthropology and cultural studies
bricoleur; *culture; *Cultural Studies; fiction; formulaic literature; *structures of feeling; *myth

Bakhtin group
assimilation; *carnival; *centrifugal-centripetal; character zone; contiguity; *dialogic; discourse; dominant; exotopy; *skaz*; *heteroglossia; horizon; hybrid; orchestration; *polyphony; refraction; semantic position; utterance

Deconstruction
agon; aporia; *arche-writing; *centre; Copernican revolution; *deconstruction; desire; *différance; dissemination; echolalia; *écriture; ephebe; erasure; *grammatology; hinge; *logocentrism; *logos; *ludism; *mise-en-abyme*; New Readers; phallogocentrism; *post-structuralism; *presence; *radical alterity; revisionism; site; subject and subjectivity; textualist; *transcendental pretence/signified/subject

Discourse analysis
*archaeology of knowledge; closure; *discourse; *dispositif*; *épistème*; exteriority; multivalent; New Historicism; *signifying practice; slippage; speech; suture; text and work; topic; *utterance

Feminism
androcentric; *androgyny; *desire; *difference; *écriture feminine; *feminism; *gender; gynocratic; *gynocritics; logic of the same; *marginality; *muted; *patriarchy; *phallocentrism; pleasure; pornoglossia; realism; *stereotype; subject and subjectivity

Linguistics
*arbitrariness; aspect; *competence and performance; cratylism; *diachronic and synchronic; *discourse; *displacement; *functions of language; idiolect; *langue and parole; linguistic paradigm; metalanguage; punctuation; register; shifter; *sign; sociolect; speech; *speech act theory; *syntagmatic and paradigmatic; text and work

Marxism
absence; aura; Copernican revolution; English; homology; ideologeme; *interpellation; literary mode of production; *Marxist literary theory and criticism; moment; myth; popular; problematic; *realism; slippage; structure in dominance; subject and subjectivity

Introduction

Media Studies
digital and analogic communication; *gatekeeping; hot and cool media; *Media Studies

Narratology
achronicity/achrony; act/actor; actualization; anachrony; analepsis; architext; aspect; cancelled character; *connotation and denotation; crisis; defamiliarization; deferred/postponed significance; deixis; deviation; *diegesis and mimesis; digital and analogic communication; *discourse; distance; duration; ellipsis; enunciation; event; fiction; figure; figure and ground; flicker; frame; *Free Indirect Discourse; frequency; function; hinge; homology; homonymy; interior dialogue; *intertextuality; interpolation; *intertextuality; intrusive narrator; isochrony; *linguistic paradigm; metalepsis; *mise-en-abyme*; mode; mood; *narratee; narration; *narrative; *narrative situation; *narratology; *narrative; order; paralipsis; *perspective and voice; power; privilege; prolepsis; repetition; semantic axis; *skaz*; slow-down; *story and plot; suspense; suture; syllepsis; synonymous characters; *text and work

New Historicism
circulation; *New Historicism; resonance

Phenomenology
epoché; *phenomenology

Pragmatics
*discourse; double bind; *politeness; *pragmatics; *speech act theory

Psychology and psychoanalysis
*condensation and displacement; contiguity; double bind; figure and ground; hommelette; *jouissance; *linguistic paradigm; *méconnaissance*; other; overdetermination; pleasure; revisionism; solution from above/below; syntagmatic and paradigmatic; *unconscious

Reader-response criticism
appreciation; code; coduction; exegesis; *interpret[at]ive community; intersubjectivity; jouissance; *meaning and significance; *open and closed texts; oppositional reading; parabolic text; *readers and reading; *reading community; *reading position; *reception theory; *self-consuming artifact; *transactional theory of the literary work

Semiotics and Information Theory
*code; *digital and analogic communication; echolalia; *epoché*; myth; sememe; *semiology/semiotics; *Shannon & Weaver model of communication; *sign

Structuralism and poststructuralism
*arbitrariness; *author; *bricolageur; convention; *diachronic and synchronic; *difference; digital and analogic communication; *écriture; *formulaic literature; *function; *functions of language; homology; *langue and parole; *linguistic paradigm; *sign; speech; structure in dominance; syntagmatic and paradigmatic; post-structuralism; *structuralism

Style and stylistics
closure; commutation (test); *connotation and denotation; deviation; kernel word or sentence; punctuation; *style and stylistics; terrorism; text and work

4 Other useful glossaries and reference books

M. H. Abrams's *A Glossary of Literary Terms* (Holt, Rinehart & Winston) appears regularly in revised editions and has intelligent entries that are both accessible and critically sophisticated. J. A. Cuddon's *A Dictionary of Literary Terms* has also appeared in a new edition published by Blackwell (1990), although the paperback edition (Penguin) is, at the time of writing, based on the earlier, revised edition (1979). It contains a much larger number of entries than the Abrams glossary, but these are, inevitably, rather less detailed than those in Abrams. *The Concise Oxford Dictionary of Literary Terms* by Chris Baldick (Oxford University Press, 1990) places its emphasis on the succinct explanation of 'those thousand terms that are most likely to cause the student . . . some doubt or bafflement'.

Also to be recommended is *The Longman Dictionary of Poetic Terms* by Jack Myers and Michael Simms (1989). *Critical Terms for Literary Study*, edited by Frank Lentricchia and Thomas McLaughlin (University of Chicago Press, 1990) contains essay-length entries on 22 central terms in use in Literary Studies, including *interpretation, figurative language, author, canon,* and *discourse.* The standard of the essays (all by different contributors) is high.

Of the more specialist sources, the following are worth noting.

The Bakhtin group
M. M. Bakhtin, *The Dialogic Imagination*, Michael Holquist (ed.), (University of Texas Press, 1981) contains a useful 11-page glossary of some of the many coinages for which Bakhtin is responsible. Tzvetan Todorov's *Mikhail Bakhtin: The Dialogical Principle* (University of Minnesota Press, 1984) contains many illuminating discussions of Bakhtin's more idiosyncratic terms.

Cultural Studies
Raymond Williams's *Keywords* (Fontana, 1976) describes itself in its sub-title as 'a Vocabulary of Culture and Society', and makes fascinating reading. The concentration upon the origins and historical changes in meaning of key terms is especially illuminating. The edition presently available was revised by Williams before his death.

Introduction

Feminism
There is not, to my knowledge, a good glossary of feminist terms which is specifically aimed at students of literature. Maggie Humm's *The Dictionary of Feminist Theory* (Harvester, 1989) covers a number of terms, but some of the entries are rather oversimplified.

Linguistics and Stylistics
Katie Wales, *A Dictionary of Stylistics* (Longman, 1989) contains useful explanations of many of the specialist terms from linguistics and stylistics which are likely to be of interest to students of literature and literary theory.

Narratology
Gerald Prince, *A Dictionary of Narratology* (Scolar Press, 1988) is highly recommended. Most of the entries are relatively short, but they are clear and detailed, and the dictionary is very comprehensive.

Media Studies
James Watson and Anne Hill, *A Dictionary of Communication and Media Studies* (Edward Arnold, 1984), gives concise definitions of most of the specialist terms from this area which are likely to be of interest to students of literature and literary theory.

Russian Formalism and the Prague School
A very useful source here is L. M. O'Toole and Ann Shukman, 'A Contextual Glossary of Formalist Terminology', which is to be found in the journal *Russian Poetics in Translation*, vol. 4, 1977, pp. 13–48. The entries consist of brief quotations from the key texts, grouped under central terms and concepts.

Structuralism and Post-structuralism
Although not a dictionary or a glossary, Richard Harland's *Superstructuralism: The Philosophy of Structuralism and Post-structuralism* (Methuen, 1987) contains useful and intelligent discussions of many of the relevant central terms.

A

Absence An interest on the part of READERS and critics in what is not to be found in a literary WORK as against what is, did not suddenly emerge in the present century: a concern to note what is lacking in one or more of an AUTHOR'S works seems to be a natural component of literary-critical discussion. But recent theorists have drawn more particular attention to this issue, and since the publication of Pierre Macherey's *Pour une Théorie de la Production Littéraire* (Paris, 1966; translated as *A Theory of Literary Production*, London, 1978) such absences have been accorded more overt theoretical attention. According to Macherey the book is not self-sufficient but is necessarily accompanied by a certain absence without which it would not exist, and he draws our attention to the fact that Freud relegated the absence of certain words to the UNCONSCIOUS. Perhaps not surprisingly, the more a critic or theorist sees the author as in less than complete conscious control over his or her creation, the more likely it is that absences from the work will be seen to be significant. At the time of writing this work Macherey was a disciple of the French MARXIST philosopher Louis Althusser, and Althusser had argued that novels could allow us to see (but not know) the ideology from which they were born and in which they bathed, from the inside (1971, 204). In like manner Macherey, and others following him, gave the concept of absence a specifically ideological importance. As it is seen by such theorists to be typical of ideologies that they are unable to confront their own conditions of existence, any ideology imposes blank spots and absences upon those in its grip. Thus by a process of logical retracing of steps it should be possible to read off the ideological underpinnings of a work by isolating its significant absences. From this perspective a work's absences are as significant as was the dog that did not bark to Sherlock Holmes.

An absence can, according to such theorists, be *determinate*. Thus using Althusser and Macherey, Graham Holderness (1982, 12) has argued that the determinate absence of D. H. Lawrence's novel *Sons and Lovers* is the bourgeois class; this is the missing element which forms and controls the novel, and which has to be perceived in order fully to understand it. No direct engagement with the bourgeoisie takes place in the novel, but the importance of that class to Lawrence ensures that its exclusion from the novel is determining. This is an absence on the level of content, but absences may also occur with regard to

1

formal and technical matters: in the final section of James Joyce's *Ulysses* or in the poetry of e e cummings we notice the absence of many conventionally expected PUNCTUATION marks.

Achronicity/achrony Achronicity is a state in which temporal relationships cannot be established; applied to a NARRATIVE it implies the impossibility of establishing an accurate chronology of events. An achrony is an EVENT in a narrative which cannot be located on a precise time scale, cannot be temporally related to other events in the narrative.

Thus the sentence, 'Both John and Albert were to have unhappy love affairs with the same woman' informs us that two unhappy love affairs will take place, but nothing about which comes first (or whether both were simultaneous).

Not to be confused with ANACHRONY.

Act/actor An actor is an agent in a NARRATIVE that performs actions, while for an agent in a narrative to act is for that agent to cause or experience an EVENT (Bal 1985, 5). An actor does not have to be an individual, or even human. Steven Cohan and Linda M. Shires (1988) suggest a main division of actors into *subject* and *object* rôles, depending upon whether they act or are acted upon. They further suggest four additional categories of actor who have an indirect relation to events: *sender*, *receiver*, *opponent* and *helper* (1988, 69). These categories clearly owe something to the influence of the SHANNON & WEAVER MODEL OF COMMUNICATION. The French terms *destinateur* and *destinataire* are, following the narrative theorist A. J. Greimas, often used instead of *sender* and *receiver*.

A number of theorists use the term *actant* rather than actor, although Prince defines an actant as a rôle rather than as an agent (1988, 1). Thus as Genette (following Spitzer) points out, any narrative in autobiographical form divides the subject of the autobiography into two actants: the narrating I and the narrated I (1980, 252).

Actualization It is a characteristic of many contemporary linguistic and literary theories that they distinguish between underlying abstract SYSTEMS and the particular implementations, manifestations, or *actualizations* which these enable or from which they are generated. Thus PAROLE can be seen as an actualization of LANGUE, performance of COMPETENCE, the particular literary READING of a general literary competence, a given folk tale of a set of possibilities contained in the set of FUNCTIONS, and so on. In a general sense PRAGMATICS can be defined as the study of actualizations.

It can be added that what generally characterizes systems and their actualizations in such subjects as Linguistics and Literary Criticism is that the implementations are much richer than the formalized system: in other words, that the real, actual system which researchers assume lies behind the actualizations is more complex and extended and has greater generative force than the formalized systems which researchers have been able to construct. No grammarian has been able to construct a grammar that can unfailingly distinguish between grammatical and non-grammatical utterances with the degree of accuracy of a native speaker of the language in question. Thus study of actualizations normally feeds back to system-construction: we refine our systems partly through abstract work, but also by adapting them to the evidence acquired from pragmatic investigations.

In the model constructed by Claude Bremond (1966), a narrative consists of functions each of which opens for two possible alternatives: actualization and non-actualization. Thus each function introduces two possible directions for the STORY to take.

In some usages *actualization* is interchangeable with CONCRETIZATION: see this entry for a more detailed account of what is meant by a reader's concretization of a literary work. Some writers have also used *actualization* as a synonym for FOREGROUNDING because of its similarity to the original Czech form of the latter term, but this usage is not common.

Addressee/addresser See FUNCTIONS OF LANGUAGE

Advance notice See PROLEPSIS

Aesthetic norm See NORM

Agon From the Greek meaning a contest: the part of a classical Greek drama in which the chorus splits in two to support two protagonists engaged in verbal debate. The term is invoked by Harold Bloom in his collection of essays of the same name (1982), especially in the chapter 'Agon: Revisionism and Critical Personality' in which he develops his ideas of misreading and misprision.

For Bloom, REVISIONISM unfolds itself only in fighting, it is a spirit which portrays itself as agonistic, and he relates this to 'the American religion of competitiveness 'which is at once our glory and (doubtless) our inevitable sorrow' (1982, viii). Revisionism, then, for Bloom, carries on a tradition of struggle that goes back to the beginning of our CULTURE and our literature.

Alterity See EXOTOPY

Anachrony Also, following Bal (1985), *chronological deviation*. Any lack of fit between the order in which events are presented in the PLOT or SJUŽET and that in which they are reported to have taken place in the STORY or FABULA is termed an anachrony. Both ANALEPSIS and PROLEPSIS are examples of anachrony.

Bal isolates two sorts of anachrony: *punctual anachrony*, when only one instant from the past or future is evoked, and *durative anachrony* when a longer span of time or a more general situation is evoked.

See also DURATION.

Analepsis Also, following Prince (1988), *flashback*, *retrospection*, *retroversion*, *cutback* or *switchback*. An analepsis involves 'any evocation after the fact of an event that took place earlier than the point in the story where we are at any given moment' (Genette 1980, 40).

As with PROLEPSIS the inclusion of evoked as well as narrated events extends the reach of analepsis rather beyond that traditionally accorded to a term such as flashback in pre-STRUCTURALIST days. With this extension, for example, the whole 'second generation' section of Emily Brontë's *Wuthering Heights* can be categorized as an example of prolepsis as it continually evokes – to us and to characters such as Heathcliff – events that took place earlier in the novel. Again, as with the extended meaning proposed by Genette for prolepsis, it may be argued that this runs the risk of giving the term too broad and vague a scope.

An *internal analepsis* does not go back beyond the chronological point at which the STORY started, while an *external analepsis* does. A *completing analepsis*, according to Genette, fills in a gap or ELLIPSIS left earlier on in the NARRATIVE, while a *repeating analepsis* or *recall*, repeats that which has already been narrated. Analepses can be measured according to their *extent* (how long a period of time they cover), and a *reach* (how far back in time they go) (Genette 1980, 48; Prince 1988, 5).

Genette suggests that analepses dealing with a STORY line or DIEGESIS different from the content(s) of the first narrative be termed *heterodiegetic*, while for those that deal with the same line of action as the first narrative he proposes the term *homodiegetic* (1980, 50–1).

Analogic communication See DIGITAL AND ANALOGIC COMMUNICATION

Androcentric Literally: centred on the male. The term has been coined by FEMI-NIST theorists wishing to describe a habit of mind and set of attitudes which are based upon a male perspective and which ignore female experience and interests. The opposite of androcentric is *gynocentric*: centred on the female. Gynocentricity is advocated by some feminists as a counter-balance to androcentricity, and in the field of literature requires writers and readers to attempt to ground themselves on female experience and to view the world from a female perspective.

Androcratic See GYNOCRATIC

Androgyny Technically, the union of both sexes in one individual. The original OED gives this as a biological term and equates it with hermaphrodism, but in recent FEMINIST writing the term is used to refer to CULTURALLY acquired characteristics rather than to biologically determined ones.

The writer who probably contributed most to this shift of emphasis was Virginia Woolf. Towards the end of her long essay, *A Room of One's Own* (1929), she reports the train of thought inspired in her by looking out of her window on what she claimed was a particular day (October 26, 1928) and seeing a taxi-cab stopping for a girl and young man, picking them both up, and driving off.

> [T]he sight of the two people getting into the taxi and the satisfaction it gave me made me also ask whether there are two sexes in the mind corresponding to the two sexes in the body, and whether they also require to be united in order to get complete satisfaction and happiness? . . . The normal and comfortable state of being is that when the two live in harmony together, spiritually co-operating. If one is a man, still the woman part of the brain must have effect; and a woman also must have intercourse with the man in her. Coleridge perhaps meant this when he said that a great mind is androgynous. (Woolf 1929, 147–8)

Those who have sought to use and develop Woolf's suggestion have generally paid less attention to the GENDER of writers and more to the gender of, as it were, their productions – that is to say, to the attitudes, ideologies and assumptions encoded in their writing.

Not all recent feminists have been happy with such an approach. Mary Daly, for example, commenting upon the word *androgyny*, claims that

> Experience proved that this word, which we now recognize as expressing pseudowholeness in its combination of distorted gender descriptions, failed and betrayed our thought. . . . When we heard the word echoed back by those who misinterpreted our thought we realized that combining the 'halves' offered to consciousness by patriarchal language usually results in portraying something more like a hole than a whole. (Daly 1979, 387)

And K. K. Ruthven has quoted Adrienne Rich's not unrelated objection, that 'the very structure of the word replicates the sexual dichotomy and the priority of *andros* (male) over *gyne* (female)' (Ruthven 1984, 106; quoting from Rich 1976, 30). In response to such criticisms, Sandra Gilbert and Susan Gubar have suggested the alternative term *gyandry*, but this coinage has not succeeded in displacing *androgyny*.

Anisochrony See ISOCHRONY

Anticipation See PROLEPSIS

Anxiety of influence See REVISIONISM

Apophrades See REVISIONISM

Aporia From the Greek for an apparently irresolvable logical difficulty, this term was traditionally used to describe statements by characters in just that state – normally in soliloquy. (Hamlet's 'To be or not to be' soliloquy, for instance.)

More recently Jacques Derrida has adopted and developed the term, and Alan Bass, the English translator of *Writing and Difference*, glosses Derrida's usage of it as follows: 'once a system has been "shaken" by following its totalizing logic to its final consequence, one finds an excess which cannot be construed within the rules of logic, for the excess can only be conceived as *neither* this *nor* that, or both at the same time – a departure from all rules of logic' (Derrida 1978, xvi). For Derrida, according to Bass, this excess is often posed as an aporia.

In the wake of Derrida the term has become more popular as a way of referring to those irresolvable doubts and hesitations which are thrown up by the READING of a TEXT. The term is not normally used (by those who normally use it) in a pejorative sense or to indicate disapproval, but rather to point to SITES within a reader's experience of a text in which he or she is given the freedom to play with the text by the irresolvability revealed at its stress points or fault lines.

Appreciation The critic Stein Haugom Olsen has given this term a rather more central and carefully defined function than it perhaps enjoyed before. According to him, 'appreciation involves an experience of value, positive or negative, that does not come into understanding. . . . Appreciation *is* the apprehension of a type of value, and the experience *consists in* and *is defined in* the apprehension' (Olsen 1987, 152). He suggests that an analysis of appreciation 'is a way of identifying that core in criticism which is constitutive of our concept of literature' (1987, 137). Thus a person who reads a literary WORK may understand it without appreciating it, following Olsen; that is to say he or she will comprehend what the words mean but will not recognize or respond to the aesthetic features of the work.

Appropriateness conditions See SPEECH ACT THEORY

Arbitrary In Linguistics a SIGN is arbitrary if the relationship between it and whatever it stands for or represents is fixed by CONVENTION rather than by any intrinsic or inherent resemblance beyond the scope of the particular sign system to which it belongs. Thus human word language typically rests primarily upon arbitrary signs. The French word *chien*, the German *Hund*, and the English *dog* are all used in their respective languages to represent the same animal; none of these words in spoken or written form resembles a dog independently of the conventions governing the use of the three languages in question. A Chinese person speaking no European language would have no way of knowing what these words mean, or that they are all used to represent the same animal. In contrast, speaking onomatopoeic words such as *pop* and *hiss* may be said to produce a noise not dissimilar to the sounds the words are used to represent. As signs, therefore, it can be said that these words are not totally arbitrary. Different writing systems can be more or less arbitrary: *pictographs*, for instance, are less arbitrary than words written in *phonetic script*.

The linked terms *motivated* and *unmotivated*, or *natural* and *conventional* are sometimes used to convey a similar point: a motivated or natural sign is one which is linked to that which it represents by a resemblance or connection existing independent of the conventions of the sign system to which the sign belongs. These terms also have application outside of formal sign systems. A motivated or natural symbol, for example, is a symbol which has some natural, extra-systemic resemblance to or connection with that for which it stands.

Ferdinand de Saussure's insistence upon the arbitrary relationship between SIGNIFIER and SIGNIFIED has been very influential in the present century, partly – it is arguable – as a result of misunderstandings of Saussure's point. Certainly some followers of Saussure have used the arbitrary nature of this relationship (between, on the one hand, a sound image or its written equivalent and, on the other, the concept to which it refers) as a basis for seeing language as a self-enclosed system with no necessary connection with extra-linguistic reality. But this is to misunderstand Saussure's point. As Thomas G. Pavel has observed, the principle of arbitrariness maintains only that there is no motivated link between the conceptual and the phonetic sides of a linguistic sign, 'it does not deny the stability of linguistic meaning, once the semiotic system has been established' (1986, 8).

Archaeology of knowledge The title of an influential book by Michel Foucault in which the author attempts to describe DISCOURSES (as he defines this term), their internal rules and structures, interrelationships, continuities and discontinuities, rules of transformation, and the conditions of their emergence, development and decline. He stresses that he does not want to suggest, by his use of the word archaeology, that he is concerned with something frozen and out of time. He sums up: 'The domain of things said is what is called the *archive*; the role of archaeology is to analyse that archive' (back cover note to Foucault 1972).

For Foucault the *archive* is a particular level that comes between the LANGUE that defines the system of constructing possible sentences, and the *corpus* that passively collects the words that are spoken. The archive is 'a practice that causes a multiplicity of statements to emerge as regular events', it is '*the general system of the formation and transformation of statements*' (1972, 130). The job of uncovering the archive 'forms the general horizon to which the description of discursive formations, the analysis of positivities, the mapping of the enunciative field belongs'. And the term archaeology is given to the totality of all these searches (1972, 131).

Arche-writing Also *archi-trace, archi-writing, proto-writing*. A term invented by the French philosopher Jacques Derrida and derived in particular from Sigmund Freud's essay 'Note on the Mystic Writing Pad'. The writing-pad in question was a toy sold for children on which messages could be written with a hard stylus, but apparently removed by detaching its double covering sheet from the wax slab on which this rested. What interested Freud was that although this operation rendered the writing in question invisible, it did not remove it utterly. The written message was still there, imprinted on the wax, hidden but not completely erased. Thus the wax base could be compared with the UNCON-SCIOUS, from which (as Freud repeated on several occasions) nothing was ever completely erased, while the outer layer of celluloid and translucent waxed paper would accordingly be taken to represent the conscious mind which sends information on to the Unconscious without retaining it.

Moreover, the writing that becomes visible on the pad as a result of the use of the stylus was already there, in the sense that the use of the stylus only makes visible part of the wax block that pre-existed the act of writing. This development of Freud's analogy thus involves a conceptualizing of the unconscious mind as constituted by *writing* (see ÉCRITURE) in the form of an arche-writing or ur-writing in the brain which precedes all physical writing and, even, all speech – both phylogenetically and ontogenetically. As Derrida puts it,

> Writing supplements perception before perception even appears to itself [is conscious of itself]. 'Memory' or writing is the opening of that process of appearance itself. The 'perceived' may be read only in the past, beneath perception and after it. (1978, 224)

From this perspective no perception is virginal or direct, but is given MEANING by a pre-existing arche-writing. The theory has points of contact (but only points) with Noam Chomsky's theory of a Language Acquisition Device (LAD) which, because it must predate the actual learning of any language, has the effect of situating language (again in the form of an ur-language or set of language universals) in the biological brain rather than on a social or CULTURAL terrain.

Derrida takes his use of the word TRACE from the same source in Freud. When the words written on the writing pad are removed, a slight scratch or trace of them remains on the surface. Freud sees this to be representative of the manner in which a trace 'is left in our psychical apparatus of the perceptions which impinge upon it' (quoted by Derrida 1978, 216). But the perceptions themselves are more than this trace: they are constituted by the relation between this trace and that which makes them visible (in the writing pad, the pressure of the wax slab behind: in the human mind the coming together of trace and the Unconscious – the two linked by Freud in a passage quoted by Derrida [1978, 225]).

Derrida then moves to apply this to writing (or, perhaps more properly, écriture). Freud 'performs for us the scene of writing', according to Derrida, but Freud's concept of the trace must nevertheless be 'radicalized and extracted from the metaphysics of presence' (1978, 229). For Derrida, the trace would thus be the erasure of selfhood, of one's own presence, and is constituted by the threat or anguish of its irremediable disappearance, of the disappearance of its disappearance. An unerasable trace is not a trace, it is a full presence . . .

(1978, 220)

Architext Following Gérard Genette's book *L'introduction à l'architexte* (1979), that ideal TEXT implied by the generic tradition to which a particular text belongs.

Archive See ARCHAEOLOGY OF KNOWLEDGE

Askesis See REVISIONISM

Aspect According to Mieke Bal the aspects of a given STORY are those traits which are specific to it and which distinguish it from other stories (1985, 7). Gerald Prince, in contrast, defines aspect as the vision or point of view in terms of which a story is presented (1988, 7), while Gérard Genette's definition of the same term is 'the way in which the story is perceived by the narrator' (1980, 29). As with many recent terms within NARRATIVE theory, *aspect* is borrowed from Linguistics, and its use rests upon an argued HOMOLOGY between the STRUCTURE of narratives and the structure of sentences.

What grammarians categorize as aspect is, in Genette's terminology, known as FREQUENCY (1980, 113).

Assimilation In Mikhail Bakhtin's theories of DIALOGUE: the process whereby an individual temporarily adopts the viewpoint or ideology of another person, or *assimilates* these to his or her own consciousness. Such assimilation will be more or less complete, more or less whole-hearted, to the extent that the individual's viewpoint or ideology are or are not at odds with those of the interlocutant. The concept can be seen as comparable in certain ways to Samuel Coleridge's 'willing suspension of disbelief', although Bakhtin seems to move more in the direction of 'adoption of belief'.

Associative See SYNTAGMATIC AND PARADIGMATIC

Aura The German MARXIST Walter Benjamin used the term aura (adj. auratic) to describe the mystical sense that surrounds artistic or ritual objects like a halo, an aura that, according to him, is ultimately destroyed by techniques of mechanical reproduction such as photography.

Author The concept of authorship has been a relatively unproblematized one until comparatively recently. But subsequent to the publication of two essays in particular – Roland Barthes's 'The Death of the Author' (1977) and Michel Foucault's 'What is an Author?' (1980b) – the term *author* has, from being one of the least problematic of terms, become the SITE of much complex discussion.

Clearly on a simple level an author is a person who writes a WORK: Emily Brontë is the author of *Wuthering Heights*. But as Foucault reminds us, one cannot be an author by writing anything: a private letter may be signed by the person who wrote it, but it does not have an author, nor do we normally speak of the author of a scientific theory: such writing is seen to have a different sort of relationship to the person who wrote it from a literary work.

In other words, the term *author* does more than attach a piece of writing to its individual human origin: it has to be a special sort of writing, and the relation thus posited is more than a certificate of origin. As Foucault puts it, 'The author-function is therefore characteristic of the mode of existence, circulation, and functioning of certain discourses within a society' (1980b, 148). To talk of an author is to appeal to a shared knowledge of these DISCOURSES and of the CONVENTIONS governing their transmission and circulation.

Foucault states that the concept of authorship comes in the train of what he calls 'penal appropriation': it is when writers become subject to punishment for what they have written that works start to acquire authors, and he dates the emergence of authorship at the point at which writers entered the 'system of property that characterizes our society' (1980b, 149). Barthes makes a very similar point, claiming that the author is a modern figure,

> a product of our society insofar as, emerging from the Middle Ages with English empiricism, French rationalism and the personal faith of the Reformation, it discovered the prestige of the individual, of, as it is more nobly put, the 'human person'. (1977, 142–3)

Perhaps the most challenging of Foucault's arguments is that *author* and *living person who wrote the work* are not to be equated, as the author function can give rise to several selves, several subjects, 'positions that can be occupied by different classes of individuals' (1980b, 153). When we talk of an author, in other words, we have in mind a range of characteristic actions and relationships which we do not attribute to every writing individual. What these are is, of course, a complex matter – especially as (according to both Barthes and Foucault), the author function is not a historically stable one.

Barthes in particular is keen (as the title of his essay suggests) to *challenge* the power of the author, a power to which he attributes a range of specifically ideological functions. For him, to seek to explain a work by reference to the person who wrote it is (by implication) to be in thrall to a pernicious sort of individualism, and to imprison the work in the imagined self of its individual producer. The alternative view involves moving from work to TEXT, seen not as personal statement from author-God but as 'a tissue of quotations drawn from the innumerable centres of culture' (1977, 146). Clearly here the author is seen in representative POST-STRUCTURALIST manner as site rather than originating PRESENCE.

Barthes's view here is intimately tied up with theories of ÉCRITURE, translated rather less than satisfactorily in the English version of his essay as 'writing'. For him, writing

> is the destruction of every voice, of every point of origin. Writing is that neutral, composite, oblique space where our subject slips away, the negative where all identity is lost, starting with the very identity of the body writing. (1977, 142)

A similar theoretical basis underlies Barthes's claim that, for Mallarmé, it is language which speaks, not the author. 'The death of the author' is, then, an aspect of the POSTMODERNIST and POST-STRUCTURALIST attack on *origins*, on the belief that we can explain (or even help to understand) anything by referring it to where we think that it comes from or to any process of cause and effect. And (as both proponents and opponents of such recent critical positions have argued), to reject such a belief involves an acceptance of the impossibility of arriving at a final meaning or interpretation of a text. Barthes closes his essay by claiming that the birth of the READER must be at the expense of the death of the author: in other words, to allow the reader unlimited interpretative play, the text must be removed from the author's control.

A textual critic such as Jerome J. McGann (1983) has drawn attention to the gap between the author seen as sole creator of the work, and the real process of literary composition involving negotiation between historically located individual author and a range of other individuals and institutions – publishers, editors, censors, collaborating friends, critics, and so on.

The term *implied author*, along with the matching term *implied reader*, comes from Wayne C. Booth's *Rhetoric of Fiction* (1961). The term has entered into current critical vocabulary and is used to refer to that picture of a creating author behind a literary work that the reader builds up on the basis of an image put in the work by the author him or herself. The implied author may be very different from the real-life individual responsible for writing the work in question.

Authorial See NARRATIVE SITUATION

Authoritative discourse See DISCOURSE

Autodiegetic See DIEGESIS AND MIMESIS

Automization See DEFAMILIARIZATION

Avant-garde See MODERNISM AND POSTMODERNISM

Axiological horizon See HORIZON

B

Backgrounding See DEFAMILIARIZATION

Base and superstructure (also basis and superstructure) Central to the traditional MARXIST analysis of society and history is the analytical distinction between base and superstructure. The most famous statement of this distinction is to be found in Karl Marx's *A Contribution to the Critique of Political Economy*, in which he states that

> In the social production of their existence, men inevitably enter into definite relations, which are independent of their will, namely relations of production appropriate to a given stage in the development of their material forces of production. The totality of these relations of production constitutes the economic structure of society, the real foundation, on which arises a legal and political superstructure and to which correspond definite forms of social consciousness. The mode of production of material life conditions the general process of social, political and intellectual life. It is not the consciousness of men that determines their existence, but their social existence that determines their consciousness. (1971, 20–21)

On the basis of this position traditional Marxists have distinguished between elements in society which, with regard to their emergence and their historical effect, are either primary and secondary. On the one hand the *economic structure of society, the real foundation* (seen as primary), and on the other the *superstructure* (seen as secondary). Along with law and politics (mentioned by Marx), the superstructure has generally been taken to include other cultural and intellectual phenomena such as (in some accounts) literature.

Such an analytical position leads inexorably to the view that to understand literature one must understand the primary phenomenon of which it is the secondary reflection: the economic base of society. Thus Terry Eagleton has suggested that 'Marxist criticism is part of a larger body of theoretical analysis which aims to understand *ideologies*', and he locates ideologies firmly within the superstructure (1976, viii, 4).

However, it needs to be remembered that the 'material forces of production' do not just consist of machines and factories, but also of human skills. To take a relevant example: a wholly or largely illiterate society is less able to produce wealth in the modern world than one possessed of a literate workforce. Clearly, then, literacy is an element in the forces of production. Following Marx's comment in the first volume of *Capital* that the difference between the worst architect and the best of bees is that, 'the architect raises his structure in imagination before he erects it in reality' (1970a, 178), it can be inferred that human imagination is implicated in the productive forces. Thus if literature contributes to the development of literacy and imagination it is hard to relegate it lock stock and barrel to Marx's superstructure.

More recently Richard Harland has coined the term *superstructuralism* to refer a range of recent theorists who 'invert our ordinary base-and-superstructure models until what we used to think of as superstructural actually takes precedence over what we used to think of as basic' (1987, 1–2). Harland has in mind not just STRUCTURALISTS and POST-STRUCTURALISTS but also SEMIO-TICIANS, Foucaultians and Althusserian Marxists.

Belatedness See REVISIONISM

Biocriticism Criticism (normally but not necessarily) FEMINIST which considers biological elements to be preeminent amongst those factors which cause or condition the production or reception of literary WORKS. Feminist biocriticism typically places a very high premium upon DIFFERENCE of biological GENDER. See also ÉCRITURE FÉMININE.

Bricoleur In his *The Savage Mind* Claude Lévi-Strauss distinguishes between the SIGN systems of modern man and those of primitive man. Modern man, like an engineer, makes use of specialized and custom-made tools and materials, whereas primitive man resembles an odd-job man or *bricoleur*, who makes use of those odds and ends of material which he has to hand to construct pieces of *bricolage*.

> The characteristic feature of mythical thought is that it expresses itself by means of a heterogeneous repertoire which, even if extensive, is nevertheless limited. It has to use this repertoire, however, whatever the task in hand because it has nothing else at its disposal. Mythical thought is therefore a kind of intellectual 'bricolage' . . . (1972, 17)

As a literary example of a bricoleur Lévi-Strauss points to the character Wemmick, from Charles Dickens's *Great Expectations*, because Wemmick creates a sort of MYTH from the raw materials at hand: the parts of his suburban villa are mythically transformed into a castle (1972, 17 and 150n).

Lévi-Strauss argues, accordingly, that the sign SYSTEMS of primitive man tend to be less ARBITRARY or unmotivated, more MOTIVATED than those of modern man. This, he continues, reflects back upon systems and habits of thought, as whereas modern man is able to separate the abstract sign systems he uses from the CONCRETE realities to which they refer, for primitive man the motivated nature of his sign systems means that reality and sign systems are perceived as more interdependent and involved in each other. For Lévi-Strauss this leads, paradoxically, to the position that the thought of primitive man is both concrete and abstract, and that separating the concrete from the abstract is much easier for modern man.

In the course of the same discussion of bricolage Lévi-Strauss suggests that it 'is common knowledge that the artist is both something of a scientist and of a "bricoleur"', and that art 'lies half-way between scientific and magical or mythical thought' (1972, 22). He further suggests that art is to be distinguished from myth in as much as whereas the artist starts with objects and events, and attempts to reveal a common structure in them by means of aesthetic creation, myths 'use a structure to produce what is itself an object consisting of a set of events (for all myths tell a story)' (1972, 26). The distinction is worth comparing with attempts made by various writers to distinguish between the epic or other pre-novelistic NARRATIVES, and the 'novel proper'. Such attempts have typically pointed to the fact that what is revolutionary about the novel is that it uses as its starting-point concrete (and 'novel') particulars, not traditional stories or characters. With the novel the aesthetic structure, as Lévi-Strauss calls it, is found or created, whereas with the epic it is the initial given.

Jacques Derrida has attempted to DECONSTRUCT the opposition between bricoleur and engineer by claiming that if by *bricolage* one refers to the necessity of borrowing one's concepts from 'the text of a heritage which is more or less coherent or ruined, [then] it must be said that every discourse is *bricoleur*' (1978, 285). This clearly attracts Derrida because it is easier to argue against the unity or absolute source of a bricolage than of some other TEXTS – unless, of course, *all* texts are bricolages in which case no text can be possessed of such a unity or absolute source – or PRESENCE, CENTRE, or any other hierarchically organizing discipline.

Those writing about the phenomena of MODERNISM and POSTMODERNISM have also considered the notion of bricolage to be useful, for it seems to have a relevance to the typically (post)modernist incorporation of 'found' objects together in new STRUCTURES which celebrate their diversity and heterogeneity.

brisure See HINGE

C

Cancelled character A term coined by Brian McHale to describe a technique whereby a literary character is exposed as textual function and no longer seen as 'integral creature' possessed of self-identity. McHale gives as example Tyrone Slothrop, from Thomas Pynchon's *Gravity's Rainbow*, who

> demonstrates this textualized concept of character: beginning as at best a marginal self, he literally becomes *literal* – a congeries of *letters*, mere words. The zone in which he is lost and scattered is not only a heterotopian projected space but, literally, a space of writing, and his disassembly 'lays bare' the absorption of character by text. (1987, 105)

According to McHale, this example lays bare what is more or less implicit in a range of other POSTMODERNIST characters: 'the ineluctable writtenness of character' (1987, 105). The technique can be seen implicit in MODERNIST portrayals of character, such for example as that of Klamm in Kafka's *The Castle*.

Canon The term originates in debate within the Christian Church about the authenticity of the Hebrew Bible and books of the New Testament. That which was termed canonical was accepted as having divine authority within the Church, while writing of no, or doubtful, authority was termed apocryphal. Thus the Protestant canon and apocrypha differ slightly from those of the Catholic Church.

The term in ecclesiastical use, then, refers both to *origin* and *value*. By extension the term in literary-critical usage came to be applied (i) to WORKS which could indisputably be ascribed to a particular AUTHOR, and (ii) to a list of works set apart from other literature by virtue of their literary quality and importance. By the middle of the present century such a decision was to a large extent decided institutionally: just as the church (or different churches) decided upon the Biblical canon, so the universities decided of which literary works the literary canon consisted. This is not to say that there were no disagreements concerning the canon: many of the disputes in which F. R. Leavis was involved during the 1930s and 1940s were essentially concerned with the canon. Leavis's view of the canon was highly restrictive: his novelistic Great Tradition consisted essentially of some of the work of just four novelists.

When certain literary critics began to speak of canon*s* (cf. Robert von Hallberg, 1985) the move had important theoretical implications. After all, although the Protestant and Catholic Churches may disagree about canon and apocrypha, they all agree that only one of them can be correct. But were a church suddenly to state that no one canon had absolute authority, then the idea of the canon as somehow linked to divine origin and authority would inevitably be opened to question.

This at any rate is what appears to have happened in literary-critical circles. For when FEMINIST critics started to construct a rival canon or canons, not always as a *replacement* for the 'official' canon but also as an *alternative* to it, then this struck at the *claim to universality* that lay behind the idea of a single canon. For, in the traditional sense, if there were several canons then there was no canon.

The implication was clear. Literary value judgements could no longer lay claim to being justified by reference to a single standard of literary quality or excellence; they reflected the needs and values of particular groups. And clearly as these groups changed over time so too would their needs and values. Thus literary evaluations and rankings could no longer lay claim to timelessness; not only were they CULTURE-bound, class-bound, perhaps GENDER-bound: they were also time-bound. In defence of this argument certain critics pointed to the fact that membership of the canon had never been that uncontested or uncontroversial at any point in history: Shakespeare's position seems the most unassailable, yet it is hard to accept that the view of his plays current in eighteenth-century England was the same as that current today, for we would hardly be happy to go on performing a rewritten version of *King Lear* which ends with Cordelia's marriage with Kent. And what about Johnson's view of the Metaphysical poets, or of *Tristram Shandy*, or the plays of Addison?

For Mikhail Bakhtin, *canonization* is a process towards which all literary genres have a tendency, in which temporary norms and CONVENTIONS become hardened into universal ones so that evaluations too are considered to reflect universal rather than culture- or time-bound values. Thus Bakhtin suggests that in its own time the HETEROGLOSSIA in a novel will be readily recognized, but as the work recedes in time this heteroglossia is more and more obscured by the process of canonization, which standardizes and reduces the ways in which the work can be read (1981, 417–8).

In recent years we have witnessed a growing interest in the investigation of *the* (historical) canon, along with attempts to explain it by reference to those groups whose interests it has been seen to reflect or to further. But these views have not gone unchallenged. There are still many critics who, while accepting that the concept of a single canon is more problematic (particularly at the edges) than was previously assumed, nonetheless insist that certain works are distinguished by a quality and importance that is not diminished by time, and that such works still merit a central place in the field of literary education and critical discussion.

John Guillory has argued, interestingly, that the establishment and modification of the canon are intimately connected with the pedagogy of language teaching, and that those works that have been canonized have been so chosen – at least in part – because they have been found suitable for the more or less sophisticated needs of language teaching at different educational levels and at different periods of history (Lentricchia & McLaughlin 1990, 240–3).

A few critics have attempted – covertly or overtly – to restrict the term *literature* to works within the canon, thus necessitating the use of other terms to describe non-canonical poetry, fiction and drama. The term *paraliterature* has been coined to describe such work which is seen to be 'literary' in a broad sense but non-canonical, such as crime fiction, romantic fiction, the sort of poetry published in mass-circulation magazines, and so on. The emergence of such new terms is associated with a historical development which alters the scope of 'literature' from that of being a broad descriptive term to the far narrower, honorific term favoured by critics such as F. R. Leavis. In recent years, however, a counter-movement to expand the scope of this term and to reject what have become to be seen as élitist attempts to narrow its scope has become apparent.

Carnival In the writings of Mikhail Bakhtin the significance of the carnival in the Renaissance and Middle Ages assumes a representative importance, indicative of a particular form of POPULAR counter-culture. During this period, according to Bakhtin, 'A boundless world of humorous forms and manifestations opposed the official and serious tone of medieval ecclesiastical and feudal culture' (1968, 4). No matter how variegated and diverse these forms and manifestations they nonetheless, claimed Bakhtin, belonged to a single CULTURE of folk carnival humour (1968, 4). Bakhtin sees this culture as existing on the borderline between art and life, 'life itself, but shaped according to a certain pattern of play' (1968, 5). There is no firm distinction between actors and spectators, and during the period of the carnival it embraces all the people and there is no life outside of it.

By extrapolation Bakhtin dubs as *carnivalesque* all manifestations of a comparable counter-culture which is popular and democratic, and in opposition to a formal and hierarchical official culture. Important here is the idea of unity-in-diversity, of the heterogenic unison or POLYPHONY of the many voices that make up the carnival. In more recent usage, then, *carnival* and *carnivalesque* refer to traditional, often spontaneous, cultural phenomena which, although assuming many different surface forms, are nonetheless deemed to express a common oppositional or counter-culture. For Bakhtin, a sure distinguishing feature of the carnivalesque is laughter, which is never allowed in official celebration – something that Bakhtin, writing in the Soviet Union under Stalin, knew all about.

In his study of Dostoevsky Bakhtin suggests that the influence of carnival is responsible for a set of 'genres of the serio-comical', and that these have three main defining features. First, that 'their starting point for understanding, evaluating, and shaping reality, is the living *present*'; second that they do not rely on *legend* but, *consciously*, on *experience* and *free invention*; and third, that they are deliberately 'multi-styled and hetero-voiced' (1984, 108).

To what extent such manifestations offer genuine opposition to the official culture has been the topic of some debate. Is the carnival like the licensed fool, the permitted safety-valve which reinforces the culture it mocks and parodies? Or is it the unassailable SITE to which a genuine oppositional force retreats when more overt challenges to official culture (and the political power that lies behind them) are not possible?

Bakhtin argues that the carnival is the place for working out,

> in a concretely sensuous, half-real and half-play-acted form, a *new mode of interrelationship between individuals*, counterposed to the all-powerful socio-hierarchical relationships of non-carnival life. (1984, 123)

He further suggests that the *eccentricity* legitimized by carnival permits 'the latent sides of human nature to reveal and express themselves' (1984, 123), a suggestion that obviously has a bearing upon his interest in Dostoevsky's use of eccentrics in his fiction.

Such debates have a clear relevance to current discussions of popular culture and popular literature, and to debates about the distinction between 'of the people' and 'for the people', or folk and commercial culture.

Catalyses See EVENT

Centre In the work of Jacques Derrida the term *centre* is used to represent 'a point of presence, a fixed origin' (1978, 278) which imposes a limit on the play of the STRUCTURE in which it is found or placed. Following Derrida, then, much of the energy of DECONSTRUCTIVE criticism is directed towards freeing structures from the tyranny of whatever centre or centres to which they are seen to be subject. Derrida also uses a range of other terms, including *origin*, *end*, *archē*, and *telos* as roughly equivalent to centre.

When such critics talk of decentering the SUBJECT they should be understood to be extending this argument to the human subject. The human subject is thereby denied a unity underwritten and orchestrated by a controlling centre which, like an all-powerful micro-chip in a super-computer, brings the whole system into synchrony with and through its all-pervasive PRESENCE and discipline. In the light of such an approach the human subject becomes SITE rather than point of origin, and a site, moreover, on which unrelated campers come and go (and sometimes fight) rather than one united by an all-powerful scoutmaster.

See also COPERNICAN REVOLUTION; LOGOCENTRIC; TRANSCENDENTAL SIGNIFIED.

Centrifugal/centripetal Mikhail Bakhtin uses these terms which describe the impulse either outwards or inwards, from or towards the centre, to refer to social and ideological rather than physical forces. (Bakhtin's use of the word CENTRE is different from that of Jacques Derrida: see the separate entry for this term.)

Both of these forces, for Bakhtin, are to be found in language: there is the impulse and pressure towards a standardization imposed and maintained by a central authority, and at the same time the urge towards diversity and POLYPHONY. Every language, he claims in his essay 'Discourse in the Novel',

> participates in the 'unitary language' (in its centripetal forces and tendencies) and at the same time partakes of social and historical heteroglossia (the centrifugal, stratifying forces). (1981, 272)

For him certain literary genres have a centripetal force, driving READERS towards a centre of conformity and uniformity, whereas others have the opposite effect, urging people away from conformity and towards diversity and heterogeneity. He accords poetry an essentially centripetal tendency, while the novel is granted the opposite, a centrifugal force. Not surprisingly, he argues that the novel flourishes during times of diversity and the slackening of central control.

Character zone According to Mikhail Bakhtin, character zones are formed from the characters' semi-discourses, from various forms of hidden transmission for the discourse of the other, by the words and expressions scattered in this discourse, and from the irruption of alien expressive elements into authorial discourse (ellipsis, questions, exclamation). Such a zone is the range of action of the character's voice, intermingling in one way or another with the author's voice. (Quoted in Todorov 1984, 73)

In other words, the READER of a novel builds up a picture of the character's identity not just from direct descriptions of her or her actions or from 'transcriptions' of his or her speech, but from a wider zone of verbal implication.

Chinese box narrative See FRAME

Chronological deviation See ANACHRONY

Circulation A term favoured by the NEW HISTORICIST writer Stephen J. Greenblatt to describe the manner in which CULTURAL artifacts or ideological meanings (for example) are transmitted from place to place by means of 'practical strategies of negotiation and exchange' (1990, 154). Greenblatt acknowledges the influence of Jacques Derrida in his use of the term, and what seems to be important is the way in which it presupposes a sequence of *transformations* of the artifact or meaning as it is passed on by means of the aforesaid strategies. (Thus an object in a museum has been transformed from what it was when it was, for example, an item in daily use.)
    See also RESONANCE.

Cleavage See HINGE

Clinamen See REVISIONISM

Closed texts See OPEN AND CLOSED TEXTS

Closure All literary WORKS come to some sort of close or conclusion, but such conclusions do not always provide the same sense of satisfaction or inevitability. According to Barbara Herrnstein Smith, closure 'may be regarded as a modification of structure that makes *stasis*, or the absence of further continuation, the most probable event'. She further adds that closure allows the READER to be satisfied by the failure of continuation or, to put it another way, it creates 'the expectation of nothing' in the reader (1968, 34).
    Closure, in other words, is more than ending, more than the discontinuation of a literary work: it requires that the ending or discontinuation have a certain aesthetic force. On the other hand, a lack of closure is frequently associated with MODERNIST or experimental works. Such works are often described as *open-ended* or lacking closure. This can refer not just to matters of STORY or PLOT, but also to aesthetic and ideological issues.

Code The influence of Linguistics and SEMIOTICS has led to an increased recourse to the term *code* on the part of literary critics and theorists during the past two decades. This may be at least in part because the term implies that writer and READER are linked by their common possession of a set of CONVENTIONS governing systematic transformations, an implication which appeals to many contemporary theorists interested in issues raised by the sociology of literature and by the concept of LITERARINESS. The term also, of course, suggests that the literary work contains that which is hidden to those not possessed of the right code-book. (In this context, see also INTERPRET[AT]IVE COMMUNITY.)

In one of the more influential examples of the development of a theory of literary codes, Roland Barthes has suggested five codes of reading which allow readers to recognize and identify elements in the literary work and to relate them to specific functions. The five codes are as follows.

The *proairetic code* controls the manner in which the reader constructs the PLOT of a literary work.

The *hermeneutic code* involves problems of interpretation, particularly those questions and answers that are raised at the level of plot.

The *semic code* is related to the textual elements which develop the reader's perception of literary characters.

The *symbolic code* governs the reader's construction of symbolic meanings.

The *referential code* is made up by textual references to CULTURAL phenomena. (Based on Barthes 1990, 19–20; The codes are also discussed in Barthes 1975.)

Few critics apart from Barthes himself have put these terms to extended literary critical use, although one who has is Robert Scholes in his book *Semiotics and Interpretation*. The book contains a chapter dealing with James Joyce's short story 'Eveline', in which Barthes's various codes of reading are pressed into explanatory service (1982, 99–104).

Elsewhere in his work Barthes uses references to a variety of other codes. Thus in the course of two pages of his 'Textual Analysis of Poe's "Valdemar"' (1981b) there are references to the metalinguistic code, the socio-ethnic code, the symbolic code, the social code, the narrative code, the cultural code, the scientific code, the scientific-deontological code and the symbolic code. The use of the word code by literary critics has an important relevance with regard to debates about INTERPRETATION. To decode a SIGN or sequence of signs is to return to a MEANING or MESSAGE that pre-existed sign or signs, whereas to engage in interpretation (at least according to certain theorists) is to generate something new.

Given that a key dispute between rival theories of interpretation centres on whether or not the interpreter is in part creator of something original, use of terms such as *code* or *decoding* tends to ally one with those who do not see interpretation as a creative activity. Jonathan Culler thus raised an important and early objection to the use of these terms when he remarked that 'listeners interpret sentences rather than decode them' (1975, 19). Although his objection concerns the study of natural languages, it would appear to have even greater force in the field of literary criticism.

Umberto Eco has coined the term *overcoding* to refer to a process of meta-communication about an expression. According to him, overcoded rules tell the reader whether a given expression is used rhetorically: thus the opening statement 'Once upon a time' is deemed by him to convey the facts (i) that the events take place in an indefinite nonhistorical epoch, (ii) that the reported events are not 'real', (iii) that the speaker wants to tell a fictional story (1981, 19).

The term *delayed decoding* was coined by Ian Watt in his *Conrad in the Nineteenth Century* (1980) to describe a particular impressionist technique of Joseph Conrad's whereby the experiences of a character who understands what is happening to him or her only in the course of, or after, these experiences, is recreated in the reader. Thus in Conrad's *Heart of Darkness* we share Marlow's belief that lots of little sticks are dropping on the ship, up to the point when Marlow realizes that the 'sticks' are in fact arrows, and that the ship is being attacked.

See also FUNCTIONS OF LANGUAGE.

Coduction A term coined by Wayne Booth to describe a process of evaluation which is not purely personal but a communal enterprise which places a due reliance upon 'the past experiences of many judges who do not have even a roughly codified set of precedents to guide them' (1988, 72). He explains,

> Coduction will be what we do whenever we say to the world . . .'Of the works of this general kind that I have experienced, *comparing my experience with other more or less qualified observers*, this one seems to me among the better (or weaker) ones, or the best (or worst).' (1988, 72)

Coloured narrative See FREE INDIRECT DISCOURSE

Commissive See SPEECH ACT THEORY

Commutation test Commutation involves the substitution of one thing for another; the commutation test involves investigating the function or significance of one thing by substituting it with another.

In literary analysis one might, accordingly, substitute a first-person NARRATOR for an omniscient one, or substitute Direct Speech for FREE IN-DIRECT DISCOURSE, in order to assess what the substituted element contributed to the passage or WORK in question.

Competence and performance A distinction introduced into Linguistics by Noam Chomsky which separates those language rules internalized by a native speaker which enable him or her to generate and understand grammatically correct sentences (competence), from the actual generation of particular correct sentences by such a speaker (performance). Competence also enables a native speaker to recognize whether or not a particular sentence is or is not grammatically well-formed.

The distinction has been extended to literary criticism by a number of theorists who have sought to draw an analogy between the internalized rules of a language and the internalized rules or CONVENTIONS which enable competent READERS to read and understand literary WORKS. The analogy has the virtue of reminding us that there is a difference between literacy and the ability satisfactorily to read and respond to literary works, but it has some shortcomings too. First, that whereas Chomsky's competence is mainly concerned with the *generation* of correct sentences, the posited literary competence has often been concerned mainly or exclusively with the *reading or reception* of literary works. And second, that literary competence seems to be CULTURALLY rather than biologically planted in the human individual (there is no literary equivalent to Chomsky's genetically transmitted 'language acquisition device'). And third, literary competence is not universally present in adult human beings. We do not have to go to university to learn how to speak.

Umberto Eco suggests a formulation which may go some way to resolving these problems, when he argues that the well-organized TEXT both presupposes a model of competence coming from outside of itself, but that it also attempts to build up such a competence by merely textual means (1981, 8).

The distinction has something in common with that between LANGUE and PAROLE.

Conative See FUNCTIONS OF LANGUAGE

Concretization *Concrete* was a favourite word of the New Critics and of F. R. Leavis, used honorifically to distinguish literature (mostly poetry) which called particulars to mind, often by means of direct evocations of the recalled testimony of the senses. Take for example Leavis's discussion of four lines from John Keats's 'Ode to Melancholy':

> Then glut thy sorrow on a morning rose,
> Or on the rainbow of the salt sand-wave,
> Or on the wealth of globed peonies;
> Or if thy mistress some rich anger shows . . .

Leavis comments: 'That "glut", which we can hardly find Rossetti or Tennyson using in a poetical place, finds itself taken up in "globed", the sensuous concreteness of which it reinforces; the hand is round the peony, luxuriously cupping it' (1964, 214).

In Roman Ingarden's *Das literarische Kunstwerk* (published in German in 1931 and in English translation as *The Literary Work of Art* in 1973) we find a use of *concretize* as verb which has exerted considerable influence subsequent to the appearance of this work in English. According to Ingarden there are two types of concretization if one speaks purely ontically (i.e. 'of or having real being or existence'): on the one hand, 'the purely intentional concretization, ontically heteronomous in form and relative to the subjective operation' and on the other hand, 'the objectively existing concretization, characteristic, in form, of the respective ontic sphere and thus, in a state of affairs that exists in the real world, in the form of an ontically autonomous realization of the corresponding essences or ideas' (1973, 162). The distinction is, it will be seen, a complex one, but it allows Ingarden to talk about the way in which the literary WORK is concretized by being read. Central to his argument is that because literary works typically contain 'spots of indeterminacy', 'the reader usually *goes beyond* what is simply presented by the TEXT (or projected by it) and in various respects *completes* the represented objectivities, so that at least some of the spots of indeterminacy are removed and are frequently replaced by determinacies that not only are not determined by the text but, what is more, are not in agreement with the positively determined objective moments' (1973, 252). READING is a creative process in this view of things, one in which the reader not only concretizes that which is in some sense 'there' in the text but also adds to and goes beyond what the AUTHOR has provided or even intended.

In Brian McHale's account,

> The complexity of the literary artwork, [Ingarden] tells us, lies first of all in its being *heteronomous*, existing both autonomously, in its own right, and at the same time depending upon the constitutive acts of consciousness of a reader. (1987, 30)

The Prague School theorist Felix Vodička adopts and develops Ingarden's category in his essay 'The History of the Echo of Literary Works'. For Vodička the study of the concretization of past and present literary works involves 'the study of the work in the particular form in which we find it in the conception of the period (particularly its concretization in criticism)' (1964, 73). Vodička stresses the key point that

> since there is . . . no single correct esthetic norm, there is also no single valuation, and a work may be subject to multiple valuation, during which its shape in the awareness of the perceiver (its concretization) is in constant change. (1964, 79)

Ingarden's 'spots of indeterminacy' lead directly to some of Wolfgang Iser's theories about the creative rôle of the reader; see the entry for PHENOMENOLOGY.

See also ACTUALIZATION; NORM.

Condensation and displacement According to Freud a comparison of the dream-content with the dream-thoughts reveals that 'a work of *condensation* on a large scale has been carried out. Dreams are brief, meagre and laconic in comparison with the range and wealth of the dream-thoughts' (1976, 383). In other words, a large amount of MEANING is *condensed* into a relatively small size by making individual signs or images signify more than one thing: the dream-thoughts are thus OVERDETERMINED. Freud's INTERPRETATIONS accordingly involve a work of unpacking; out of a single scene or figure in a dream a number of different meanings can be salvaged. As Freud also points out, the interpretation of a dream may occupy six or twelve times as much space when written out as does the written account of the dream itself (1976, 383). Dreams involve extreme *concentration* of meaning. Freud suggests a number of ways in which the process of condensation can be carried out – by means of collective figures (one known person in a dream standing for a number of different people, for example), of composite structures (a dream person who combines the appearance and characteristics of a number of different people, for example), or by verbal means (puns, for instance, which unite a number of different words). All of these argued techniques have been of interest to literary critics, and particularly critics of poetry, who have found points of comparison with the concentrated nature of the poetic image or symbol, and indeed many aspects of Freud's dream ANALYSES are remarkably similar to, for example, aspects of New Critical analyses of lyric poems.

For Freud, condensation is typically associated with *displacement*, and he argues that '*Dream-displacement* and *dream-condensation* are the two governing factors to whose activity we may in essence ascribe the form assumed by dreams' (1976, 417). Freud sees displacement as a means whereby censorship is outmanoeuvred; for example, if a person cannot consciously admit his or her hatred of another as a result of the operation of the censor, this hatred may be transferred to something associated with the person in question, *displaced* from one object protected by the censor to another one about which the censor is unconcerned. This again has been of interest to literary critics who have used the concept (often in association with that of condensation) to explore the way symbolism functions in literary WORKS.

Linguisticians use the term DISPLACEMENT in a rather different way: see separate entry. See also the discussion of *metaphor* and *metonymy* in the entry for SYNTAGMATIC AND PARADIGMATIC: following Lacan, a number of commentators have observed that the condensation-displacement distinction has much in common with Roman Jakobson's distinction between metaphor and metonymy (see the discussion in Scholes 1982, 75–6).

Conjuncture See MOMENT

Connotation and denotation The two terms distinguish between two forms of reference: the word 'military' as defined in the dictionary involves that which is connected to armies or soldiers (denotation), but it carries with it a range of associations which spring to the minds of those who share a common CULTURE – uniforms, marching, discipline, force, masculinity, rigid collectivity – and these are the *connotations* of the word. Denotations are almost invariably more fixed than connotations, changing only over much longer periods of time than it takes for a word's connotations to alter.

Roland Barthes points out in the introductory comments to his *S/Z* that the precise relationship between connotation and denotation is a matter of dispute. There are thus those for whom denotation is primary and connotation either secondary or non-existent. Some ('the philologists, let us say')

> declaring every text to be univocal, possessing a true, canonical meaning, banish the simultaneous, secondary meanings to the void of critical lucubrations. On the other hand, others (the semiologists, let us say) contest the hierarchy of denotated and connotated; language, they say, the raw material of denotation, with its dictionary and its syntax, is a system like any other; there is no reason to make this system the privileged one, to make it the locus and the norm of a primary, original meaning . . . (1990, 7)

Such objections have not generally undermined a widespread belief in the utility of the distinction.

A number of recent theorists have suggested that there are similarities between the connotation/denotation distinction and the METONYMY/METAPHOR distinction. This is because both connotation and metonymy involve relations of CONTIGUITY, whereas denotation and metaphor involve relations mediated by CONVENTION. (The difference is, however, that whereas denotation involves unmotivated relations, metaphor normally relies upon MOTIVATED relations, or upon some aspect of similarity which is external to the system of MEANING involved. Warmongers and peacemakers bear some resemblances to hawks and doves which are external to any single language, whereas the denotation of 'war' as 'armed conflict' is specific to the English language and is therefore unmotivated.)

Connotation and denotation are not exclusively linguistic phenomena: the sign of the cross, uniforms, expressive bodily actions, representations of the physical landscape – all these can have both connotations and denotations.

See also SYNTAGMATIC AND PARADIGMATIC.

Consonant psycho-narration See FREE INDIRECT DISCOURSE

Constatives See SPEECH ACT THEORY

Construction See DECONSTRUCTION

Contact See FUNCTIONS OF LANGUAGE

Context See FUNCTIONS OF LANGUAGE

Contiguity Literally, the relation of touching or adjoining. METONYMY is defined as that relation based on contiguity, and has led to important theoretical work in both SEMIOTICS and Literary Criticism. The Freudian concept of DISPLACE-MENT also relies to some extent on relations of contiguity: thus my fears about my boss may be displaced in a dream on to a fear of the colour blue if that is the colour of the suits he wears. The process of displacement follows a path based on the contiguous relation: boss → blue.

Mikhail Bakhtin distinguishes between relations of contiguity and those of mutual reflection; merely contiguous lives, he writes,

> are self-enclosed and deaf; they do not hear and do not answer one another. There are not and cannot be any dialogic relationships among them. They neither argue nor agree. (1984, 70)

See also CONNOTATION AND DENOTATION.

Convention In traditional usage, either the allowances made by READERS and audiences required by certain GENRES, or the framework of formal requirements imposed by the same genres or sub-genres. Thus it is a theatrical convention that the actors normally face towards the audience, while other conventions place a certain pressure on both poet and reader with regard to a poem's formal STRUCTURE.

Recent literary and other theory has been much occupied with the larger extent to which systems of rules or conventions underlie the production or recognition of SIGNS and MEANING. A key rôle in the more general concern with this issue has been played by STRUCTURALIST theorists and critics. As Jonathan Culler has put it,

> Structuralism is thus based . . . on the realization that if human actions or productions have a meaning there must be an underlying system of distinctions and conventions which makes this meaning possible. (1975, 4)

Generally speaking, a sign that derives its force from a system of conventions is said to be *unmotivated*, whereas one which has a force independent of any such agreed or accepted conventions is said to be *motivated*.

'Agreed or accepted' is important: conventions may be technically *artificial*, that is to say they may be drawn up, agreed upon, and abided by on the basis of conscious human planning and acceptance. Alternatively, they may be more *natural*, growing in a more unplanned manner, as particular tasks require a set of rules to enable and standardize communication. The conventions governing the presentation of academic papers are more artificial: they have been collated and regularized by a group of people or an individual, whereas those governing the behaviour of INTERPRET[AT]IVE COMMUNITIES are (to a much greater extent) natural: they have grown up through tacit consent without necessarily ever having been considered or written down.

It is typical of natural conventions that they are very often not even recognized as such, but are naturalized by those who are familiar with and accept them. Thus *changing* such conventions involves shock techniques: a good example is that of the alienation effect pioneered by Brecht to make his audiences aware of, and to reject, the theatrical conventions within the grip of which they were imprisoned. The pejorative use of the term *conventional* stems from the recognition that when conventions are applied mechanically and unfeelingly in literature and art then they have a deadening effect: if we describe a play as 'merely conventional', we mean that its conventions have become clichés, and far from being invisible are more like bare bones gaping through the flesh of the work.

See also REGISTER.

Conversational implicature/maxims See SPEECH ACT THEORY

Co-operative principle See SPEECH ACT THEORY

Copernican revolution A favoured metaphor of much recent theory, used to suggest a range of decentring processes allegedly comparable to the way in which the theories of Copernicus rendered untenable a belief in the earth as the CENTRE of the universe. In his essay 'Freud and Lacan' Louis Althusser refers to Sigmund Freud's comparison (on more than one occasion) of 'the critical reception of his discovery with the upheavals of the Copernican Revolution'. Since Copernicus, Althusser continues,

> we have known that the earth is not the 'centre' of the universe. Since Marx, we have known that the human subject, the economic, political or philosophical ego is not the 'centre' of history – and even, in opposition to the Philosophers of the Enlightenment and to Hegel, that history has no 'centre' but possesses a structure which has no necessary 'centre' except in its ideological misrecognition. (1971, 201)

He adds that, in like manner, since Freud we know that the real SUBJECT, 'the individual in his unique essence', has not the form of ego which is centred on consciousness or existence, but rather that 'the human subject is decentred' (1971, 201). A similar use of Freud's comments on the Copernican revolution can be found in the work of Jacques Lacan, and to this list of 'decenterers' Catherine Belsey has added the name of Ferdinand de Saussure, who, according to her, decentered language and thus put into question the metaphysics of PRESENCE which had dominated western philosophy (1980, 136).

The relevance of all this for students of literature is that Belsey reaches the conclusion that the epoch of the metaphysics of presence is doomed, 'and with it all the methods of analysis, explanation and interpretation which rest on a single, unquestioned, pre-Copernican *centre*' (1980, 137). In particular, the TEXT (literary or otherwise) is no longer seen as source and centre of its own MEANING; instead, the meaning of the text is detached from a fixed centre and thus deprived of that fixity that comes from self-identity. Such a position ties in with a number of other arguments which have a direct relevance to interpretation: the death of the AUTHOR and the movement from WORK to text, for example.

See also *ÉPISTÈME*; PARADIGM SHIFT; PROBLEMATIC.

Covert plot See STORY AND PLOT

Cratylism From Plato's dialogue *Cratylus*, in which the participants discuss whether names are motivated or not: the theory that the relationship between words and what words refer to is existential rather than CONVENTIONAL.

See also *motivated* and *unmotivated* in the entry for ARBITRARINESS.

Crisis In traditional usage, the point at which the fortunes of the hero change. More recently, Mieke Bal (1985) distinguishes between *crisis* and *development*: the former a short span of time into which many events are compressed, the latter a longer span of time in which, as the name suggests, a development takes place.

Critics of consciousness See PHENOMENOLOGY

Cultural code See CODE

Cultural materialism See CULTURE

Cultural Studies CULTURE, it should be clear from the separate entry for this term, is itself an extremely complex concept – one which has involved related but nonetheless separate traditions of research and theory in a range of different academic disciplines (Anthropology, Social History, Linguistics, Sociology, and Literary Studies, among others). Cultural Studies has emerged as a separate field of interdisciplinary study during the past three decades, initially in Britain, but more recently in the United States and in other countries.

Perhaps the most important institutional decision in the emergence of Cultural Studies was the foundation of the Centre for Contemporary Cultural Studies at Birmingham University in 1964. The Centre was initially a graduate research group within the English Department, although it now has the status of an autonomous department. The association with the English Department was not fortuitous: the key figure in the setting-up of the Centre was Richard Hoggart, whose main academic/institutional affiliation had been with English Literary Studies, however much his own work (*The Uses of Literacy* [1957], for example) had moved beyond a concern with CANONICAL literature by the early 1960s. Hoggart and Raymond Williams were undoubtedly the most influential figures in the formation of Cultural Studies in the 1960s. Although very different, they had much in common. Both had a background in English Literary Studies, but both were drawn outside the then accepted limits of this academic area, to larger historical, cultural, and political issues of both a pragmatic and a theoretical nature.

Right from its inception, then, Cultural Studies was academically expansionist if not downright colonialist, basing itself upon some of the methods and principles developed within Literary Studies but applying them in new ways to different objects of study. Thus by 1970 Richard Hoggart was able to write an essay entitled 'Contemporary Cultural Studies: An Approach to the Study of Literature and Society' – which had echoes from the debates between F. R. Leavis and the MARXIST critics of the 1930s – while referring to the fourth Occasional Paper published by the Centre, 'Lévi-Strauss and the Cultural Sciences', by Tim Moore. Hoggart's article is prefaced by a bibliographical note, the composition of which is interesting. It starts with references relevant to what Hoggart calls the English 'culture and society' debate, including of course Raymond Williams's *Culture and Society* (1958), but also L. C. Knights's *Drama and Society in the Age of Johnson* (1937), Lionel Trilling's *Beyond Culture* (1966), Georg Lukács's *The Historical Novel* (English translation, 1962), and other work on 'the sociology of literature'. This is one important branch in Cultural Studies' family tree: literary criticism that is antiformalist and that seeks to establish connections with History and with theories of society. In the opening part of his essay Hoggart argues that what Raymond Williams has termed 'the culture and society debate' 'runs from Blake to T. S. Eliot through Coleridge, Arnold, Carlyle, Ruskin, Morris and many others' (1970, 155–6).

The bibliography then moves to list material concerned with the analysis of POPULAR literature, starting with Q. D. Leavis's *Fiction and the Reading Public* (1932) and ending with *The Popular Arts* by Stuart Hall and Paddy Whannel (1964). There are then works on mass communication, and works related to the social sciences, including Psychology. Works on STRUCTURALISM and SEMIOTICS follow, along with texts concerned with 'mass culture' and with the sociology of knowledge. And finally, at the bottom of this complex family tree, are the Centre's own publications.

Referring to 'the culture and society debate' mentioned above, Hoggart argues that

> 'Culture' there means the whole way of life of a society, its beliefs, attitudes and temper as expressed in all kinds of structures, rituals and gestures, as well as in the traditionally defined forms of art. (1970, 156)

This urge towards a totalizing and inclusive perspective, towards the tracing of connections, relationships and influences, along with a concomitant rejection of academic wall-building, has continued to characterize Cultural Studies, and makes it hard to pigeon-hole the area by means of traditional academic category distinctions such as that between the social sciences and the humanities. Thus in an article published in 1976 entitled 'Cultural Studies at Birmingham University', Michael Green is able to list six main areas in which research at the Centre is clustered: *the mass media*; *cultural history*; *women's studies*; *art and politics* (particularly Marxist and semiological); *subcultures*; and *work*. As

Green admits, by this time the activities of the Centre have broadened out considerably beyond the early concentration on the popular arts and the recovery and assessment of forms of working-class culture (1976, 140). (Another important influence which should be mentioned is the *Mass Observation* movement of the 1930s.)

In the 1970s and 1980s courses in Cultural Studies developed outside Birmingham, with full or part degree courses (both undergraduate and postgraduate) on offer in a number of British polytechnics. In general such courses have been characterized by similar commitments to those of the Birmingham Centre, along with a strong interest in theory and a generally radical flavour.

Cultural Studies has drawn much from Literary Studies, but it has also repaid much. Work within Cultural Studies has often fed back into Literary Studies, particularly with regard to the study of popular, non-canonical writing, the drawing of relationships between literature and the wider culture, and the development of specialized bodies of theory.

Culture According to Raymond Williams's *Keywords*, *culture* is 'one of the two or three most complicated words in the English language' (1976, 76). Williams attributes this complexity partly to the word's intricate historical development in several European languages, but mainly to the fact that it is now used for important concepts in several different intellectual disciplines. His discussion of the word should be consulted in its entirety, but his isolation of three interrelated modern usages is worth summarizing here. These are, first: 'a general process of intellectual, spiritual and aesthetic development'; second: 'a particular way of life', of either a people, a period or a group; third: 'the works and practices of intellectual and especially artistic activity' (1976, 80).

In recent literary-critical discussion the term has undoubtedly been used by those who wish to set literature in a socio-historical context without the use of terms which might invoke a specifically MARXIST methodology or analytical framework, although to this one should add the point that Marxists have offered their own definition of the term. In an article published first in 1937, Edgell Rickword claimed that for the Marxist

> culture is not a mass of works of art, of philosophical ideas, of political concepts accumulated at the top of the social pyramid by specially-gifted individuals, but the inherited solution of problems of vital importance to society. (1978, 103)

This certainly distinguishes culture from, for example, the related terms BASE and SUPERSTRUCTURE, but it also restricts culture to *solutions*. More recent usages, many associated with the newly emergent academic area of CULTURAL STUDIES, have seen culture in terms of inheritance, not just of solutions, but of elements from all three of Raymond Williams's alternative definitions. For FEMINISTS it has been important to be able to attribute some or all GENDER characteristics and rôles to cultural rather than to biological influences.

The term *popular culture* refers to the culture of a subordinate group or class which is distinct from the dominant culture of a particular society, dominant in the sense either of more widely disseminated or valued, or in the sense of belonging to and reflecting the interests of a dominant group or class. The term POPULAR is itself problematic, invoking either that which is *of*, or that which is *for* the people (for which the term *folk culture* has sometimes been reserved). Thus novels by Robert Tressell and Agatha Christie could either or both be included in or excluded from the categories of popular culture or popular fiction depending upon one's definition of these terms.

In the past decade the term *cultural materialism* has been brought into use to describe a particular approach to the study of culture and cultural texts, including literary ones. Cultural materialism is something of an umbrella term, and sheltering under it at varying times can be found Marxists, POST-STRUC-TURALISTS, Althusserians, Foucaultians and Bakhtinians. What all appear to have in common is a view of culture as a system of DISCOURSES which may or may not represent class interests (like ideologies) and may or may not be the product of productive forces and relations (see the entry for BASE AND SUPERSTRUCTURE), but which certainly have greater explanatory power *vis-à-vis* works of art than do attempts to relate works of art to their origin in individual artists or artistic inspiration. This sounds very similar to Marxist criticism, and some who call themselves cultural materialists are Marxists, but others see cultural formations and discourses as self-validating and self-reproducing rather than as the creation of productive forces and relations.

See also POPULAR; STRUCTURES OF FEELING.

Cutback See ANALEPSIS

D

Daemonization See REVISIONISM

Data driven See SOLUTION FROM ABOVE/BELOW

Death of the author See AUTHOR

Decentering of the subject See CENTRE

Declarations See SPEECH ACT THEORY

Deconstruction The term originates in the writings of the French philosopher Jacques Derrida, and implies, as Jonathan Culler puts it, that the hierarchical oppositions of Western metaphysics are themselves constructions or ideological impositions (1988, 20). Deconstruction thus aims to undermine Western metaphysics by undoing or deconstructing these hierarchical oppositions and by showing their LOGOCENTRIC reliance upon a CENTRE or PRESENCE, which reflects the idealist desire to control the play of signifiers by making them subject to some extra-systemic TRANSCENDENTAL SIGNIFIED. As will be seen, Derrida is a great coiner of neologisms, and to avoid the necessity for repetition the reader is advised to look up these separate terms – along with DIFFÉRANCE, DISSEMINATION, and PHONOCENTRISM. Deconstruction is generally taken to represent an important – even dominant – element in POST-STRUCTURALISM.

There is no absolute agreement concerning what implications Derrida's more general positions hold for literary criticism and theory. At one extreme its implications can appear modest: Jonathan Culler quotes Barbara Johnson to the effect that deconstruction is 'a careful teasing out of warring forces of signification within the text' (Culler 1981, ix) – a statement with which the New Critics would surely have been in full accord. In an interview with Imre Salusinszky Johnson has further commented that

> if it is indeed the case that people approach literature with the desire to learn something about the world, and if it is indeed the case that the literary medium is not transparent, then a study of its non-transparency is crucial in order to deal with the desire one has to know something about the world by reading literature. (Salusinszky 1987, 166)

This, one may be forgiven for noting, is so buttressed with qualifications that it would be hard to disagree with – although it does hedge its bets on whether it really is possible to learn something about the world through literature or whether this is a delusion experienced by 'people' who can be relieved of their inappropriate 'desire' through a study of the literary medium's non-transparency.

Johnson does, however, go on to distance herself and deconstruction from the 'self-involved textual practice of "close reading"' of the New Critics mentioned by her interviewer, suggesting that deconstruction necessarily involves a political attitude, one which examines authority in language, and she notes that Karl Marx was as close to deconstruction as are a lot of deconstructors – particularly by virtue of his bringing to the surface of the hidden inscriptions of the economic system, uncovering hidden presuppositions, and showing contradictions (Salusinszky 1987, 167).

It would certainly seem that deconstruction involves one inescapable implication for the process of interpretation – literary or otherwise. This is that the interpretation of a TEXT can never arrive at a final and complete 'meaning' for a text. As Derrida himself remarks about a READING of the Marxist 'classics',

> These texts are not to be read according to a hermeneutical or exegetical method which would seek out a finished signified beneath a textual surface. Reading is transformational. (1981b, 63)

Not just reading, but (clearly implied) each reading. Thus for Derrida the MEANING of a text is always unfolding just ahead of the interpreter, unrolling in front of him or her like a never-ending carpet whose final edge never reveals itself. Introducing a volume of essays entitled *Post-structuralist Readings of English Poetry*, the volume's editors, Richard Machin and Christopher Norris note that post-structuralist readings tend to 'feature the text as active object' (1987, 3): the AUTHOR is no longer seen as the source of meaning, and deconstruction is guilty of being an accessory after the fact with regard to the death of the author. Later on in their introduction they seek to establish that whereas each reading in the collection 'develops an insistent coherence of its own that drives towards conclusive and irrefutable conclusions', the possibility is nonetheless held open of 'a multitude of competing meanings, each of which denies the primacy of the others' (1987, 7). The possibility of such a paradoxical blending of linear rigour and pluralistic co-existence has not always convinced the sceptical, however, and one of the most recurrent criticisms of the readings or interpretations generated by deconstruction is that they are not subject to falsification. Another objection is that these same readings and interpretations have a tendency to end up all looking the same, all demonstrating the ceaseless play of the signifier and nothing much else, just as crude psychoanalytic readings of the 1930s and 1940s tended all to end up demonstrating certain recurrent items of Freudian faith. And indeed the more a criticism holds that interpretations are not subject to the control of textual meaning (however defined), the more it has to cope with the problem that the choice of text necessarily becomes a matter of less and less moment. How can one talk about rigorously grappling with a text if there is said to be nothing fixed 'in' the text?

Deep structure See STRUCTURE

Defamiliarization From the Russian meaning 'to make strange', the term originates with the Russian Formalists and, in particular, the theories of Viktor Shklovsky. In his essay 'Art as Technique', Shklovsky argues that perception becomes automatic once it has become habitual, and that the function of art is to challenge automization and habitualization, and return a direct grasp on things to the individual perception.

> Habitualization devours works, clothes, furniture, one's wife, and the fear of war. 'If the whole complex lives of many people go on unconsciously, then such lives are as if they had never been.' And art exists that one may recover the sensation of life; it exists to make one feel things, to make the stone *stony*. (1965, 12; the quotation is from Leo Tolstoy's *Diary*)

The Prague School theorist Bohuslav Havránek provides useful definitions of both *automization* and *foregrounding* in his essay 'The Functional Differentiation of the Standard Language'.

> By *automization* we . . . mean . . . a use of the devices of the language, in isolation or in combination with each other, as is usual for a certain expressive purpose, that is, such a use that the expression itself does not attract any attention . . .

> By *foregrounding* . . . we mean the use of the devices of the language in such a way that this use itself attracts attention and is perceived as uncommon, as deprived of automization, as deautomized, such as a live poetic metaphor (as opposed to a lexicalized one, which is automized). (1964, 9, 10)

For Shklovsky the purpose of art is to impart the sensation of things as they are perceived and not as they are known, and the technique used to achieve this end is that of making objects *unfamiliar*. One variant of this technique which Shklovsky attributes to Tolstoy is that of not naming an object but of describing it as if one were seeing it for the first time (1965, 13). This technique actually predates Tolstoy by many years: think for example of the Lilliputian descriptions of the contents of Gulliver's pockets in Jonathan Swift's *Gulliver's Travels*. Boris Tomashevsky, one of Shklovsky's fellow Russian Formalists, refers to Swift's defamiliarizing techniques in *Gulliver's Travels* in his essay 'Thematics' (1965, 86).

It is important to note that members of the Prague School believed that automization could occur at various levels: a CANON, for instance, could become automized, and subsequently defamiliarized by a work which forced readers to recognize this fact.

Theories of defamiliarization base themselves upon the assumption that outside the realm of art perceptual evidence is often overridden by what we know, such that we end up with familiar STEREOTYPES instead of knowledge constructed from the concrete information given to us by our senses. Mikhail Bakhtin, arguing along similar lines, suggests that by creating an extraordinary situation it is possible to 'cleanse the word of all of life's automatism and object-ness', thus forcing a person to reveal the deepest layers of both his personality and his thought (1984, 111).

In as much as defamiliarization involves challenging existing habits and assumptions, the view of art associated with the concept grants art – to a greater or lesser extent – a revolutionary rather than a reflectionist rôle, although for the Russian Formalists in general defamiliarization relates more to the challenging of linguistic than of political or ideological habitualization (although there is no reason why the latter could not to some extent at least be seen to be involved in the former). There are interesting points of similarity here with Brecht's alienation effect, although for Brecht the defamiliarization process is certainly accorded a much more overtly political and ideological function.

The term *foregrounding* represents a development of the concept of defamiliarization which builds on 'figure-ground' theories developed by researchers into perception. Nowadays, *foregrounding* and *defamiliarization* are often used interchangeably. Both concepts are related to the view that 'poetic language' is to be sharply distinguished from other forms of language; according to Jan Mukařovský, the 'function of poetic language consists in the maximum of foregrounding of the utterance', while the 'foregrounding of any one of the components is necessarily accompanied by the automatization of one or more of the other components' (1964, 19–20). *Foregrounding* has led to the coining of a complementary term: *backgrounding* – meaning the process whereby certain elements in a literary WORK are presented in such a way as not to stand out or be noticed. The most overt example of backgrounding is probably to be found in detective novels, in which part of the AUTHOR's skill lies in blending in crucial clues with the unperceived background of the work so that the reader only fully understands the full significance of the clue later on. (See also the entry for ELLIPSIS for Gérard Genette's comments on *hypothetical ellipses*; and also the entry for DEFERRED/POSTPONED SIGNIFICANCE.)

The verb *to naturalize*, which also gives us the process of *naturalization*, is often used as an alternative term in English for automization. According to Gérard Genette, for Roland Barthes the 'major sin of petty-bourgeois ideology' is the naturalization of culture and history (1982, 36). By this is meant that CULTURE and history are made so familiar that their historico-cultural specificity, and thus the possibility of changing them, is obscured. Anne Cranny-Francis has argued that part of the formation of subjectivity of men and women involves the naturalization of sexist DISCOURSE 'as the obvious mode of representation and self-representation of women and men' (1990, 2).

See also FIGURE AND GROUND; LITERARINESS.

Deferred/postponed significance Also referred to as *enigma* by Roland Barthes. Any element in a NARRATIVE the full significance of which is only appreciated at a stage later in the telling than that at which it appears.

Compare *delayed decoding* in the entry for CODE.

Deformation In Roman Jakobson's essay 'On Realism in Art' the term *deformation* is given a meaning very similar to that given to the term DEFAMILIARIZATION by the Russian Formalists. According to Jakobson, as artistic traditions develop, 'the painted image becomes an ideogram, a formula, to which the object portrayed is linked by contiguity' (1971, 39). (Compare what is said about *automization* in the entry for defamiliarization.) To break into this STEREOTYPED encoding of reality in art, according to Jakobson, the ideogram 'needs to be deformed' (1971, 40), and he outlines a number of different ways in which this can be done. He thus makes REALISM a relative term, dependent

upon the operation of processes of disruption which prevent artistic CONVEN-
TIONS from hardening into what he calls ideograms, or stereotypes.

For the Prague School theorists deformation is, in like manner, linked to
the concept of *foregrounding* (see the entry for defamiliarization). According
to them, deformation can be used either to make an element stand out so that
it is foregrounded, or (as Yuri Tynyanov in particular argues), in the opposite
manner: so as to reduce non-foregrounded elements to the status of neutral
props.

See also DEVIATION; DOMINANT.

Degree zero (writing) See ÉCRITURE

Deixis Those features of language which fasten utterances temporally or spatially:
'here', 'now', for example. *Deictics*, or *deictic elements* (*deictic* can perform
as either noun or adjective) play an important rôle in NARRATIVE; they
constitute an important token of FREE INDIRECT DISCOURSE, for example.

See also SHIFTER.

Delayed decoding See CODE

Denaturalize See NATURALIZE

Denotation See CONNOTATION AND DENOTATION

Desire Both as noun and as verb *desire* indicates a central but diffuse and by no
means unified concept or set of concepts in a cluster of different contemporary
theories, very often in connection with attempts to DECONSTRUCT or theorize
the SUBJECT or subjectivity. According to Michel Foucault, the more recent
researches of psychoanalysis, linguistics and ethnology have 'decentred the
subject in relation to', among other things, 'the laws of his desire' (1972, 13),
and the concept of desire has assumed an important but varied function within
theories concerned to see the subject as more SITE than determining origin or
PRESENCE. For Jacques Lacan, because the subject is split between a conscious
mind the contents of which are unproblematically retrievable, and an unconscious set of drives and forces (*Trieb*), and because the subject knows that what
it knows is not all that it is, desire for the *other* is a constituting part of the
subject. This is my own précis of a notoriously difficult author's position; those
wishing to check it against the original should consult, among other sources,
Lacan 1977, 292–325. The following quotation should illustrate the difficulty
involved:

> For it is clear that the state of nescience in which man remains in relation to his
> desire is not so much a nescience of what he demands, which may after all be
> circumscribed, as a nescience as to where he desires.

This is what I mean by my formula that the unconscious is *'discours de l'Autre* (discourse of the Other), in which the *de* is to be understood in the sense of the Latin *de* (objective determination): *de Alio in oratione* (completed by: *tua res agitur*).

But we must also add that man's desire is the *désir de l'Autre* (the desire of the Other) in which the *de* provides what grammarians call the 'subjective determination', namely that it is *qua* Other that he desires (which is what provides the true compass of human passion). (1977, 312)

For Lacan, moreover, desire is necessarily linked to PHALLOCENTRISM because the child desires the mother's desire and thus identifies himself (Lacan's gendered term) 'with the imaginary object of this desire in so far as the mother herself symbolizes it in the phallus' (1977, 198).

It should not surprise anyone who has read this far to discover that FEMINIST critics have displayed both interest in and suspicion towards the concept of desire, variously defined. Catharine A. MacKinnon, for example, states that she has selected 'desire' as a term parallel to 'value' in MARXIST theory, 'to refer to that substance felt to be primordial or aboriginal but posited by the theory as social and contingent' (1982, 2). MacKinnon distances herself forcefully from the use of the term 'desire' to be found both in Jean-Paul Sartre's *Existential Psychoanalysis* and in *Anti-Oedipus: Capitalism and Schizophrenia* by Gilles Deleuze and Felix Guattari. In these works, Mac-Kinnon argues, the concept of desire entails sexual objectification, which for her is 'the primary process of the subjection of women' (1982, 27). To substantiate her case she quotes first Sartre: 'But if I desire a house, or a glass of water, or a woman's body, how could this glass, this piece of property reside in my desire and how can my desire be anything but the consciousness of these objects as desirable?' (Sartre 1973, 20), and then Deleuze and Guattari's view of man as 'desiring-machine'. She insists: 'Women are not desiring-machines' (1982, 27).

See also SYNTAGMATIC AND PARADIGMATIC (metonymy as desire).

Destinataire See ACT/ACTOR

Destinateure See ACT/ACTOR

Determinant absence See ABSENCE

Deviation The more stress is laid upon norms and CONVENTIONS in a given theory or approach, the more significance is likely to be accorded to deviation from these norms and conventions. (We can only confidently refer to 'deviates' in a CULTURE in which we have, or think we have, a firm sense of what constitutes normality.) Clearly deviation is closely related to the Russian Formalist concept of DEFAMILIARIZATION, in which the LITERARINESS of language consists in the extent to which it deviates from extra-literary language, or to which it encourages deviation from everyday habits of perception. In the context of the Russian Formalists, then, deviation and DEFORMATION are well-nigh interchangeable as terms.

Deviation is also closely related to various usages of the terms DIFFERENCE and DIFFÉRANCE, as a deviation is significant as much (if not more) in terms of what it is *not* as in terms of what it *is*. Deviation has also become an important term in the fields of STYLISTICS and NARRATOLOGY: a style may be constituted at least in part by deviations from a linguistic norm, and according to Gerard Génette, Marcel Proust's *À la Recherche du Temps Perdu* deviates from then-accepted laws of NARRATIVE by its manipulation of the *singulative* and the *iterative modes* – basing the narrative rhythm of this work not, as in the classical novel, on alternation between the summary and the scene, but on alternation between the iterative and the singulative mode (1980, 143). (For an explanation of these terms see the entry for FREQUENCY.)

Device See FUNCTION

Diachronic and synchronic A diachronic study or analysis concerns itself with the evolvement and change over time of that which is studied: thus diachronic linguistics is also known as historical linguistics, and is concerned with the development of a language or languages over time. A synchronic study or analysis, in contrast, limits its concern to a particular moment of time. Thus synchronic linguistics takes a language as a working system at a particular point in time without concern for how it has developed to its present state. One of the main reasons why Ferdinand de Saussure is credited with having revolution-ized the study of language early in this century is that he drew attention to the possibility of studying language synchronically, and thus established the possibility of a STRUCTURAL linguistics. It is, however, not clearly the case that, as David Lodge has suggested, 'Saussure argued that a scientific linguistics could never be based on such a "diachronic" study but only by approaching language as a "synchronic" system' (1988, 1). Many recent commentators on Saussure's work have made similar claims, but if we turn to the only evidence we have for Saussure's own position – the posthumous reconstruction of his lectures by students of his which was published as the *Course in General Linguistics* – we find a more nuanced position. There are strong grounds for attributing a belief in the necessity of both the diachronic and the synchronic study of language to Saussure; at the start of the second chapter on the *Course*, outlining what the scope of linguistics should be, he includes the task of describing and tracing the history of all observable languages (1974, 6), and later on he suggests that

> the thing that keeps language from being a simple convention that can be modified at the whim of interested parties is not its social nature; it is rather the action of time combined with the social force. If time is left out, the linguistic facts are incomplete and no conclusion is possible. (Saussure 1974, 78)

(It is, additionally, worth mentioning that this comment also tends to the invalidation of another present-day 'Saussurean' myth – that the ARBITRARINESS of language means that words can mean anything one wants them to mean.)

Most conclusively, in the *Course* Saussure speaks directly of the reasons for distinguishing 'two sciences of language', *evolutionary linguistics* and *static linguistics* (1974, 81).

The extent to which synchronic study really does as it were take a frozen slice of history for study is itself not absolute: to talk of a SYSTEM is necessarily to imply movement and interaction, and movement and interaction can only take place in time. Thus the synchronic studies of complete CULTURES carried out by the anthropologist Claude Lévi-Strauss involved investigation of, for instance, symbolic exchanges which were consecutive rather than simultaneous, so that the element of temporal sequence is still present in such STRUCTURALIST investigations.

There have been attempts to study literature synchronically (diachronic literary study has, of course, a long pedigree). Roman Jakobson, for example, has argued that the synchronic description of literature concerns itself not just with present-day literary production, but also with that part of the literary tradition which has either remained vital or has been revived (1960, 352). Gérard Genette, taking up this suggestion from Jakobson, suggests that the structural history of literature 'is simply the placing in diachronic perspective of these successive synchronic tables' (1982, 21). This of course leaves unanswered (or unacknowledged) the question of whether there are isolable laws of transformation governing the replacement of one synchronic table by its successor, as to whether, in other words, historical development itself is capable of being analysed in terms of cause and effect. (There is also the question of the interaction between different, co-temporal structures, which may only be observable historically.)

The concept of 'structural history', indeed, implies that the fundamental reality is that of the synchronic structure, and that history is a secondary reality formed by successive structures.

Dialect See IDIOLECT

Dialogic Along with *dialogue, dialogism, dialogical,* and *dialogism,* dialogic owes its current technical use to the influence that the writings of Mikhail Bakhtin have had in the West following their translation into English during the 1970s and 1980s. Bakhtin wrote under difficult conditions in the Soviet Union of the 1920s and, especially, the 1930s (his first published work was in 1919 and he was still writing at the time of his death in 1975). As a result of these difficult circumstances it has been claimed (and disputed) that some of his writings were published under the names of his friends V. N. Vološinov and P. N. Medvedev. In what follows I shall attribute opinions to the person whose name was associated with them on initial publication.

Dialogue in its everyday usage means verbal interchange between individuals, especially as represented in literary writing. Vološinov (1986) builds upon this familiar usage in a number of ways. First, he suggests that verbal *interaction* is the fundamental reality of language: both in the history of the individual and also in the history of the human species, language is born not within the isolated human being, but in the interaction between two or more human beings. The recent development of PRAGMATICS – both in Linguistics and Literary Studies – may make this obvious to the present-day reader, but highly influential theories of language have obscured this truth. Second, however, Bakhtin was increasingly to argue that even in DISCOURSE or UTTERANCE which was not overtly interactive, dialogue was to be found. Because all utterances involve the, as it were, 'importing' and naturalization of the speech of others, all utterances include inner tensions, collaborations, negotiations which are comparable to the process of dialogue (in its everyday sense). For Bakhtin, words were not neutral; apart from neologisms (of which he was, not surprisingly, rather fond) they were all second-hand and had belonged to other people, and in incorporating them into his or her own usage the individual had to engage in dialogue with that other person, struggle to wrest possession of them from their previous owner(s). Discussing language, Bakhtin habitually makes use of terms such as 'saturated'; 'contaminated'; 'impregnated'; a word for Bakhtin is like a garment passed from individual to individual which cannot have the smell of previous owners washed out of it. Spoken or written utterances are like palimpsests: scratch them a little and hidden meanings come to light, meanings which are very often at odds with those apparent on the surface.

The Bakhtinian view of the dialogic connects with the topics of INTERTEXTUALITY and transtextuality, and with Harold Bloom's concept of the ANXIETY OF INFLUENCE. For in using a word or an expression, an author will engage in some sort of dialogue with the text in which he or she first encountered this word, or the text in which the word has had a particular meaning embossed upon it.

The opposite of dialogue for Bakhtin is, logically, *monologue*. According to him,

> Ultimately, *monologism* denies that there exists outside of it another consciousness, with the same rights, and capable of responding on an equal footing, another and equal *I (thou)*. . . . The monologue is accomplished and deaf to the other's response; it does not await it and does not grant it any *decisive* force. (Quoted in Todorov 1984, 107)

Polyglossia is Bakhtin's term for the simultaneous existence of two national languages within a single CULTURAL system; in contrast, *monoglossia* indicates that a culture contains but one national language.

See also INTERIOR DIALOGUE.

Diegesis and mimesis Both of these terms are to be found in the third book of Plato's *Republic*, in which Socrates uses them to distinguish between two ways of presenting speech. For Socrates, diegesis stands for those cases where the poet himself is the speaker and does not wish to suggest otherwise, and mimesis stands for those cases in which the poet attempts to create the illusion that it is not he who is speaking. Thus a speech spoken by a character in the play would represent mimesis, whereas if the writer spoke 'as him- or herself' about characters, we would have a case of diegesis. Of course recent concepts such as that of the implied AUTHOR complicate this issue considerably.

Aristotle, in the *Poetics*, extended use of the term mimesis to include not just speech but also imitative actions, and as these could of course be rendered in indirect speech this extension had the effect of blunting Plato's rather sharper distinction.

In his Appendix to Aristotle's *Poetics* (Oxford, 1968), D. W. Lucas notes that it is clear that not just poetry, painting, sculpture and music are forms of mimesis for both Plato and Aristotle, but so too is dancing. Lucas further adds that the word mimesis has an extraordinary breadth of meaning which makes it difficult to discover just what the Greeks had in mind when they used it to describe what poet and artist do, and he suggests that to translate it we may at different times need to use words such as 'imitate', 'indicate', 'suggest' and 'express', although all of these words are related to human action ('praxis').

Since Aristotle, both terms have been incorporated into different systems of terminology, and their original, clear-cut meanings have been extended into new usages and more complex distinctions. The term 'mimesis' has been pressed into service to describe the more general capacity of literature to imitate reality, and has on occasions accumulated a somewhat polemical edge as a result of its use by those wishing to establish imitation as central or essential to art – by MARXIST critics intent on stressing that literature and art 'reflect' extra-literary reality, for example.

With the growth of modern NARRATIVE theory in recent years, diegesis in particular has been given something of a new lease of life. A number of theorists have equated diegesis and mimesis with telling and showing, a distinction which can be traced back to Henry James, and which was both adopted and simplified by Percy Lubbock. This actually makes rather a large difference in the meaning of diegesis. For if one takes a novel such as, for example, Jane Austen's *Pride and Prejudice*, what the READER learns he or she learns through a *telling*, a *narration*, rather than as a result of a *performance* as in a play. One could thus defend referring to the work *in toto* as an example of diegesis, because even the direct speech of characters is *told* to the reader through a narrating. But any reader of the novel will recognize that such passages in the novel, in which dialogue and character interaction give a dramatic effect, cause the reader to forget about the NARRATOR and to feel as if he or she is witnessing the characters in dramatic interaction. (Note that we have now moved from a concern with the author to a concern with the narrator.) From a Jamesian perspective such passages would be categorized as examples of showing rather than telling, so that if diegesis and mimesis are to be treated as equivalent to telling and showing, then clearly *Pride and Prejudice* is not an example of pure diegesis, but includes both diegetic and mimetic elements. Gérard Genette comments:

> no narrative can 'show' or 'imitate' the story it tells. All it can do is tell it in a manner which is detailed, precise, 'alive,' and in that way give more or less the *illusion of mimesis* – which is the only narrative mimesis, for this single and sufficient reason: that narration, oral and written, is a fact of language, and language signifies without imitation. (1980, 164)

Modern narrative theory has introduced another use of these terms which is related to those discussed already, but which actually represents a significant change and extension of their meaning. Instead of relating them to telling and showing, it has equated them with PLOT and STORY, such that the diegetic level is the level of the 'story reality' of the events narrated, while the mimetic level is the level of the 'narrator's life and consciousness'. Both Genette and Rimmon-Kenan, for example, use *diegesis* as 'roughly equivalent to my "story"' (Rimmon-Kenan 1983, 47). This extension can lead us into some terminological contradictions. For if diegesis is equivalent to story, then *extra-diegetic* must mean 'outside the story', and therefore could refer us to the actual *telling* of the story, the comments from a narrator who is not a member of the world of the story. But this is exactly the opposite of what we started with: for Socrates, we may remember, diegesis referred to those cases where the poet himself is the speaker, roughly what we have just termed *extra-diegetic*! In narrative theorists such as Shlomith Rimmon-Kenan and Gérard Genette then, an extradiegetic narrator is a narrator who, like the narrator of *Pride and Prejudice*, exists on a different narrative level from the level of the events narrated or the story, whilst an intradiegetic narrator is one who is presented as existing on the same level of reality as the characters in the story he or she tells: Esther Summerson in Charles Dickens's *Bleak House*, for example. Non-personified narrators introduce an additional problem here, but it is still possible to refer to 'extra-diegetic narrative' even in these cases, for the narrative 'knows' things which the characters do not and could not. 'Dear Reader . . .' would be an example of the diegetic level; 'Mary felt fear grip her heart' of the mimetic level, even though it is indisputably narrated and thus, from a Platonic perspective, a straightforward example of diegesis.

To add to the confusion (as he himself admits), in his *Narrative Discourse* Gérard Genette uses the term *metadiegetic* to describe 'the universe of the second narrative', and the term *metanarrative* to refer to 'a narrative within the narrative' (1980, 228n). This is confusing because a METALANGUAGE is a language about a language – in other words, a 'framing' language and not a 'framed' one. For this reason Genette's terminology has not caught on (as can be confirmed by reference to François Lyotard's definition of the postmodern as 'incredulity towards metanarratives', by which he means narratives *about* and not *within* other narratives: see the entry for MODERNISM AND POSTMODER-NISM). Indeed, Genette himself is not consistent, and in essays collected in his *Figures of Literary Discourse* he uses a different terminology: he defines a *metalanguage* here as a 'discourse upon a discourse' (he defines criticism as a metalanguage) and a metaliterature as 'a literature of which literature itself is the imposed object' (1982, 3–4). Rimmon-Kenan's alternative term for the level of the embedded narrative – *hypodiegetic* – avoids these confusions (1983, 92).

A number of recent narrative theorists have suggested that, rather than considering mimesis and diegesis as two mutually exclusive categories, it is more productive to think of them as representing a continuum with minimal narrator colouring at one end and maximal narrator colouring at the other.

The terms *homodiegetic* and *heterodiegetic*, coined by Gérard Genette, introduce additional complications. Genette applies both terms to distinguish different types of ANALEPSIS or flashback: whereas a homodiegetic analepsis provides information about the same character, or sequence of events or milieu that has been the concern of the text up to this point, a heterodiegetic analepsis refers back to some character, sequence of events, or milieu *different from* that/those that have been the concern of the preceding text.

Différance A portmanteau term coined by Jacques Derrida, bringing together (in its French original) the senses of DIFFERENCE and deferment. For Derrida *différance* is the opposite of and alternative to LOGOCENTRISM; while logocentrism posits the existence of fixed MEANINGS guaranteed by an extra-systemic PRESENCE or origin, *différance* sees meaning as permanently deferred, always subject to and produced by its difference from other meanings and thus volatile and unstable. Meaning is always relational, never self-present or self-constituted. Derrida uses and discusses the term throughout his writing, but perhaps the most accessible of his discussions is in *Positions* (1981b, 26ff), in which he identifies three main meanings for the term:

> *First, différance* refers to the (active *and* passive) movement that consists in deferring by means of delay, delegation, reprieve, referral, detour, postponement, reserving. . . . *Second*, the movement of *différance*, as that which produces different things, that which differentiates, is the common root of all oppositional concepts that mark our language, such as, to take only a few examples, sensible/intelligent, intuition/signification, nature/culture, etc. . . . *Third*, *différance* is also the production, if it can still be put this way, of these differences, of the diacriticity that the linguistics generated by Saussure, and all the structural sciences modeled upon it, have recalled is the condition for any signification and any structure. . . . From this point of view, the concept of *différance* is neither simply structuralist, nor simply geneticist, such an alternative itself being an 'effect' of *différance*. (1981b, 8–9)

Derrida has suggested a number of alternative terms for différance, including (in *Positions*) gram.

Difference

It should be apparent from what has been said that the attempt to provide a neat, glossary definition of this term raises certain logical problems, for if one accepts Derrida's argument then the meaning of différance, like that of any other term, is deferred and subject to difference: there is no firm or fixed presence that can guarantee or underwrite the meaning of the term. If there were, then the theory on which the term depends would be in error.

Difference In an essay on the varied meanings attributed to this term within FEMINIST theory alone, Michèle Barrett expresses surprise at 'what can be fitted into this capacious hold-all of a concept', and admits to a lack of clarity concerning the term's meaning within different contexts (1989, 38). If we seek to explain the rise to prominence of the term in the last couple of decades then the best place to start is with Ferdinand de Saussure's *Course in General Linguistics*. Absolutely fundamental to Saussure's approach is the view that language works as a system of differences – that, as he puts it, 'in a language-state everything is based on relations' (1974, 122). He points out, for example, that the modern French *mouton* and the English *sheep* have the same significa-tion but not the same value, because the single French word is roughly equivalent to *two* English ones: *sheep* and *mutton*. Thus the value of *sheep* is partly conditioned by its being *not-mutton* – by being *different* from *mutton*.

Saussure adds that 'everything said about words applies to any term of language, e.g. to grammatical entities' (1974, 116). It is certainly true of the phonemic system, where it is not necessary that all speakers of a language produce identically sounding phonemes, but that the same set of phonemically significant *differences* between sounds can be recognized. On the syntactical level, Saussure draws attention to the importance of SYNTAGMATIC AND PARADIGMATIC choices, thus providing two key axes of meaning-generating difference in the syntax of the sentence.

Given the significance of Saussure's work for the development of important theoretical movements such as STRUCTURALISM, the idea that it is difference rather than identity or PRESENCE that is important has won widespread accept-ance in a range of theoretical fields. Jacques Derrida's coinage DIFFÉRANCE is a development of a Saussurean theme – even though one which deconstructs its own parent. The idea that where signification is concerned, what something *is* is dependent upon what it *is not*, that meaning is generated at least in part by a difference from what is *not meant*, has clear points of contact with theories of determinate ABSENCE in the interpretation of complex TEXTS – including literary ones. MEANING in literary and CULTURAL texts is in part (those who believe that systems of signification are closed would say wholly) generated by PARADIGMATIC exclusions, by a difference from the not-meant. A smart three-piece suit has significance at least in part because of what it is not, as a result of its displayed difference from other possible styles of dress – just as sheep is sheep partly by virtue of being not-mutton.

Jonathan Culler suggests one way in which some of these insights can be applied to literature:

If in language there are only differences with no positive terms, it is in literature that we have least cause to arrest the play of differences by calling upon a determinate communicative intention to serve as the truth or origin of the sign. We say instead that a poem can mean many things. (1975, 133)

Michèle Barrett's essay, mentioned at the start of this entry, provides some representative examples of the appropriation and development of this term within feminist theory. Barrett isolates three main feminist usages of the concept of difference: (i) the 'sexual difference' position, seen for example in psychoanalytic discussion which invokes an ESSENTIALIST conception of GENDER identity and gendered subjectivity, and which explicitly refuses the sex/gender distinction; (ii) a more Saussurean view of meaning as positional or relational which, in the form of a POST-STRUCTURALIST and anti-MARXIST critique of totality, sees gender, race and class as SITES of difference (rather than, as Barrett points out, sites of the operation of power), and which DECONSTRUCTS the idea of gendered subjectivity, and (iii) a more diffuse usage which stresses plurality and diversity within, say, feminism. Barrett suggests that these different usages may not be reconcilable, and that the use of the same word to cover all three may therefore be unwise.

Digital and analogic communication The distinction between digital and analogic communication is illustrated by Watzlawick *et al.* through reference to the difference between the basic modes of operation of the central nervous system and of the humoral system. In the central nervous system

the functional units (neurons) receive so-called quantal packages of information through connecting elements (synapses). Upon arrival at the synapses these 'packages' produce excitatory or inhibitory postsynaptic potentials that are summed up by the neuron and either cause or inhibit its firing. (1968, 60)

Thus the central nervous system works by means of the DIGITALIZATION of information via a mass of binary possibilities: a neuron either fires or it does not: there are no shades of grey. The humoral system, in contrast, works in a completely different manner, by means of the release of discrete quantities of particular substances into the bloodstream. Releasing either more or less of a particular substance can lead to a significantly different effect. Watzlawick *et al.* point out that these two systems 'complement and are contingent upon each other'.

A perhaps more familiar example of the same distinction would be that between the two sorts of loudness indicator on a tape recorder. The traditional moving-needle indicator is an analogue system: each slight variation in noise produces a variation in the position of the needle. In contrast, the LED system consists of a series of lights which either fire or they do not. Modern computer systems are based upon the digitalization of information.

Theories based upon the digitalization of information have assumed a considerable importance in Linguistics in recent years. In phonetic systems, for example, research may reveal that different members of a language community may actually produce rather different sounds to represent a particular phonetic units, but so long as these sounds produce recognizable *oppositions* or binary distinctions, the system works. The Linguistics of Ferdinand de Saussure relies heavily upon the recognition of DIFFERENCES between binary oppositions.

All this would seem to be a long way away from literature and literary criticism. But Jonathan Culler has pointed out that the linguistic model has encouraged STRUCTURALISTS to think in binary terms and to search for functional oppositions in whatever material they are studying (1975, 14), and this has had a direct influence upon such fields of knowledge as NARRATIVE and literary criticism.

It has, for example, created an awareness that the READER's perception of a set of binary oppositions may play a necessary function in the READING of a WORK of literature, alongside the operation of more subtle, 'analogic' responses. This is true at the macro-level of genre and generic classification (for example, the opposition between tragedy and comedy sets up certain either-or expectations which exert a strong influence on our literary responses), and also at micro-levels within particular TEXTS. An example here would be Claude Bremond's narrative theory in which each function opens for two possibilities: ACTUALIZATION or non-actualization.

Certainly in FORMULAIC literature response seems to be conditioned by the operation of simple binary distinctions: 'If this blonde, shy girl is the heroine, then this dark, self-confident girl must be the attractive but treacherous rival.'

Directives See SPEECH ACT THEORY

Discourse This word has experienced a relatively sudden rush of fashionability in the past couple of decades in a number of different academic and intellectual fields. According to the OED, *discourse* as noun can mean (sense 4) 'Communication of thought by speech', and Johnson's definition is quoted: 'Mutual intercourse of language.' Interestingly, the use of the noun to mean 'talk' or 'conversation' is described as archaic.

In Linguistics a renewed reliance upon the term is related to the growth in importance of PRAGMATICS; discourse is language in use, not language as an abstract system. But even within Linguistics there are varieties of meaning. Michael Stubbs comments on the use of the terms TEXT and *discourse*, and states that this is often ambiguous and confusing. He suggests that the latter term often implies greater length than does the former, and that *discourse* may or may not imply interaction (1983, 9). Thus if we take an academic seminar, for some linguisticians the whole process of verbal interaction would constitute a discourse, whereas for others an extended statement by one participant would qualify as a discourse. Yet others would be prepared to accept even short statements by individuals as discourses. Moreover, for some linguisticians discourse is uncountable, for others it is not, and for yet others it appears to be countable at some times but not at others. If discourse *is* countable, the next problem is to decide what constitute(s) the defining borders of a single discourse: Michael Stubbs notes that the unity of a particular discourse can be defined in either structural, semantic or functional ways (1983, 9).

Gerald Prince isolates two main meanings for the term within NARRATIVE theory: first, the expression plane of a narrative rather than its content plane, the narrating rather than the narrated. Second, following Benveniste, *discourse* is distinguished from *story* (*discours* and *histoire* in the original French) because the former evokes a link between 'a state or event and the situation in which that state or event is linguistically evoked' (Prince 1988, 21). Contrast 'John's wife was dead' (story) with 'He told her that John's wife was dead' (discourse). (Compare the distinction between *énonciation* and *énoncé* in the entry for ENUNCIATION.) Some writers on narrative in English prefer to retain *discours* in untranslated form when using the term in Benveniste's sense.

The work of Michel Foucault has been highly influential across a number of disciplines so far as the term discourse is concerned. For Foucault discourses are 'large groups of statements' – rule-governed language terrains defined by what Foucault refers to as 'strategic possibilities' (1972, 37), comparable to a limited extent to one possible usage of the term REGISTER in Linguistics. Thus for Foucault at a given moment in the history of, say, France, there will be a particular discourse of medicine: a set of rules and CONVENTIONS and SYSTEMS of MEDIATION and transposition which govern the way illness and treatment are talked about, when, where, and by whom. Clearly we meet a similar problem here to that mentioned in a different context above: how does one define the boundaries of a particular discourse?

Foucault also uses the term *discursive formation* in a way that seems interchangeable with *discourse*: *discursive* here represents the adjective form of discourse, not the adjective meaning 'round-about, meandering'. According to Foucault

> Whenever one can describe, between a number of statements, such a system of dispersion, whenever, between objects, types of statement, concepts, or thematic choices, one can define a regularity (and order, correlations, positions and functionings, transformations), we will say, for the sake of convenience, that we are dealing with a *discursive formation* . . . (1972, 38)

All societies, following Foucault, have procedures whereby the production of discourses is controlled, selected, organized and redistributed, and the purpose of these processes of discourse control is to ward off 'powers and dangers' (1981, 52). These procedures govern, variously, what Foucault terms *discursive practices*, *discursive objects*, and *discursive strategies*, such that in all discourses *discursive regularities* can be observed. As Paul A. Bové puts it in his discussion of Foucault's use of the term, discourse 'makes possible disciplines and institutions which, in turn, sustain and distribute those discourses' (Lentricchia & McLaughlin 1990, 57). Lynda Nead, however, argues that Foucault is not consistent in his use of it, and that consequently there is some uncertainty about the precise meaning of the term as it is used even in a single work of Foucault's (she cites *The History of Sexuality*) (1988, 4).

The work of Mikhail Bakhtin gives us yet further examples of the pressing of the word *discourse* into new services. According to the glossary provided in Bakhtin (1981), *discourse* is used to translate the Russian word *slovo*, which can mean either an individual word, or a method of using words that presumes a type of authority (1981, 427). This is quite close to the usage argued for by Foucault, and this similarity can also be seen in some cognate terms used by Bakhtin. Thus *authoritative discourse* is the privileged language that 'approaches us from without; it is distanced, taboo, and permits no play with its framing context' (1981, 424). In contrast, *internally persuasive discourse* is discourse which uses one's own words, which does not present itself as 'other', as the representative of an alien power. *Ennobled discourse* is discourse which has been made more 'literary' and elevated, less accessible. Tzvetan Todorov gives a number of brief quotations from Bakhtin which show, however, that even his use of the term (or its Russian near-equivalent) has its variations: 'Discourse, that is language in its concrete and living totality'; '*discourse*, that is language as a concrete total phenomenon'; '*discourse*, that is utterance (*vyskazyvanie*)' (1984, 25). In his *Problems of Dostoevsky's Poetics*, Bakhtin refers to '*discourse*, that is, language in its concrete living totality, and not language as the specific object of linguistics, something arrived at through a completely legitimate and necessary abstraction from various aspects of the concrete life of the word' (1984, 181). This associates discourse with PAROLE rather than LANGUE, and the UTTERANCE rather than the sentence. In the same work, Bakhtin also refers to 'double-voiced discourse', which he claims always arises under conditions of dialogic interaction (1984, 185).

It seems clear that ideology, variously defined, is a near neighbour to discourse in both Foucault's and Bakhtin's understanding of the term, and in his own definition Roger Fowler mentions ideology directly:

> 'Discourse' is speech or writing seen from the point of view of the beliefs, values and categories which it embodies; these beliefs (etc.) constitute a way of looking at the world, an organization or representation of experience – 'ideology' in the neutral, non-pejorative sense. Different modes of discourse encode different representations of experience; and the source of these representations is the communicative context within which discourse is embedded. (1990, 54)

If from Fowler's perspective 'beliefs, values and categories' are embodied in discourse, Foucault appears to go further and to suggest that discourses may force these beliefs, values and categories on to others, implying that the rules of particular discourses do not just allow certain things to be said, but impose certain ways of looking upon the world on participants while excluding alternatives. Thus it is not surprising that a MARXIST or quasi-Marxist use of the term has emerged in recent years, one which owes something to some or all of the sources suggested above, but perhaps most to Foucault (who is not, incidentally, a Marxist). In a letter to the *London Review of Books* which is critical of this development, James Wood sums up his own understanding of this current usage.

> Discourse, according to the cultural materialists, is a network of meanings, signs, rhetoric; and like ideology, it works to legitimize the status quo . . . The text – the poor text – lies at 'the intersection' of these various discourses, and is in fact 'the site' on which these conflicting discourses have it out with each other. The text's rôle in this is seen as entirely passive. (Wood 1990, 4)

Wood's main objection to the literary criticism which he claims is underwritten by such assumptions is that it is deeply conservative and deterministic. Whether or not one accepts his criticisms, it is of note that he locates a current use of the concept of discourse at the heart of a particular sort of literary criticism (cultural materialist [see CULTURE]).

For *monovalent discourse* and *polyvalent discourse* (Todorov), see the entry for REGISTER.

See also ARCHAEOLOGY OF KNOWLEDGE; ENUNCIATION; FREE INDIRECT DISCOURSE, and the discussion of the difference between text and discourse in the entry for TEXT AND WORK.

Discursive practice See DISCOURSE

Displacement Within Linguistics, displacement refers to the human ability to refer to things removed from the utterer's immediate situation, either in time or in space. This ability seems to distinguish human beings from other living creatures, and it is language-dependent: it is human language which allows us this unparalleled freedom to refer beyond our geographical, social, CULTURAL or historical here-and-now. Thus a statement such as 'Do you remember the nice time we had on holiday in Bulgaria last year?' may appear trivial, but it exemplifies a resource not available in any significant way to other species. In one sense literature is one of the most sophisticated exemplifications of this ability: members of other species can sham and mislead, but FICTION seems a specifically human resource. This should perhaps lead us to consider whether or not literature and other imaginative arts actually play a more important rôle in human development than has sometimes been accorded them. It may also suggest that reductionist views of literature as merely a form of reflection of the life-situation of the writer or his or her society are inadequate: clearly what we imagine is based upon what we know, but in important respects it is not limited to it. Our ability to imagine 'what may be the case' or 'what might have been the case' have arguably increased our chances of survival (as well as having given us a much greater ability to endanger ourselves and our future).

Dispositif

Sigmund Freud's use of this term is rather different: see CONDENSATION AND DISPLACEMENT.

Displayed See DEFAMILIARIZATION

Dispositif A term used by Michel Foucault to describe the totality of 'the said and the unsaid' in its heterogeneity. Foucault includes under this heading DIS-COURSES, institutions, architectural forms, regulatory decisions, laws, administrative measures, scientific statements, and philosophical, moral and philanthropic propositions (1980a, 194). Sometimes rendered into English as *apparatus*.

Disruption See DEFORMATION

Dissemination From Jacques Derrida's book *Dissemination* (1981a), the term describes that state of endless seeding and potential growth of MEANING said to characterize the play of SIGNIFIERS in the absence of SIGNIFIEDS. According to Gayatri Chakravorty Spivak, the translator of Derrida's *Of Grammatology*, the term refers to 'the seed that neither inseminates nor is recovered by the father, but is scattered abroad' (Derrida 1976, xi). Dissemination differs from Empsonian ambiguity to the extent that the flow of new meanings can never be exhausted, nor can these be in any way attached to an AUTHOR: they are the product of language itself.

Dissonant psycho-narration See FREE INDIRECT DISCOURSE

Distance A term used with a range of related meanings in literary criticism, mostly within the theory of NARRATIVE. The most general meaning refers to READER involvement in a literary WORK. Thus whereas readers of Dickens's novels typically became (and become) very involved in the fate of characters in the course of reading (gathering on the quay in the United States to meet the latest instalment of *The Old Curiosity Shop* to learn of the fate of Little Nell, for example), much of Joseph Conrad's fiction encourages the reader to observe characters and events more dispassionately, at more of an emotional distance.

This is not unrelated to more specific usages of the term within narrative theory. The reader of Conrad's 'An Outpost of Progress' feels relatively distanced from the fates of the characters of the work, but this is in part because the NARRATOR also seems detached and, if pitying, at a distance from the characters. Distance can, therefore, refer to the gap between STORY and NARRATION, and this gap can be temporal, geographical, or emotional – or traceable to a clash between the value-systems associated with characters and with the narrative. It can also be attributed to more technical matters: the more anonymous and covert the narration, the less distance there is between story and narration; the more the narrative draws attention to itself as narrative (through, for example, a personified narrator), then the greater the story-narrative distance. It should be remembered, however, that it is possible for the technical distance between narrative and story to be very small without necessarily producing very much reader or NARRATEE involvement in the work on an emotional level.

Mieke Bal uses distance as a measure of types of ANACHRONY: the more an event presented in an anachrony is separated from the 'present' (that is, the moment at which the story is interrupted by the anachrony), the greater the distance (1985, 59).

See also ANALEPSIS.

Dominant According to the Prague School theorist Jan Mukařovský:

> The systematic foregrounding of components in a work of poetry consists in the gradation of the interrelationships of these components, that is, in their mutual subordination and superordination. The component highest in the hierarchy becomes the dominant. All other components, foregrounded or not, are evaluated from the standpoint of the dominant. (1964, 20)

And Roman Jakobson proposes that

> The dominant may be defined as the focusing component of a work of art: it rules, determines, and transforms the remaining components. It is the dominant which guarantees the integrity of the structure. (1971, 82)

Jakobson goes on to suggest that one may seek a dominant not only in an individual artist's poetic WORK or in the poetic CANON, 'but also in the art of a given epoch, viewed as a particular whole (1971, 83), and he suggests that in Renaissance art 'such an acme of the aesthetic criteria of the time, was represented by the visual arts' (1971, 83).

Brian McHale has pointed out that it is thanks to Roman Jakobson that the concept is known today, but that Jurij Tynjanov is probably the person who deserves to be credited with its invention (1987, 6).

Mikhail Bakhtin makes very extensive use of the concept, especially in his study of Dostoevsky (Bakhtin 1984).

See also CULTURE (dominant culture); DEFAMILIARIZATION; DEFORMATION.

Dominant discourse See DISCOURSE

Double-bind A term from interpersonal psychology. In their book *Pragmatics of Human Communication* Paul Watzlawick *et al.* give the following definition.

A double-bind is a message so structured that it both (i) asserts something, and (ii) asserts something about its own assertion such that (iii) assertion *i* contradicts assertion *ii*. Furthermore, it is necessary that the recipient of the message be incapable of stepping outside the FRAME of contradiction set up by these conflicting assertions, such that he or she oscillates between them but cannot resolve the contradiction by means of some sort of meta-assertion (1968, 212).

This sounds complex, but relates to a very simple and not uncommon situation. The parent who says to a child, 'If you loved me you wouldn't misbehave' will double-bind the child if it is incapable of stepping out of the enclosing frame of the double-bind and responding 'My misbehaving does not affect the fact that I *do* love you.' To give another illuminating example: according to Gilles Deleuze and Félix Guattari in their *Anti-Oedipus: Capitalism and Schizophrenia*, '*the "double bind" is none other than the whole of Oedipus*' (1983, 80, their emphasis).

The theory of the double-bind has been made use of by literary critics in two rather different ways. A number of critics have made use of the theory to throw light on what it is claimed are depictions of unhealthy or pathological human relationships. Thus in their book *Families under Stress* (1975), Tony Manocchio and William Petitt use a number of psychological concepts including that of the double-bind to analyse family relations in WORKS by Terence Rattigan, Shakespeare, Eugene O'Neill, Arthur Miller and Edward Albee. The experiment has points of interest for students of literature, but the failure fully to take account of the fictional and artistic aspects of the works studied leads to a number of shortcomings in the analyses.

A rather different use can be found in Harold Bloom's *The Anxiety of Influence*, in which Bloom invokes the double-bind concept to characterize 'the paradox of the precursor's implicit charge to the ephebe'. For Bloom, what the precursor's poem says to its descendant poem (here Bloom shifts the ground of his argument a little), is, 'Be like me but unlike me' (1973, 70). The EPHEBE'S relation to his precursor, then, is for Bloom essentially neurotic and pathological in nature.

For a more detailed account of Bloom's position see the entry for REVISIONISM.

Duration In NARRATIVE theory, duration can refer either to the time covered by the STORY or part of it (an EVENT), or to the 'time' allotted to either by the TEXT (story-time and text-time). As Rimmon-Kenan points out, the latter concept is a highly problematic one as 'there is no way of measuring text-duration' (1983, 51). 'Pages' do not give a particularly reliable measure: not only do some READERS read more quickly than others, the same reader will read more or less quickly depending upon such factors as textual complexity, reader involvement and tension, and so on.

Gerald Prince points out that as a result many writers on narrative find *speed* or *tempo* more fruitful concepts in the analysis of narrative texts (1988, 24).

According to Gérard Genette, the four basic forms of narrative movement are ELLIPSIS, pause, scene and summary. These constitute four different ways of varying duration (1980, 94).

E

Echolalia A term intended to convey the ceaseless echoing back and forth between SIGNS whose significance is determined only relationally and not by any over-riding PRESENCE or fixed authority.

Écriture French-English dictionaries give 'writing' as the equivalent of écriture, and in an article on DECONSTRUCTIVE criticism M. H. Abrams has glossed écriture as 'the written or printed text' (1977, 428), but the fact that many critics writing in English continue to use the French term suggests that this equivalence is very incomplete. We need to understand that the contemporary critical use of this term dates from Roland Barthes's extension of the meaning of the French term in his *Le Degré Zéro de L'écriture*, which was published in 1953. The English translation (Barthes 1967b) has what, given the following comments, is arguably the misleadingly title *Writing Degree Zero*. In an article on écriture, Ann Banfield has named other 'landmark texts' which have contributed to the establishment of this term: Maurice Blanchot's 'The Narrative Voice' (1981); Michel Butor, 'L'Usage des Pronoms Personnels dans le Roman' (1964), and Michel Foucault, 'What is an Author?' (1980b, first published 1977) (Banfield 1985, 2). Barthes's translators point out in a note that although in everyday French écriture normally means only 'handwriting', or 'the art of writing', 'It is used here in a strictly technical sense to denote a new concept' (Barthes 1967b, 7). This 'new concept' has to be explained by reference to Barthes's setting of écriture in opposition to *littérature*, a distinction related to that which he makes between *lisible* and *scriptible* or, as rendered in English translation, READERLY AND WRITERLY TEXTS. As Banfield points out, the distinction between écriture and littérature is the more striking in French because prose fiction in French has appropriated to itself certain *grammatical* characteristics which distinguish it from other forms of writing, notably the *passé simple* and the third person NARRATIVE (Banfield 1985, 4). If *littérature* is characterized by these overt grammatical markers, and by less overt and related ideological ones, *écriture* seeks to escape from 'LITERARINESS' by a 'zero style' first, and most strikingly, seen in the French novel in Albert Camus's *L'Étranger*, a novel told in the first and not the third person, and using not the *passé simple* but the *parfait composé*, a grammatical choice which has (or had) a shock effect in French but which is lost in English translation. For Barthes, 'writing degree zero' is a 'colourless writing, freed from all bondage to a pre-ordained state of language' (1967b, 82), it represents an attempt 'to go beyond Literature by entrusting one's fate to a sort of basic speech, equally far from living languages and from literary language proper' (1967b, 83).

What, then, is the significance of this for non-French readers? Banfield argues that although the grammatical markers of écriture are not so apparent in English, nonetheless the term points to a writing characterized by ABSENCE, an absence of the marks of literature, of human agency, which is not limited to French language or CULTURE. Écriture as substantive, says Banfield, 'is a product now divorced from the person and activity of its producer', it is 'the name for the coming to language of a knowledge which is not personal' (Banfield 1985, 13), and she links it with the use of *style indirecte libre*, or FREE INDIRECT DISCOURSE in the novel.

The same loss of complexities can accompany the translating of Jacques Derrida's use of the term *écriture* by the English term *writing*. In an interview with Henri Ronse, published in *Positions*, Ronse puts a case for this complexity to Derrida, who does not reject Ronse's argument.

> *Ronse*: In your essays at least two meanings of the word 'writing' are discernible: the accepted meaning, which opposes (phonetic) writing to the speech that it allegedly represents (but you show that there is no purely phonetic writing), and a more radical meaning that determines writing in general, before any tie to what glossematics calls an 'expressive substance'; this more radical meaning would be the common root of writing and speech. The treatment accorded to writing in the accepted sense serves as a revelatory index of the repression to which archi-writing is subject. (Derrida 1981b, 7–8)

For *archi-writing*, see the entry for ARCHE-WRITING. It seems clear that for Derrida, *écriture* and *arche-writing* can on occasions perform almost interchangeable rôles.

It would be a mistake to conclude from the above that the term was now possessed of a relatively fixed set of meanings: because of the centrality of the rôle played by the term in a range of actively developing contemporary theories, its meanings seem to be characterized more by continued expansion than by finality or fixity. Even in the writings of the theorists referred to above, the term is rarely accorded the same meaning from one work to another.

Theories of écriture clearly appealed to STRUCTURALISTS who were keen to stress the depersonalized systematics of LANGUE and eager to reject views which saw language always in terms of (normally individual) human origins or PRESENCE. So far as literature is concerned, an adoption of the term seems typically to stem from impulses similar to those which lie behind the belief in the death of the AUTHOR, and its use often betokens a commitment to a writerless writing, or at least to a writing seen as intransitive and self-regarding.

See also ÉCRITURE FÉMININE.

Écriture féminine According to Elaine Showalter, 'the inscription of the feminine body and female difference in language and text' (1986, 249). Showalter's discussion of the concept is worth consulting in its entirety. The term was coined by French FEMINISTS, and represents more a description of an ideal, future achievement than of a particular type of writing of which there already exist many examples.

The concept has interesting forebears. The following comment from Virginia Woolf's essay 'Women and Fiction', was first published in 1929.

> But it is still true that before a woman can write exactly as she wishes to write, she has many difficulties to face. To begin with, there is the technical difficulty – so simple, apparently; in reality, so baffling – that the very form of the sentence does not fit her. It is a sentence made by men; it is too loose, too heavy, too pompous for a woman's use. (1966b, 145)

Woolf concludes that a woman must 'alter and adapt' the current sentence until she can write one that 'takes the natural shape of her thought without crushing or distorting it' (1966b, 145).

In another essay she makes it clear that it is not just the shape of a woman's thought but the reality of her body that manifests itself as a problem of writing for her. In 'Professions for Women', which was first read as a paper to the Women's Service League, she pictures for her listeners a girl sitting with pen in hand, and notes that the image that this picture brings to mind is that of a fisherman 'lying sunk in dreams on the verge of a deep lake with a rod held out over the water'.

> Now came the experience that I believe to be far commoner with women writers than with men. The line raced through the girl's fingers. Her imagination had rushed away. It had sought the pools, the depths, the dark places where the largest fish slumber. And then there was a smash. There was an explosion. There was foam and confusion. The imagination had dashed itself against something hard. The girl was roused from her dream. She was indeed in a state of the most acute and difficult distress. To speak without figure, she had thought of something, something about the body, about the passions which it was unfitting for her as a woman to say. (1966a, 287–8)

More recent feminist accounts of *écriture féminine* suggest that this sense of one's own body may become the source from which the new writing must stem. Madeleine Gagnon, for example, after noting that she has to take over a language which, although it is hers, is foreign to her, argues that there is an alternative.

> All we have to do is let the body flow, from the inside; all we have to do is erase, as we did on the slate, whatever may hinder or harm the new forms of writing; we retain whatever fits, whatever suits us. (1980, 180)

Some feminist commentators have, however, suggested that the process may not be so easy as is here assumed, pointing out that women's sense of their own bodies may already be saturated with ideologically foreign elements: what flows from the inside of the body may thus be more than body alone.

55

Ellipsis Alternatively *gap*. The omitting of one or more items in a NARRATIVE series: any gap of information in a temporal or other sequence. We never learn anything concrete, for example, of Heathcliff's history prior to his discovery in Liverpool by Mr Earnshaw, nor of what he does to become rich between the time of his disappearance and re-appearance in *Wuthering Heights*. In this case the ellipsis is relatively *unmarked* (or implicit), as it covers information not known to the personified NARRATORS. But when in Charles Dickens's *Bleak House* Esther Summerson seeks to explain why she finds Mrs Woodcourt irksome, and breaks off with the words, 'I don't know what it was. Or at least if I do, now, I thought I did not then. Or at least – but it don't matter', then we have a clearly *marked* (or explicit) ellipsis. Few readers are concerned to ask the above question about Heathcliff in reading *Wuthering Heights*, and L. C. Knights, in a famous article, certainly thought that a correct response to Shakespeare's *Macbeth* should *not* lead one to ask how many children had Lady Macbeth. Examples of the FANTASTIC, in contrast, draw the reader's attention to certain explanatory gaps which cause them to hesitate between natural and supernatural explanations of events.

Gérard Genette characterizes certain ellipses as *hypothetical*; these are those ellipses which are impossible to localize or – on occasions – to place in any spot at all, but which are revealed after the event by an ANALEPSIS (1980, 109).

Ellipses can be permanent or temporary: in most detective novels certain marked gaps are sustained until the end of the WORK only to be filled in the course of the final pages.

See also ABSENCE; analepsis; CONCRETIZATION; narrative movements (entry for DURATION); PARALIPSIS.

Embedded event See EVENT

Embedded narrative See FRAME

Emotive See FUNCTIONS OF LANGUAGE

Empirical/ism See SOLUTION FROM ABOVE/BELOW

Empirical reader See READERS AND READING

Empiricist fallacy See NORM

Enchained event See EVENT

English This has long been considered to be an ideologically loaded or, at least, coloured word by those who have argued that the tendency within and outside Britain to substitute it for the more accurate *British* compromises its use as a neutral descriptive term in other contexts (the 'English language', for example).

This suspicion of the word seems to have been at least partly responsible for the emergence of a new usage, current in British rather than American contexts, which can be summed up as 'That complex of attitudes and exclusions which accompanies the rôle played by English language and literature in the educational system, and which functions as a part of the dominant ideology'. The usage owes much to Louis Althusser's theory of the Ideological State Apparatuses (see the entry for ideology), and has been backed up by arguments which appeal to the evidence of public examinations and the syllabuses and teaching associated with them. Such arguments typically involve reference to the ideologically determined element in CANON-formation. The usage can be confusing – especially, it seems, to non-British users – as it is often difficult to tell whether the word is intended as a neutral, descriptive term or as a term with a specifically political thrust behind it.

*Énoncé/Énonciation/*Enunciatee See ENUNCIATION

Enunciation Along with cognate words such as *enunciatee, enunciator* and *enunciated,* enunciation has now begun to replace the French loan-words *énonciation, énonciateur,* and *énoncé,* but such translations often fail to carry the more specific meanings of the French originals. (The translator of Roland Barthes's article 'To Write: an Intransitive Verb?', for example, regularly includes the French original terms alongside the English translation, and *énonciation* is translated on one occasion as *utterance* and on another as *statement.* Umberto Eco, in contrast, renders énoncé and énonciation as *sentence* and *utterance* [1981, 16].)

What is central to use of the various French terms is a distinction between the particular, time-bound *act* of making a statement, and the *verbal result* of that act, a result which escapes from the moment of time and from the possession of the person responsible for the act. We can note that the important distinction between *utterance* and *statement* is that the former term links that uttered to its human originator, whereas the latter term concentrates attention on to the verbal entity itself. When *énonciation* is used in French it more usually has the meaning we attribute to *utterance,* that is to say, it calls to mind the *act* of producing a form of words which involves a human SUBJECT. In contrast, when *énoncé* is used the intention is normally to consider a form of words independently from their association with a human subject.

In addition, the French terms generally include the idea of a human target or audience (whereas a statement or UTTERANCE can be made in the absence of these). Thus some writers in English prefer to translate the term *énonciateur* as *addresser,* a usage which inevitably perhaps also brings with it *addressee* – the person at whom an utterance is aimed. When one meets with the term *enunciation* in English care should therefore be taken. This often implies the precise act-in-a-context which produces a person-oriented utterance, but it can also have a more restricted sense of the *evidence* remaining in an utterance that it stems from a *subject's act-in-a-context.*

See also the distinction between DISCOURSE and STORY in the entry for discourse.

Ephebe According to the OED, in Classical Greece a young citizen aged between 18 and 20 years who was chiefly involved in garrison duty. The term has been pressed into new service by Harold Bloom to describe the 'young citizen of poetry' or 'figure of the youth as virile poet' (1973, 10, 31). Bloom's ephebe, it should be said, seems to be engaged more in storming the paternal garrison than in defending it.

Episodic narrative See STRING OF PEARLS NARRATIVE

Épistème (Sometimes written *epistēmē*.) A term coined by Michel Foucault and widely used by, among others, Jacques Derrida, to indicate the totality of relations and laws of transformation uniting all discursive practices (see the entry for DISCOURSE) at any moment of time.

The term can, alternatively, refer to a given historical period during which the above-mentioned relations and laws of transformation are constant and stable. Thus *épistème* has points of contact with Marx's *ruling ideas* and with the MARXIST sense of ideology, but it has a more all-embracing, totalizing sense: an *épistème* leaves no room – or attempts to exclude the space – for any ways of producing or arranging knowledge apart from its own. As Richard Harland points out, one problem caused for Foucault by the theory of the *épistème* is that the theorist of the concept (i.e. Foucault himself) must be part of the *épistème* if indeed the *épistème* is all-embracing (Harland 1987, 123). A further set of problems involves the reason why – and manner whereby – one *épistème* gives way to and is replaced by another.

For comparable concepts, see PARADIGM SHIFT and PROBLEMATIC.

Epoché In PHENOMENOLOGICAL criticism, that suspension of all pre-existing beliefs and attitudes which must precede the analysis of consciousness. According to Gérard Genette,

> when the semiologist has operated the semiological reduction, the *epoché* of meaning on the object-form, he is presented with a matte object, cleansed of all the varnish of dubious, abusive significations, with which social speech had covered it, restored to its essential freshness and solitude. (1982, 39)

Erasure In recent theoretical usage, normally associated with a practice popularized by Jacques Derrida and the bane of typesetters and proof readers, of leaving deleted words 'under erasure' (*sous rature*) in his writings – that is, of leaving them crossed out but not removed. By so doing Derrida enjoys a certain simultaneous having and eating of his cake: he makes use of words and terms which he feels to be inadequate but for which he finds no viable alternatives. Derrida apparently adopted the practice after noting Martin Heidegger's use of it. The erasure marks thus act in a manner similar to what are known colloquially as scare quotes; that is, quotation marks placed round a word with the similar intention of drawing attention to their inadequacy or questionable validity.

See also the entry for ARCHE-WRITING.

The term is sometimes given a more general meaning in discussion of MODERNIST and POSTMODERNIST techniques whereby achieved verisimilitude or REALISM is subsequently denied. Thus an erased character would be a character who the reader accepted as 'real' according to realist CONVENTIONS, but who was shown later to be not-real in some sense, either within the achieved world of the fiction or by a transference of the character from this world to the extra-fictional world of the text. (See the discussion in McHale 1987, 64–6.)

Erlebte Rede See FREE INDIRECT DISCOURSE

Essentialism The belief that qualities are inherent in objects of study, and that therefore the contexts in which these exist or are studied are irrelevant. Essentialism is therefore to be distinguished from dialectical, contextual or relational theories and approaches. The term often carries with it the implication that the qualities of objects of study are self-evident and do not themselves need to be sought for or explained (see Cameron 1985, 187).

Event According to Mieke Bal an event is 'the transition from one state to another state' in a NARRATIVE (1985, 5).

Steven Cohan and Linda M. Shires distinguish between *kernel* and *satellite* events: the former 'advance or outline a sequence of transformations' while the latter 'amplify or fill in the outline of a sequence by maintaining, retarding, or prolonging the kernel events they accompany or surround' (1988, 54). They further argue that events are *enchained* when they are found in back-to-back succession with each other, whereas it is, alternatively, possible for one event to be *embedded* in another (1988, 57). Finally, they point out that an event can be *singular*, *repeated*, or *iterative* (1988, 86).

Roland Barthes (1975) makes a similar distinction between *catalyses* and *nuclei*: the former denotes events that are not logically essential to the narrative, and the latter those that are.

Compare *kernel function* in the entry for FUNCTION, and see also the entry for FREQUENCY.

Exegesis Stemming from a tradition of Biblical study, exegesis traditionally involved a range of activities from the elucidation of textual cruces and difficulties through commentary on the implications and applications of textual meanings. The Roman exegetes had as official function the interpretation of such things as dreams, laws, omens and the pronouncements of the Oracle, so that in some usages exegesis is more or less interchangeable with interpretation.

In current usage, however, the term is normally reserved for more careful commentary or *close reading* which stays near to the words on the page.

Tzvetan Todorov distinguishes between *literal exegesis*, which seeks to elucidate the meanings or words, supply references to allusions, and so on; and *allegorical exegesis*, which seeks a further meaning for a TEXT or part of a text which already has one (1984, xxii).

Exotopy The word suggested in the English translation of Tzvetan Todorov's *Mikhail Bakhtin: The Dialogical Principle* (1984) to represent a coinage of Bakhtin's which describes an AUTHOR's movement outside of and away from his or her character subsequent to an earlier, initial stage of identification and empathizing with the character.

Both movements are important to Bakhtin: the novelist must understand his or her character from within, as it were, but in order to understand the character fully it must be perceived as OTHER, as apart from its creator and in its distinct *alterity*. Moreover, DIALOGUE is only possible with an 'other': one can only talk to oneself if one estranges oneself from part of oneself and treats this part as other.

Expressive; expressives See FUNCTIONS OF LANGUAGE; SPEECH ACT THEORY

Extent See ANALEPSIS

Exteriority In Michel Foucault's usage, rejecting the procedure whereby the investigator proceeds from DISCOURSE to its 'interior, hidden nucleus, towards the heart of a thought or a signification supposed to be manifested in it', and instead, adopting the alternative procedure whereby the investigator proceeds on the basis of discourse itself, 'its appearance and its regularity, [and moves] towards its external conditions of possibility, towards what gives rise to the aleatory series of these events, and fixes its limits' (1981, 67).

This recommendation ties in with a number of movements in recent theory which reject the search for a hidden, inner, CENTRE or PRESENCE and instead seek to explain the object of study in terms of the possibilities engendered by its existence in a complex of shifting relations. In literary criticism an analogous movement would be represented by the rejection of ESSENTIALIST views of the literary TEXT in favour of a study of the literary text's 'conditions of possibility' in different READING or INTERPRET[AT]IVE COMMUNITIES.

Extradiegetic See DIEGESIS AND MIMESIS

F

Fabula See STORY AND PLOT

Fabulation See MODERNISM AND POSTMODERNISM

Fantastic An early concern with the fantastic can be found in the work of the Russian Formalists. In his essay 'Thematics', for example, Boris Tomashevsky quotes an interesting passage from Vladimir Solovyev's introduction to Alexey Tolstoy's novel *The Vampire*, which Tomashevsky describes as 'an unusually clear example of fantasy'. According to Solovyev, the distinguishing characteristic of the genuinely fantastic is that

> it is never, so to speak, in full view. Its presence must never compel belief in a mystic interpretation of a vital event; it must rather point, or *hint*, at it. In the really fantastic, the external, formal possibility of a simple explanation of ordinary and commonplace connections among the phenomena always remains. This external explanation, however, finally loses its internal probability. (Tomashevsky 1965, 83–4)

Does the fantastic constitutes an independent genre, and, if so, what are its defining characteristics? Perhaps the most influential contribution to the view that the fantastic constitutes such an independent genre is Tzvetan Todorov's *The Fantastic: A Structural Approach to a Literary Genre* (1973). Christine Brooke-Rose has made a useful summary of the three conditions which Todorov believes to be more or less standard components of the 'pure' fantastic. The READER must hesitate between natural and supernatural explanations of what happens in the WORK up to its conclusion; this hesitation may be represented – that is, it may be shared by a leading character in the work (this, according to Todorov, is normal but not essential); and the reader must reject both a poetic and an allegorical reading of the work, as both of these destroy the hesitation which is fundamental to the pure fantastic (Brooke-Rose 1981, 63). If there is no hesitation, then either we are in the realm of some variant of the *uncanny* (the events are seen by the reader to have a natural explanation), or of the *marvellous* (the events are seen by the reader to have a supernatural explanation).

Brooke-Rose points out that Todorov's rather demanding conditions leave us with very few examples of the pure fantastic – that is, works in which a hesitation between natural and supernatural explanations lasts until the very end of the STORY. She suggests that the pure fantastic is 'not so much an evanescent *genre* as an evanescent *element*' (1981, 63).

Kathryn Hume, in her *Fantasy and Mimesis* (1984), provides an extended discussion of the problems of defining the fantastic, and in her summary of attempted definitions she categorizes these as either one-, two-, three-, four-, or five-element definitions. The elements involved range from the choice of subject matter, the changing of 'ground-rules' as with Alice's discovery of the new rules governing Wonderland (Erik Rabkin), the 'persuasive establishment and development of an impossibility' (W. R. Irwin), satisfying readers' desire for recovery, escape, consolation (J. R. R. Tolkien), and tracing 'the unsaid and the unseen of culture: that which has been silenced, made invisible' in a way that is fundamentally subversive (Rosemary Jackson) (Hume 1984, 13–17).

Some commentators make an overt or implied distinction between *fantasy* and *the fantastic*. Thus, for example, Anne Cranny-Francis uses *fantasy* as an umbrella-term containing three different sub-types: 'other-world fantasy', 'fairy-tale', and 'horror' (1990, 77). It is clear that in this usage fantasy is different from (if related to) the fantastic.

Felicity conditions See SPEECH ACT THEORY

Female See FEMINISM

Femininity See FEMINISM

Feminism Toril Moi makes a useful distinction between three cognate terms which provides a good starting point: *feminism* is a political position, *femaleness* a matter of biology, and *femininity* a set of CULTURALLY defined characteristics (Moi 1986, 204). It should be recognized, of course, that Moi's suggested definitions here have a political edge: she is as much arguing for how these terms *should* be used as describing an actual, existing usage. Phrases such as 'the eternal feminine' make it clear that non-feminist usages can define femininity in universal, biological rather than cultural terms – nor is it that uncommon to find 'female' used to refer to culturally acquired characteristics. (The OED definitions of femininity make interesting reading in this context.)

However good a starting point this is, it is not unproblematic – not least because Elaine Showalter, in her *A Literature of Their Own*, suggests a different way of using these three terms in the narrower field of women's writing. For Showalter, the feminine stage of women's writing involves a prolonged phase of imitating the prevailing modes of the dominant tradition and internalizing its standards of art; the feminist stage involves the advocacy of minority rights and values; and the female stage is the phase of self-discovery and search for identity (1982, 13).

Of the three terms, feminism is probably the most complex. The OED describes the word as 'rare', and defines it as 'the qualities of females', giving an example from 1851. But from the end of the nineteenth century the word comes increasingly to be applied to those committed to and struggling for equal rights for women – including men: in Joseph Conrad's *Under Western Eyes* (first book publication 1911), for example, the character Peter Ivanovitch is repeatedly referred to as a feminist. Moreover, not all those women fighting for women's rights accepted the term. In Virginia Woolf's *Three Guineas*, first published in 1938, Woolf writes

> What more fitting than to destroy an old word, a vicious and corrupt word that has done much harm in its day and is now obsolete? The word 'feminist' is the word indicated. That word, according to the dictionary, means 'one who champions the rights of women'. Since the only right, the right to earn a living, has been won, the word no longer has a meaning. (1977, 117)

Woolf goes on to describe a symbolic burning of the 'dead' and 'corrupt' word, and declares that, once this has been done the air is cleared, and that we can see men and women working together for the same cause. Woolf argues, too, that the word *feminist* was one which was applied to those fighting 'the tyranny of the patriarchal state', 'to their great resentment' (1977, 118) – in other words, that the word was imposed on rather than chosen by women fighting for the rights of women.

Woolf's argument has not been successful in burying the word in question, however, and to a very large extent women (and men) fighting for women's rights have been happy to call themselves, and be called, feminists. But doubts about the term have remained. In an interview published in *The Guardian*, 18 May 1987, Margaret Atwood responds as follows when her interviewer suggests that in her book *Bluebeard's Egg* she seems mellower about men than in her other books.

> 'It depends how you count. (I was in market research,' she adds, very deadpan.) 'If we all vote if women have souls, I vote on that side, if it's kill all the men, I'm not for it. I don't know what feminism means.' (Nadelson 1987, 10)

The importance of such doubts should not be exaggerated. In general usage the term feminism is usually treated as an umbrella term to describe those (normally women but sometimes also men) who disagree with Virginia Woolf that there are no more rights to be achieved for women, and who think that it is necessary to struggle against the oppression of women on a number of different planes: social, economic, and ideological.

Feminism as socio-political movement experienced a resurgence in the late 1960s and early 1970s, especially in Western Europe and the United States, one which is still continuing, which has established a number of seemingly permanent changes in the developed countries and which has not been without an effect in the developing world. Since that time feminism has become more and more of an international movement, with increasing contacts between activists and sympathizers in different parts of the world. From the start of this movement, the rôle of literature was considerable. This is partly because literary writing was less closed to women than most of the other arts, and other forms of writing, but also because the literature of the past written (especially) by women offered itself as a record and analysis of the past oppression of women.

It should also be remembered that the modern resurgence of feminism had its most important source in the universities and colleges of the developed world, amongst a group of widely read women.

Radical feminism is a term still current but perhaps more in use in the 1960s and 1970s. It is in its insistence upon the fundamental and all-embracing significance of gender differentiation that radical feminism's radicalness is normally taken to consist – along with (often but not always) a rejection of most or all forms of collaboration with men or with organizations containing men. Radical feminism is often (but again, not always) associated with a commitment to Lesbianism, and if it is possible for a man to be a feminist it seems impossible (or at the very least extremely difficult) for one to be a radical feminist. Radical feminism tends to be universalizing rather than to focus upon the socially, culturally, and historically specific characteristics of PATRIARCHY, although to this it needs to be added that radical feminists have led important campaigns against specific forms of oppression. Of perhaps most specific interest to students of literature has been their analysis of patriarchal and sexist elements in language. Representative radical feminists are Adrienne Rich, Mary Daley and Shulamith Firestone.

Fiction Literary critics have traditionally used the term *fiction* to denote imaginative writing (normally NARRATIVE) which occupies a category distinct both from writing which purports to be true and also from forms of deceit and lying. The fact that certain early works now defined as novels were passed off on their initial readers as historical and true accounts complicates but does not invalidate this usage.

In recent years the word has been yoked into more extended applications by literary and CULTURAL critics. One of the first to comment upon this extension was Gerald Graff, who entitled chapter 6 of his *Literature Against Itself* (1979) 'How not to Talk about Fictions'. Graff summarized the extension of meaning given to the term as follows: not just the action and PLOT of literary works, but the ideas, beliefs and themes embodied in the action or plot and the 'message' or 'world view' conveyed in their presentation were often now described as fiction by those critics whose position Graff was concerned to attack (generally speaking STRUCTURALIST and POST-STRUCTURALIST and new left sympathizers). Nor was this the end of the matter, Graff added:

> Going a step farther, critics now sometimes suggest, by a kind of tautology, that literary meanings are fictions because *all* meanings are fictions, even those of nonliterary language, including the language of criticism. In its most extreme flights, this critical view asserts that 'life' and 'reality' are themselves fictions. (1979, 151).

Graff further suggests that Jonathan Culler's use of the term MYTH is very close to the (mis)use of the term fiction with which he is concerned (1979, 153).

Fictograph Also *fictogram*. A term coined by the Nigerian writer Wole Soyinka to describe a false picture of (in this case African) society which has been culled from a (mis-)reading of works of fiction. Soyinka argues that 'certain European critics proceed from the abyss of ignorance on which they must erect a platform', and that these construct a BRICOLAGE which has the fictogram as its basic unit. As example he cites the critic Gerald Moore,

> late developer currently knocking at the portals of the Nigerian leftocracy . . . [who] takes one look at the following lines –

> > I watch my dreams float vaguely through the streets, lie at the bulls' feet. Like the guides of my race on the banks of Gambia or Saloum.

> – and, from them, constructs this 'fictograph' of an African world-view: 'Senghor, in any case, has expressed unforgettably *the classical view* of the dead as the principal force *controlling* the living, benevolent and watchful.' (Soyinka 1984, 45, Soyinka's emphases)

Figural See NARRATIVE SITUATION

Figure According to Gérard Genette, there is a gap between what the poet has written and what he has thought. Like all gaps, Genette continues, this gap has a form, and the form is called a figure (1982, 47). Genette thus relates the term to some of the traditional concerns of rhetoric; indeed, he rejects the term *figure of thought* on the ground that a figure pertains not to *thought* but to *expression* (1982, 54; compare the more idiomatic English expression *figure of speech*).

See also ABSENCE; FIGURE AND GROUND.

Figure and ground Experiments have confirmed that the process of visual perception typically involves a sorting of the information received by the brain from the eye into two categories, which psychologists name figure and ground. This process of sorting prevents the brain from being swamped by too much information, and allows for concentration upon certain aspects of incoming messages at the expense of other aspects.

R. L. Gregory has cited the Dane, Edgar Rubin, as the psychologist whose name is associated with the first experiments involved with figure-ground reversal. In 1915 Rubin published a study, *Synoplevende Figurer*, describing his use of line drawings which were ambiguous and could be perceived in two ways: the best-known example of these (much pirated for book jackets!) is that of the picture which can be seen either as an elegant urn or vase, or as two human faces turned towards each other. Gregory points out that such trick pictures tell us something about the active nature of perception and of the principles on which the brain sorts out incoming information (1970, 15–18). What is achieved by Rubin's pictures, or a conjuror's sleight-of-hand, is a disturbing of the perceptual process either in the interests of illustrating some of the principles which govern it, or of trickery.

According to Irvin Rock (1983), the essence of the figure-ground concept

> is not, contrary to popular opinion, that one or another region stands out from the background (although that is true) but that the contour dividing two regions ends up *belonging to* the region that becomes figure. It therefore gives that region rather than the other a specific shape. (1983, 65)

Both Rubin and Rock are concerned with the processes of visual perception, but many recent commentators on the Russian Formalist concepts of FORE-GROUNDING and DEFAMILIARIZATION (which have, potentially, a much wider application) have associated both with figure-ground separation; just as we pay only passing attention to what we perceive as 'ground', reserving our attention and concern for what we single out as 'figure', so too there are things – concepts, ideas, attitudes as much as objects – which we perceive as STEREO-TYPES in a 'familiarized' manner. And just as Rubin's diagrams upset the fixed categories with which the brain sorts information received from the eye, so literary defamiliarization upsets other fixed categories which allow us to skip over certain information without scrutinizing it at length or in detail. Many MODERNIST and POSTMODERNIST writers have attempted to disturb READERS' familiar responses in comparable ways: breaking those artistic rules and CONVENTIONS which are dominant at any given period.

One of the reasons why some literary WORKS give new READING experiences time and time again may well be that we make different figure-ground distinctions on successive readings. Experimental psychologists have demonstrated that although there may be some innate predispositions in the making of figure-ground distinctions, personal and CULTURAL experience, motivation, and varying needs are also powerful factors. Thus as a reader's background and experience alter, his or her figure-ground distinctions will also change.

See also FRAME.

First-person See NARRATIVE SITUATION

Flashback See ANALEPSIS

Flashforward See PROLEPSIS

Flicker The effect achieved by a certain sort of ambiguity, in which rather than having two clear alternatives between which to choose, the READER is disturbed by flashes of alternative meanings. The term is Brian McHale's, and he relates it to Roman Ingarden's concept of *iridescence* or *opalescence*, found where two alternative worlds are struggling for supremacy in a TEXT but neither is capable of achieving it (1987, 32).

Focalization See PERSPECTIVE AND VOICE

Folk See POPULAR

Foregrounding See DEFAMILIARIZATION

Foreshadowing See PROLEPSIS

Formulaic literature A concern with the formulaic element in art and literature during the present century is closely connected with investigations into POPULAR and folk art, but has spread beyond the boundaries of such investigations. A key figure here is that of the Russian Vladimir Propp, whose *Morphology of the Russian Folktale* was first published in Russian in 1928. Propp based his work on the study of a corpus of nearly two-hundred Russian folk tales, and attempted to abstract common elements from these, elements which he named FUNCTIONS. Propp's work was ground-breaking, but it focused attention on to what is rather an obvious point, that folk tales rely very heavily on elements that recur from tale to tale – formulae.

It seems that *oral* performance typically involves a heavy reliance upon the formulaic, and that the advent of writing leads to a lessening of the verbal artist's reliance upon formulaic elements. Just as those who must frequently speak in public without notes in our own time tend to rely upon formulaic expressions (think of politicians and the tellers of jokes), so too the oral poet or story-teller needed formulae to act as props to the memory, while his or her listeners also found them useful as they injected familiar elements into that which could not be read a second time and thus made it easier to assimilate. This does not mean to say that formulaic elements have no aesthetic significance; as Max Lüthli puts it

> The esthetics of production and the esthetics of reception are parallel, just as mnemetic technique, the basis of oral narration in general, and esthetic effect are connected to one another. . . . Formulas are memory props and transition aids for the narrator. They are useful to him and comfortable, but they are additionally agreeable to him – just as the hearer is also delighted – when they turn up time and again, because he feels the organizing effect they have, and also simply because they are familiar to him. (1984, 44)

Moreover, in a situation in which an audience is very familiar with a range of formulae, the slightest variations in these will be perceived by the audience. This provides the opportunity for very subtle aesthetic effects based on such variation.

The research led by Propp and others into material which was unambiguously either oral in nature or closely related to oral material led, however, to an interest in formulaic elements in non-oral productions. The classic film Western, popular romantic fiction, and television soap operas certainly appeared to rely more heavily upon formulaic elements than did CANONICAL literature. Put crudely, we know what will happen on the last pages of a Barbara Cartland novel before we have started it, but even three-quarters of the way through *Wuthering Heights* on a first reading we will be in doubt as to its final conclusion.

John Cawelti has defined a formula as a 'combination or synthesis of a number of specific cultural conventions with a more universal story form or archetype' (1977, 181; quoted in Yanarella & Sigelman 1988, 7). Cawelti finds a particular CULTURAL significance in such formulae because through many repetitions they become the conventional way in which particular images, symbols, MYTHS and themes are represented, and from which inferences concerning collective fantasies can be hazarded. This perhaps suggests that formulaic elements involve an ideological element through an association with the STEREOTYPE: the reader or TV viewer faced with a familiar formula is released from the need to confront a problem but merely swallows a preformed 'truth' without examining it. This seems to be true of certain formulaic elements in popular literature, but Max Lüthli argues, interestingly, that the formula's lack of individualization and concretization – what he calls its 'quasi-abstract generality' – actually leaves the reader's imagination more free to plump out the bare-bones of the formula as he or she wishes (1984, 21). (Compare Umberto Eco's argument in the entry for OPEN AND CLOSED TEXTS.) This leads to the unusual idea that formulaic literature and art may actually allow for greater rather than lesser reader creativity. The negative side of such freedom, however, may be that the work offers fewer aesthetically productive constraints to the reader's fantasizing..

Frame 1. According to Mieke Bal, 'the space in which the character is situated, or is precisely not situated, is regarded as the *frame*' (1985, 94).

2. In her book *Reading Frames in Modern Fiction* (1985) Mary Ann Caws applies the term *frame* to the phenomenon whereby many READERS find that certain passages in works of prose fiction 'stand out' from their surroundings. These passages are as it were *framed* by the surrounding TEXT, and this framing has important effects upon the manner in which they – and the WORK as a whole – are read. Caws suggests that such framing assumes an especial form in modernist fiction as the idea of framing is called attention to or, we might say, FOREGROUNDED (1985, xi).

3. Following Erving Goffman's *Frame Analysis* (1974) the term is also used to denote various ways in which works of art (among other things) are aesthetically bounded and, thus, require or invite a range of different possible relationships with the art-consumer, with other works of art, or generally with extra-artistic reality.

A framed (or nested) NARRATIVE is a narrative containing within itself at least one other narrative, such as Henry James's *The Turn of the Screw*. With reference to such a work the term *frame narrator* refers to the NARRATOR of the outer narrative (alternatively, the term *outer narrator* is often used). Inner, or framed narratives are also known as *embedded narratives* or *Chinese Box narratives*.

4. Umberto Eco adopts definitions from Eugene Charniak and Michael Riffaterre in order to suggest a distinction between common frames – which are the rules for practical life possessed by ordinary individuals – and INTER-TEXTUAL frames, which are existing literary *topoi* or narrative schemes (1981, 21). (The Greek *topoi* means 'a commonplace'.)

In P. N. Furbank's *Reflections on the Word 'Image'* there is an interesting discussion of what Furbank sees as the peculiarly modern tendency of 'abolishing the frame', a tendency he relates to a revolt against the idea of standards of reference and to an egalitarian desire to oppose the isolation of art in separated-off compartments (1970, 128–9).

5. In his *Framing the Sign*, Jonathan Culler explains why he prefers the term *frame* to the more conventional *context*. Most important, perhaps, is the argument that whereas the assumption is that a context is given, he avers that the truth is that 'context is not given but produced', and that

> The expression *framing the sign* has several advantages over *context*: it reminds us that framing is something we do; it hints of the frame-up . . ., a major use of context; and it eludes the incipient positivism of 'context' by alluding to the semiotic function of framing in art, where the frame is determining, setting off the object or event as art, and yet the frame itself may be nothing tangible, pure articulation. (1988, ix)

In his introductory comments to an essay by Barbara Johnson, Robert Young discusses briefly Jacques Derrida's use of the terms *parergon* (a term Derrida finds in Kant) and *ergon* as substitutes for *frame* and *work*:

> In the visual arts, the parergon will be the frame, or drapery, or enclosing column. The parergon could also be a (critical) text, which 'encloses' another text. (1981, 226)

He goes on, however, to note that Derrida's terms are connected with a more complex relationship than that of a simple inside/outside dichotomy, a complexity (we may add) which relates to Derrida's interest in the paradoxical nature of MARGINALITY.

According to Brian McHale, *frame-breaking* is characteristic of much POST-MODERNIST fiction: as, for instance, the statement of the narrator of John Fowles's *The French Lieutenant's Woman* that 'This story I am telling is all imagination. These characters I create never existed outside my own mind' (McHale 1987, 197).

See also FIGURE AND GROUND.

Free Indirect Discourse. Also *Free Indirect Speech* or *Style*; *Narrated Monologue*; *Erlebte Rede*; *Style Indirecte Libre*; *Quasi-Direct Discourse* or

Substitutionary Narration. In some usages these all represent the same general NARRATIVE technique, subdivisions within which are indicated by distinguishing between *Narrated Speech* and *Narrated Thought*, or between *Free Indirect Speech* and *Free Indirect Thought* (thus making the former phrase slightly ambiguous as it can either represent the umbrella term or a subdivision within it).

Usages do vary, however, and some commentators use *narrated monologue* to refer to a variety of Free Indirect Discourse in which there is indirect quotation of the words used in a character's speech or thought. This would mean that non-verbalized thought-processes could not be represented by means of narrated monologue, and thus another term is called for: *psycho-narration*. According to Steven Cohan and Linda M. Shires, psycho-narration can be either *consonant* (following a character's own self-apprehension), or *dissonant* (moving back from a character's own perspective) (1988, 100).

The traditional way of defining what we can refer to as FID makes use of grammatical or linguistic evidence. This involves seeing FID as a midway point between Direct, and Indirect (or Reported) Discourse (DD and ID), or as a combination of the two which blends their grammatical characteristics in a distinctive mix. Thus Shlomith Rimmon-Kenan provides the following example, in which one can note that the third example retains the third person 'he' and past tense from ID, but in its truncation resembles the words in inverted commas in the DD example.

DD: He said, 'I love her'
ID: He said that he loved her
FID: He loved her (1983, 111)

FID often resembles ID minus the normal accompanying tag phrases (e.g. 'he suggested', 'she thought'). The standard grammatical/linguistic signs of FID are taken to be such things as DEICTICS referring to the character's own time or place (e.g. 'Tomorrow was Christmas'), the use of colloquialisms etc. unlikely to have been used by the NARRATOR, abridgement such as is found in spoken but not, normally, written language, and the back-shift of tenses to be found in ID. When many of these characteristics are found together then a passage can be unambiguously FID, but FID may appear without any linguistic markers, such that only the semantic content of the passage in question can be adduced as evidence that one is dealing with FID.

Dorrit Cohn suggests that FID 'may be most succinctly defined as the technique for rendering a character's thought in their own idiom while maintaining the third-person reference and the basic tense of narration' (1978, 100). As already suggested, however, it is not just thought that can be represented, but also speech and, furthermore, attitudes, ideological presuppositions, and so on. And the speech and thought can be either particular acts or ITERATIVE examples, or even thoughts that are potential in a character but unactualized. And, moreover, the thought may be either verbalized or unverbalized.

A matter of some contention has been that of the 'dual voice' hypothesis, with Pascal (1977) and Banfield (1982) taking up positions for and against the suggestion that FID involves the combination of two VOICES, those of the narrator and the character.

The general advantage gained from a use of FID is probably that of an apparently dramatic and intimately direct access to a character's thoughts or speech without the distracting presence of a narrator signalled by tag-phrases such as 'he thought' or 'she said'. By mixing FID, DD and ID an AUTHOR can achieve very considerable narrative flexibility.

A related term noted by Wales (1989, 77), who attributes it to Graham Hough, is *coloured narrative*. In this case, as Wales points out, the narrative is seen to be 'coloured' by the speech of a character, whereas in FID it is the speech which is coloured by the narrative voice.

Free Indirect Speech/Thought See FREE INDIRECT DISCOURSE

Frequency Following Genette, the numerical relationship between events in a PLOT (or SJUŽET) and events in a STORY (or FABULA). This relationship can vary as follows:

i   a singular event which is narrated once (*singulative narration*)

ii   an event which occurs x times and is narrated x times (*multiple narration*)

iii an event which occurs once but is narrated more than once (*repetitive narration*)

iv a repeated event which is narrated only once (*iterative narration*)

A writer or NARRATOR's skill in varying frequency can play a crucial rôle in telling a STORY: stories which consist only of examples i and ii above can give a mechanical and unvarying impression, whereas the skilled use of REPETITION – especially forms of repetition with significant variation – can contribute to the achieving of an impression of depth and multiple PERSPECTIVE. Some writers (Genette draws particular attention to Proust) have made effective use of iterative narration to suggest underlying consistencies and patterns in a character or situation.

It will be noted that examples ii, iii and iv are all forms of repetition, although only iii is a form of *narrative* repetition. Repetition is probably one of the most common and most effective ways of building up patterns of meaning in a NARRATIVE.

Movement from frequencies i or ii to frequencies iii or iv in a narrative can be one of the means whereby an AUTHOR manipulates such things as DISTANCE, perspective, and dramatic involvement.

Genette uses the term *pseudo-iterative* to describe passages of narrative which claim to be iterative but which provide extended detail or include elements which by their very nature must be unique.

Function Probably the usage which has most relevance for Literary Studies is that to be found in Vladimir Propp's *Morphology of the Folktale*. Here Propp defines a narrative function as 'an act of a character, defined from the point of view of its significance for the course of the action' (1968, 21). Propp argued that although folk tales contain an extremely large number of different characters, they contain a relatively small number of functions, functions which constitute the 'fundamental components' of the folk tale (1968, 21).

Propp's approach is STRUCTURALIST to the extent that it assumes a grammar of the folk tale such that functions play a rôle in an individual folk tale analogous to that played by parts of speech in a well-formed sentence. Thus just as the same word can perform different grammatical functions in different sentences (compare 'I set the table' with 'You win the first set'), so too can the same act perform a different narrative function in different folk tales (the appearance of a dragon could represent struggle in one tale, pursuit in another).

We find a similar distinction in the work of the Russian Formalists between *function* and *device*. Of the two terms, device is the more neutral, and has a general reference independent of the context of a single TEXT. Thus Viktor Shlovsky writes of the device of eavesdropping in Dickens, which performs different functions in his works (Šklovskij 1971, 221). The distinction is perhaps clarified by reference to another term used by the Russian Formalists – that of *motivation*. According to Y. Tynyanov, 'Motivation in art is the justification of some single factor vis-à-vis all the others . . . Each factor is motivated by means of its connections with the remaining factors' (Tynjanov 1971, 130). This resembles Barthes's comments, referred to below, on the *chaining* of sequences of actions to form functions. For the Russian Formalists, device and function were both involved in the concept of DEFAMILIARIZATION: a device could perform the function of defamiliarization at one time, but as it became familiar to readers it could lose this ability.

Propp limited the number of functions to 31, and argued that these appear in the individual folk tale in a sequence which is fixed and invariable – although, of course, not all functions appear in every tale. As with the governing of the choice and order of words in a sentence, the choice of alternative functions in a given STORY was seen to be governed by SYNTAGMATIC and PARADIGMATIC rules. However, arguments about just how many functions there were, about the rules governing their selection and use, and about which function(s) particular acts represent, soon began to suggest that even the relatively simple narratives with which Propp was concerned might resist the systematized analysis that he brought to bear on them. In general Propp's work has been more fruitful for the study of FORMULAIC LITERATURE than for more CANONICAL works, although it is clear that even in the canonical works of high literary CULTURES structural analysis on the basis of functions may have *some* validity.

In Claude Bremond's (1966, 1973) development and modification of Propp's work, functions group together in threes to form sequences within which they punctuate three logical stages: possibility, process, outcome. For Bremond, each function opens a potentiality which can be ACTUALIZED or NON-ACTUALIZED.

In the work of Roland Barthes we find a further variation in the use of this term. In his 'Introduction to the Structural Analysis of Language'(1975),

Barthes argues that a narrative can be seen as a large sentence and a sentence as, in some sense, a small narrative. He proceeds to isolate basic narrative units, and distinguishes between the *function* and the *index*. If the narrative units can be chained in sequences of actions they are termed functions, while if they perform a less structured rôle in the story they are termed indices. Jonathan Culler has suggested that Barthes's use of the term *function* in this essay is not a happy one, and that Barthes would have done better to have stuck to the term *lexie* (in the English translation: *lexia*) used in *S/Z* (Culler 1975, 202). In *S/Z* a lexia is a minimal unit of reading, a passage which has an isolable effect on the reader which can be distinguished from the effect of other passages (Barthes 1990, 13–14).

Gérard Genette uses the word in a different sense when he argues that 'there is no literary object strictly speaking, but only a *literary function*, which can invest or abandon any object of writing in turn' (1982, 4). Genette here uses *function* as equivalent to 'system-determined set of rules' in a STRUC-TURALIST sense. Thus if one played chess with stones, one would be (according to this view) investing the stones with the chess function, a function which would subsequently abandon them if they were thrown away after the game.

A *kernel* function or type, according to some recent theorists of narrative, is one of the basic or essential components of a PLOT – or alternatively an element in a story that advances the action. (Compare HINGE, and see also *kernel event* in the entry for EVENT.)

See also FUNCTIONS OF LANGUAGE.

Functions of language In 1934, in his book *Language Theory*, Karl Bühler suggested an elegant way of classifying the different semantic functions performed by the linguistic SIGN. For him, it was illuminating to distinguish between the linguistic sign's *symbolic* function, which arose from its relation to things and states of affairs, its *symptomatic* function, which arose from its dependence upon its sender, whose inner states it expressed, and its *signalling* function, which rested upon its appeal to the listener, whose external or internal attitudes it directed much like a traffic sign. As Anders Pettersson (who refers to Bühler's distinctions) points out, Roman Jakobson's classification of the fun-ctions of language is 'a well-known further elaboration of Bühler's' (1990, 73).

Jakobson's rather more influential account is to be found in his essay 'Linguistics and Poetics', in which he claims that before the 'poetic function' is discussed, its place amongst the other functions of language must be defined. To do this, he argues, the constitutive factors in any act of verbal communica-tion must first be surveyed. In a much-quoted passage he proceeds to do just this.

> The *addresser* sends a *message* to the *addressee*. To be operative the message requires a *context* referred to ('referent' in another, somewhat ambiguous, nomenclature), seizable by the addressee, and either verbal or capable of being verbalized; a *code* fully, or at least partially, common to the addresser and

addressee . . .; and, finally a *contact*, a physical channel and psychological connection between the addresser and the addressee, enabling both of them to enter and stay in communication.

(1960, 353; small capitals in original replaced by italics)

Jakobson then moves to claim that each of these six factors determines a different function of language. An orientation towards the context involves the *referential function*, which he sees as the leading task of numerous messages. The *emotive or expressive function* is focused upon the addresser, and an example of the emotive function in a rare, pure form would be interjections such as 'Tut! tut!'. The *conative function* involves an orientation towards the addressee, typically in the vocative or imperative modes, and this function is distinguished by the fact that it is not liable to a truth test. The *phatic function* includes messages designed purely to 'keep the line open', to maintain communicative contact without actually communicating any information other than that needed to remain in such contact. The *metalingual function* involves checking that the same CODE is being used, where, for example, we ask a conversational partner to explain what he or she means by a particular word. Finally, a focusing on the message itself for its own sake, leads us to the *poetic function* of language.

Robert Scholes has explicitly adapted the diagrammatic rendering of Jakobson's functions to describe the reading of a literary text, as follows.

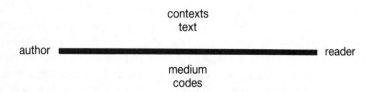

Jakobson's analysis has been influential but it has not escaped criticism. Referring to the passage quoted above R. A. Sharpe makes the acid comment that banality does not preclude falsehood, and he goes on to argue that Jakobson's ignoring of the rôle played by interpretation in the literary arts is fundamental to what is wrong with his terminology (1984, 15). It is clear that to define the poetic use of language as a focusing upon the message itself, for its own sake, rather than on any of the other 'constitutive factors' he lists, takes us near to some very familiar formalist arguments – that the literary work refers only to itself and neither comments upon the world nor communicates between human beings. It would seem to be the case that much literature encourages the READER to scrutinize the language it uses; much turns the reader's attention to specific issues in human history and perennial problems of human conduct; much directs the reader's attention to the writer of the work; and, finally, much leads the reader to think of him or herself. Literature, in other words, seems to straddle all of Jakobson's functions apart from, perhaps, the phatic.

See also the entry for the SHANNON & WEAVER MODEL OF COMMUNI-CATION, in which it is suggested that renderings of Jakobson's argument in diagrammatic form are much influenced by the Shannon and Weaver model.

G

Gap See ABSENCE; ELLIPSIS; FIGURE; PHENOMENOLOGY

Gatekeeping The concept of gatekeeping comes from MEDIA STUDIES and, more particularly, studies of the attitude-forming effects of the news media. Just as a literal gatekeeper will prevent you getting through the door to talk to an important person, metaphorical gatekeepers prevent certain news items, or opinions, or interpretations from reaching a larger public. As with the agenda-setter, the gatekeeper has power that is not only wide-ranging but is also largely invisible, and there is a disproportion between the gatekeeper's overt and covert authority.

A splendid literary example of this is the figure of ex-Pfc Wintergreen in Joseph Heller's satirical novel *Catch-22*, who has been demoted so many times that he is not even a private any longer, but who, because he is the radio operator, can decide which messages are sent and which are not. It can be argued that the formation and defence of a CANON can have a gatekeeping function, and that gatekeepers work with certain ideological presuppositions that help them to carry out their function – as much in university departments of literature as on TV news desks.

Gender In current FEMINIST usage, gender is defined as characteristics of socio-cultural origin which are attributed to the different biological sexes. Within Linguistics this usage is sometimes varied in order to avoid confusion with linguistic gender, but generally speaking feminist influence has succeeded in establishing that *gender* involves society and or culture and *sex* involves biology.

A *genderlect* is a term used to describe linguistic characteristics which in a given society or CULTURE are specific to women.

See also IDIOLECT; SOCIOLECT.

Genderlect See GENDER

Geneva School See PHENOMENOLOGY

Glissade See SLIPPAGE

Gram See DIFFÉRANCE

Grammatology In *Of Grammatology* Jacques Derrida attributes this term to Littré, from whom he quotes: 'A treatise upon Letters, upon the alphabet, syllabation, reading, and writing.' Derrida notes that to his knowledge the word has been used in the present century only by I. J. Gelb in *A Study of Writing: The Foundations of Grammatology* (1952), which book, Derrida claims, 'follows the classical model of histories of writing' (Derrida 1976, 323 n. 4). Derrida uses the word to indicate a 'science of writing' that is, he believes, showing signs of liberation all over the world (1976, 4). This should not, however, be understood in terms of a full-formed science the basic principles of which are established and final, but – he implies – a science in which everything is questioned, including its own basis and history (1976, 28). For Derrida's use of the word *writing* see the entry for ÉCRITURE.

In 'Linguistics and Grammatology' Derrida suggests that the word grammatology should replace the word semiology in the programme set out in Ferdinand de Saussure's *Course in General Linguistics*, as this will give the theory of writing the scope needed to counter LOGOCENTRIC repression and the subordination to linguistics.

Ground See FIGURE AND GROUND

Gyandry See ANDROGYNY

Gynecocratic See GYNOCRATIC

Gynocentric See ANDROCENTRIC

Gynocratic/gynecocratic That which is ruled by women. Thus a gynocratic society would be one in which women held power, in contrast to an ANDRO-CRATIC society, in which power would be – and has been – in the hands of men.

Gynocritics According to Elaine Showalter the term gynocritics is an invention of hers to describe that FEMINIST criticism which studies women *as writers*, 'and its subjects are the history, styles, themes, genres, and structures of writing by women; the psychodynamics of female creativity; the trajectory of the individual or collective female career; and the evolution and laws of a female literary tradition' (1986, 248).

See also ÉCRITURE; ÉCRITURE FÉMININE.

H

Helper See ACT/ACTOR

Hermeneutic code See CODE

Heteroglossia In the writing of Mikhail Bakhtin, that multiplicity of social voices linked and interrelated DIALOGICALLY which enters the novel through the interplay between authorial speech, NARRATOR speech, 'inserted genres', and character speech (1981, 263).

The glossary provided in Bakhtin's *The Dialogic Imagination* notes that heteroglossia is determined contextually and extra-linguistically as well as intra-linguistically: 'all utterances are heteroglot in that they are functions of a matrix of forces practically impossible to recoup' (1981, 428).

In Bakhtin's usage, according to the same source, *polyglossia* refers more specifically to the co-existence of different national languages within a single CULTURE.

See the longer entries for DIALOGUE and POLYPHONY.

Heteronomous objects See CONCRETIZATION

Heuristic reading See READERS AND READING

Hinge 1. Mieke Bal uses the term *hinge* in the context of a discussion of FOCALIZATION, suggesting that it can be applied to passages of NARRATIVE with either a double or an ambiguous focalization.

2. In the writing of Jacques Derrida *brisures* are often rendered as *hinge-words* in English, although Maud Ellmann has suggested the alternative translation of *cleavage* (Ellmann 1981, 192). These hinge-words contain, following Derrida, a paradoxical logic which must be explored by deconstructive analysis. Commenting upon Derrida's use of this term, Robert Young suggests that the effect of such hinge-words 'is to break down the oppositions by which we are accustomed to think and which ensure the survival of metaphysics in our thinking' (1981, 18).

3. What Roland Barthes refers to as *nuclei* are sometimes described as *hinge-points* in English: see the entry for EVENT.

4. Clemens Lugowski uses the term to refer to a 'crucial point in the action' of a narrative (1990, 56).

Hommelette A coinage of Jacques Lacan's which combines the senses of 'little man' and omelette, and by which he seeks to describe the pre-Oedipal psychic condition of the child. The child is a little man (the GENDER bias is impossible to avoid) in as much as it contains *in posse* the whole of the later adult, but in diffused and undistinguished form (the child has no clear sense of self distinct from non-self).

Homodiegetic See DIEGESIS AND MIMESIS

Homology Also *isomorphism* or *structural parallelism*. A correspondence or similarity which establishes a significant pattern or structural REPETITION. This can either be within a given literary WORK, or (in STRUCTURALIST theory) between the structure of a language and the STRUCTURE of, for instance, the human UNCONSCIOUS. Structuralists have also argued for the existence of homologies between the language system and other systems, from kinship relationships to literature, claiming that literature (seen as a total system of relations) is itself structured like a language.

Similarly, in NARRATIVE theory, structuralist theorists have argued that there is a homology between the syntax of a grammatical sentence and the larger narrative 'syntax' of a literary work, and have used terms from linguistics to describe particular narrative functions (e.g. MODE). Tzvetan Todorov has suggested that we think of a literary character as a noun and an action as a verb, and their combination as the first step towards narrative (1969, 84). (See the entry for LINGUISTIC PARADIGM.)

The French MARXIST critic Lucien Goldmann has made considerable use of the concept in his work, suggesting homologies between class situation, world view, and artistic form.

Fredric Jameson has implied that homology should be distinguished from MEDIATION, for whereas homology involves resemblance at a structural level, mediation involves a connective relationship which has an element of dependence or causality between the different elements linked by mediation (1981, 43). Usage tends to be less tidy than this, however, and although Jameson's suggested distinction makes good sense it does not reflect the way the terms are actually used.

Homonymy Following Brian McHale, the reappearance of an entity from one fictional world in another, but with essential changes. The extent of these changes is important: to count as a case of homonymy there must be variants in essential properties – the main characters of Samuel Richardson's *Pamela* and of Henry Fielding's parodic *Shamela*, for example. Where the changes involve only accidental qualities, then we have a case of quasi-homonymy. And where a character is arguably unchanged, as with the character Cordelia in Shakespeare's *King Lear* and Nahum Tate's rewritten version of the same play, then we have a case of *transworld identity* (McHale 1987, 35–6).

Horizon Members of the group around Mikhail Bakhtin (P. N. Medvedev, V. N. Vološinov, and Bakhtin himself) regularly used this term to suggest the borders of possibility (normally) constraining a READER. Thus we come across terms such as *ideological horizon, socio-linguistic horizon,* and *axiological horizon* (i.e. the limit of possible evaluative acts) in their work. The usage has something in common with theories concerning the manner in which ideological situations restrict interpretative possibility, and also with Michel Foucault's view of the way in which the ARCHIVE of possible DISCOURSES limits an individual's access to knowledge.

See the discussions in Todorov (1984).

Horizon of expectations See RECEPTION THEORY

Hot and cool media According to Marshall McLuhan, there is a basic principle which distinguishes hot media such as radio and film from cool media such as the telephone and TV.

> A hot medium is one that extends one single sense in 'high definition.' . . . Telephone is a cool medium, or one of low definition, because the ear is given a meager amount of information. And speech is a cool medium of low definition, because so little is given and so much has to be filled in by the listener.
>
> (1964, 22–3)

Furthermore, McLuhan argues, hot media do not leave so much to be filled in or completed by the audience, whereas cool media require the receiver of the information to fill in much. Hot media, therefore, are low-participation media, whilst cool media are high-participation media.

McLuhan's assimilation of technology and message raises a number of problems here – problems which have led to his being accused of technological determinism by many commentators. For clearly although the telephone gives a meagre amount of information compared to a film *in a purely technical sense,* the information given in a telephone conversation can be semantically very rich indeed. It is nonsense, surely, to say that a monophonic record requires more audience participation than does a stereophonic one, or that a black-and-white film requires more participation from viewers than does a colour film – and both assertions would seem to follow logically from McLuhan's premises.

Compare READERLY AND WRITERLY TEXTS, noting the difference that emphasis on a medium and emphasis on a TEXT makes.

Hybrid According to Mikhail Bakhtin a hybrid utterance is one within which two different linguistic consciousnesses co-exist. Bakhtin analyses some parodic/ironic passages in Charles Dickens's *Little Dorrit* as examples of hybrid utterances (1981, 302–7).

In more recent use, a *hybrid text* can be one formed by cutting two other texts together – in either a planned or a random manner. The term hybrid text can also be used to describe a text in which two separate, and often opposed, elements can be detected, on a thematic or an ideological level.

Hypodiegetic See DIEGESIS AND MIMESIS

Hypothesis driven See SOLUTION FROM ABOVE/BELOW

I

Ideal reader See READERS AND READING

Ideogram See DEFORMATION

Ideologeme According to Fredric Jameson, 'the smallest intelligible unit of the essentially antagonistic collective discourses of social classes' (1981, 76). Formed by analogy with such terms as *phoneme* – the smallest intelligible unit of significant sound in a language. (Compare SEMEME, STYLEME, and other such coinages.)

Ideological horizon See HORIZON

Idiolect A term used by linguisticians to describe the features of a particular person's language which mark out him or her *individually* from others. An idiolect is thus distinguished from a *dialect*, which refers to the language characteristics marking out a *community* (geographical, social, educational) from others. Linguisticians normally restrict the primary reference of both terms to speech, but they are also applied by extension to written language as well.

Thus a writer's achievement in giving a particular literary character a distinctive idiolect can be an important aspect of that writer's success in characterization. Linguistic analysis of Jane Austen's fiction has confirmed that one of the reasons why readers find her characters to be possessed of such convincing independent life is that Jane Austen is very adept at granting them distinctive idiolects.

A writer has, of course, to represent both dialect and idiolect in writing, and although this may present few problems in certain areas (vocabulary, syntax) it requires the use of special conventions of notation in others (pronunciation, for example). Additional problems stem from the symbolic weight accorded by readers to divergences from the conventions of standard written English: as Leech and Short point out, 'non-standard language often implies remoteness from the author's own language, and hence from the central standards of judgement in a novel' (1981, 170).

Roland Barthes suggests, following Jakobson, that the concept of idiolect is a problematic one as, in Jakobson's words, 'private property in the sphere of language does not exist'. This objection notwithstanding, Barthes is prepared to use the concept to describe either (i) the language of the aphasic, (ii) the style of a writer, and even (iii) the language of a linguistic community (Barthes 1967a, 21).

Compare *genderlect* in the entry for GENDER; and SOCIOLECT.

Illocutionary act See SPEECH ACT THEORY

Implicature (conversational) See SPEECH ACT THEORY

Implied author See AUTHOR

Implied reader See READERS AND READING

Indeterminacy See ELLIPSIS

Influence See REVISIONISM

Inscribed reader See READERS AND READING

Institution According to certain recent theorists, the literary WORK is 'an institutional object' and can only fully be understood in the light of this fact. As Stein Haugom Olsen puts it,

> the specifically artistic features of a literary work are defined by the institutional conventions and have no existence independently of the institution; . . . therefore the literary work has no objectively given institutional features, but . . . these features are a product of a set of descriptive and classificatory possibilities created by the institution. (1987, 22)

In common with a number of different recent theories, then, such an approach rejects the New Critical view that literary qualities are *intrinsic* to a work, although it retains the possibility of arguing that certain works are more fruitfully treated as an institutional object than are others (in other words, that we cannot make anything a literary work by institutional means in the way that more or less any object can be treated as a chess-piece). On the other hand, certain critics who have incorporated 'institutional' elements into their approaches have left open the possibility that works not written with the intent of being considered literature may, by being absorbed into the institution, become literary: as Terry Eagleton has remarked, some texts are born literary, some achieve literariness, and some have literariness thrust upon them (1983, 8–9).

Olsen's own position here has something in common with the idea of the INTERPRET[AT]IVE COMMUNITY; it differs in as much as whereas he tends to describe the literary institution in cross-cultural and cross-historical terms, a multitude of different and differing interpret[at]ive communities has been posited, even within particular CULTURES at particular times. A further difference is that whereas Olsen claims that 'the characteristic purpose of the institutional transaction which constitutes a literary work is aesthetic significance' (1987, 23), those arguing for the existence of interpret[at]ive communities have seen these to be characterized by varied and on occasions non-aesthetic purposes.

Intended reader See READERS AND READING

Intercalated dialogue See INTERIOR DIALOGUE

Interior dialogue Alternatively (in Mikhail Bakhtin's usage) *internal dialogue* or *microdialogue*. A DIALOGUE between two well-defined voices within the single consciousness of a literary character (or, in a wider usage, of a real human being), and the NARRATIVE representation of this process.

Interior dialogue involves more than the representation of a character's verbalized thought-processes in which questions are asked and answered. To count as genuine interior dialogue the questions and answers must stem from two voices which represent different and as it were *personified* attitudes, beliefs, or characteristics. A good example occurs towards the beginning of the tenth chapter of Charlotte Brontë's *Jane Eyre*, in which we have represented a long dialogue between different aspects of Jane Eyre's personality or identity. Mikhail Bakhtin gives another example from Book 11 of Part 4 of Feodor Dostoevsky's *The Brothers Karamazov* (Bakhtin 1984, 255).

Internal dialogue See INTERIOR DIALOGUE

Internally persuasive discourse See DISCOURSE

Interpellation According to the French MARXIST philosopher Louis Althusser, all ideology '*hails or interpellates concrete individuals as concrete subjects*, by the functioning of the category of the subject' (1971, 162). Althusser (possibly as a result of the influence of Lacan) is making use of a technical term used to describe what happens when the order of the day in a governmental chamber is interrupted so as to allow a Minister to be questioned. The implication is that, like the Minister, individuals are interrupted and called to account – but in this case, by different ideologies. As ideology calls them (and us) – so the argument goes – so they and we recognize who they are. In other words: individuals come to 'live' a given set of ideological assumptions and beliefs, and to identify these with their own selves, by means of a process whereby they are persuaded that that which is presented *to* them actually represents their *own* inner identity or self. For Althusser, then, the SUBJECT is the *concrete individual* after interpellation, that is, after a sort of ideological 'body snatching'. However, Althusser believes that bodies are always already snatched; he adds that individuals '*are always-already subjects*'; even before being born 'an individual is always-already a subject' (1971, 164). According to Althusser, the only way for an individual to change this is for him or her, 'from within ideology', 'to outline a discourse which tries to break with ideology, in order to dare to be the beginning of a scientific (i.e. subject-less) discourse on ideology' (1971, 162).

On the theoretical level, the discussion by Etienne Balibar and Pierre Macherey in 'Literature as an Ideological Form' (1973) should be consulted. Some literary critics have applied Althusser's concept of interpellation to the way in which a reader adopts the 'subject' of a literary narrator or character as the consciousness through which the literary WORK or events in it are experienced and assessed: Roger Webster refers to the reader's experience of Leo Tolstoy's *Anna Karenina*: 'The reader is drawn towards Levin and becomes through him the experiencing centre of the novel's organic vision: unless we resist such positioning by reading against the grain, it is hard to avoid the process' (1990, 82–3). The term has been of use not just to Marxist critics, but also to FEMINIST critics and to those exploring the ways in which, for example, a literary work can force a reader from a subject group to adopt a reading position which positions him or her in such a manner as to force acceptance of his or her own oppression.

Not to be confused with INTERPOLATION.

Interpolation To interpolate is to make insertions in something, and the term has been used in different ways by recent literary critics and theorists. The term *interpolated narration* (sometimes referred to as *intercalated narration*) is used to describe passages of NARRATIVE which come between two moments of action. Prince (1988, 44) points out that the epistolary novel provides many examples: letters are normally written in between dramatic events rather than during them, although Henry Fielding's parody of Richardson *Shamela* suggested that Richardson's characters wrote letters when they would not normally have been written in real life.

In an essay on Virginia Woolf entitled 'Virginia's Web', Geoffrey Hartman (1970) has argued that Woolf's subject is the activity of the mind, and he defines that activity as a work of interpolation: the mind is perpetually filling in gaps and adding explanatory information.

Not to be confused with INTERPELLATION.

Interpret[at]ive communities The notion of the interpretive community stems from the American critic Stanley Fish; British critics have sometimes adopted the term and modified it to *interpretative* communities so as to conform with more usual British English usage. Fish's view of the interpretive community is bound up with a related concept: that of the *interpretive strategy*:

> it is interpretive communities, rather than either the text or the reader, that produce meanings and are responsible for the emergence of formal features. Interpretive communities are made up of those who share interpretive strategies

not for reading but for writing texts, for constituting their properties. In other words these strategies exist prior to the act of reading and therefore determine the shape of what is read rather than, as is usually assumed, the other way round. (1980, 14)

From this perspective an interpretive community is rather like a speech community – unified around adherence to a common set of rules which enable meaning transformations and MEDIATIONS. An interpretive strategy is thus comparable to the transformations made possible by the rules of grammar and syntax: its possession by a group of people means that they will all share a common relation to a TEXT or an UTTERANCE because they will bring the same transformational/interpretative procedures to bear on the text-to-be-interpreted or the utterance-to-be-understood.

This leads Fish to claim that when READERS interpret a text in either the same or in varying ways this is because

members of the same community will necessarily agree because they will see (and by seeing, make) everything in relation to that community's assumed purposes and goals; and conversely, members of different communities will disagree because from each of their respective positions the other 'simply' cannot see what it obviously and inescapably there. This, then, is the explanation for the stability of interpretation among different readers (they belong to the same community). It also explains why there are disagreements and why they can be debated in a principled way: not because of a stability in texts; but because of a stability in the makeup of interpretive communities and therefore in the opposing positions they make possible. (1980, 15)

It will be seen that there is a potentially dangerous circularity here. Any group of individuals which reaches agreement concerning ground-rules necessary for the discussion of a text belong by definition to the same interpretive community, while any group which disagrees about these ground rules consists of members from different interpretive communities. This becomes more of a problem when we remember that two readers may reach such agreement with regard to one text while failing to do so with regard to another. Moreover, it is hard to see what might disprove the theory: if two readers share a common interpretation then they belong to the same interpretive community; if they disagree but can talk about their disagreement then they still belong to the same community; but if they cannot even find a common ground on which to talk about a difference then they belong to different interpretive communities.

In a section dealing with Fish's theory of the interpretive community in his book *Textual Power* Robert Scholes indicates other problems: only those who belong to the same community can discuss interpretive disagreements – but as they belong to the same community they shouldn't have any such disagreements to discuss. Thus only those who have no disagreements can settle them in a principled way! Scholes also points out that the inevitable multiplicity of interpretive communities (see my comments above) means that the interpretive community cannot be equated with Thomas Kuhn's PARADIGM or Michel Foucault's ÉPISTÈME (1985, 154–6).

Fish's argument does focus a necessary attention on to the formation of writers and readers by pre-existing CONVENTIONS, but it lacks a suitably sophisticated underpinning in the form of a detailed theory of communities – where they come from, why they change, what their internal contradictions and tensions are, and how their members communicate with and influence one another. It also seems to condemn readers to imprisonment within the conventions of the reading community to which they belong: as Fish puts it,

> In other words, there is no single way of reading that is correct or natural, only 'ways of reading' that are extensions of community perspectives. (1980, 16)

This seems to grant the individual reader about as much personal freedom as did very mechanistic MARXIST or Freudian views, and it leaves us with the problem of explaining how one reading community is ever replaced by another in the historical development of a CULTURE or a society. Fish does accept that communities change, and he attributes this to the fact that the way members of a community read 'is not eternally fixed but will vary with cultures and times' (1980, 97). This seems to contradict what he says elsewhere, for here it is changes in ways of reading which change the community, whereas elsewhere it is the community and its accepted strategies which limit ways of reading.

The concept ties in with STRUCTURALIST and other notions of literary COMPETENCE, although it perhaps suggests a greater degree of homogeneity in the community than does the former approach.

Intersubjectivity Used to suggest that SUBJECTS are not specific to the individual but – because they are formed by common forces – have much in common. In recent literary theory often associated with the view that the reader's experience of a TEXT is actively internalized through incorporation in his or her self rather than passively adopted or 'taken over'. As a result, a READER's view of a WORK becomes, in part, a view of him- or herself: the work has been structured into the reader and is no longer a merely objective fact. Such a view gives the reader more of a creative rôle than he or she is accorded by a number of other theories, in which textual MEANING is received rather than received/constructed.

Intertextuality A relation between two or more TEXTS which has an effect upon the way in which the *intertext* (that is, the text within which other texts reside or echo their PRESENCE) is read. In some usages the term *transtextuality* is reserved for more overt relations between specific texts, or between two particular texts, while *intertextuality* is reserved to indicate a more diffuse penetration of the individual text by memories, echoes, transformations, of other texts. Gérard Genette has also coined the terms *hypertext* and *hypotext* to refer to the intertext and the text with which the intertext has some significant relation. This coinage has not been adopted in general usage.

It is possible to argue that any system of genres, of generic distinctions or requirements, carries with it the idea that the individual text is read in a manner determined by its relations with other texts, and indeed commentaries on literary WORKS from the earliest times have generally involved cross-references to other texts which have served as models or contrasts. Even during the heyday of the New Criticism, when a commitment to the autonomy of the individual text was almost a *sine qua non* in certain circles, it was still common and accepted to interpret individual literary works in terms of their intertextual relations with others.

More recently, however, specific attention has been paid to the various forms that intertextuality can take. One of the most influential presences here has been that of Mikhail Bakhtin. His insistence upon the DIALOGIC element in all UTTERANCES, and the range of different dialogues to be traced in literary works, undoubtedly sparked a more overt interest in the issue of intertextuality. A good example here is his extended discussion of 'the problem of quotation' in his essay 'From the Prehistory of Novelistic Discourse' (in Bakhtin 1981). He pays particular but not exclusive attention to such forms as parody and travesty and develops a theory of the linguistic HYBRID to cover them, pointing out in passing parallels with the use of parody and travesty in the modern novel (1981, 77).

Bakhtin seems himself to be an intertextual presence in Roland Barthes's and Julia Kristeva's development of theories of intertextuality. In her *Desire in Language* Kristeva defines the text as

> a permutation of texts, an intertextuality: in the space of a given text, several utterances, taken from other texts, intersect and neutralize one another. (1980, 36)

Commenting upon the concept of intertextuality in his Introduction to *Desire in Language*, Leon S. Roudiez claims that it has been generally misunderstood. According to him, intertextuality has nothing to do with matters of influence of one writer upon another or with the sources of a literary work;

> it does, on the other hand, involve the components of a *textual system* such as the novel, for instance. It is defined in [Kristeva's] *La Révolution du Langage Poétique* as the transposition of one or more *systems* of signs into one another, accompanied by a new articulation of the enunciative and denotative position. (Kristeva 1980, 15)

Roland Barthes seems partly in agreement with this position, at least so far as the distinction between intertextuality and influence is concerned. But his usage seems significantly more diffuse and all-embracing than Kristeva's. According to him, any text is an intertext.

> Any text is a new tissue of past citations. Bits of code, formulae, rhythmic models, fragments of social languages, etc. pass into the text and are redistributed

within it, for there is always language before and around the text. Intertextuality, the condition of any text whatsoever, cannot, of course, be reduced to a problem of sources or influences; the intertext is a general field of anonymous formulae whose origin can scarcely ever be located; of unconscious or automatic quotations, given without question-marks. (1981b, 39)

It should be said, in conclusion, that the term intertext enjoys no single, agreed meaning in current usage, a fact deplored in the introduction to an edition of the journal *Texte* (2, 1983), which is wholly given over to discussion of this and related concepts.

Intradiegetic See DIEGESIS AND MIMESIS

Intrusive narrator A NARRATOR who breaks into the NARRATIVE to comment upon a character, event or situation – or even to introduce opinions not directly related to what has been narrated. The term is often reserved for situations in which the intrusion is felt to break into an established narrative tone or illusion, although it is also used in a purely technical sense to describe 'own voice' comments from a narrator which may hardly be remarked by the READER because of their homogeneity with the rest of the narrative.

Iridescence See FLICKER

Isochrony Borrowed by recent NARRATIVE theorists from a term used to describe poetic rhythm, isochrony denotes an *unvarying* or an *equal* relationship between NARRATING time and STORY time. The two are not the same: if a story covers three hours and each hour is narrated by means of five thousand words, then the relationship between narrating time and story time is unvarying. But if a story covers three hours and each hour of the story takes approximately an hour to read, then the relationship between narrating time and story time can be said to be equal. It should be clear that whereas the former relationship can be measured with some degree of precision, the latter cannot. (Different readers read at different speeds, and one's speed of reading varies according to a number of factors – level of textual difficulty or interest, for example.) As Mieke Bal puts it, real isochrony (of the second type) cannot be determined precisely, although we may 'assume that . . . a dialogue without commentary takes as long in TF [FABULA-time] as it does in TS [story-time]' (1985, 70–1).

The opposite of isochrony is *anisochrony*: either a varying or an unequal relationship between narrating time and story time – normally the former.

Isotopy See TOPIC

Iterative See FREQUENCY

J

Jouissance To the surprise of many English-speaking people, this word can be found in the OED, although classified as obsolete and with examples cited from, among others, Carew and Spenser. Of the two main meanings given, that which is nearer to the current usage found amongst critical theorists is the second: Pleasure, delight; merriment, mirth, festivity. This sounds very innocent, and is clearly different from the current usage – loaned from the French – that involves *sexual* PLEASURE. The first meaning concerns the possession and use of something affording advantage, as in the *enjoyment* of a right, and jouissance is etymologically related to the word enjoyment.

Leon S. Roudiez dates the renewed critical interest in this term from the publication of Jacques Lacan's discussion of it in his 1972–3 seminar. In its French publication this sported a cover picture of the *Ecstasy of St. Theresa*, which suggests the prominent part played by sexual orgasm in jouissance. For Lacan, Roudiez claims, jouissance 'is sexual, spiritual, physical, conceptual at one and the same time' (Kristeva 1980, 16).

In Roland Barthes's *The Pleasure of the Text* jouissance is translated as *bliss*. Barthes claims that to judge a TEXT according to pleasure means that it is impossible to say either that it is good or that it is bad, because the text is 'too much *this*, not enough *that*' (1976, 13). This suggests that textual jouissance is an orgasmic experience in which the reader is so enrapt (or enwrapped) that that objectivity and distance necessary for judgement is impossible.

K

Kenosis See REVISIONISM

Kernel event See EVENT

Kernel function See FUNCTION

Kernel word or sentence In STYLISTICS, any word possessed of such stylistic emphasis as to colour the stylistic force of a textual unit, however defined.

L

Langue and parole Perhaps the most important – and influential – distinction introduced by Ferdinand de Saussure in his *Course in General Linguistics*. It is now common to use the French words to represent these paired concepts in English, but one can find attempts to render them in English, with langue represented by *language* (sometimes *a* or *the* language, as in the English translation of Roland Barthes's *Elements of Semiology*, or as *language-system*), and parole as *speaking, speech, language-behaviour*, or, on occasions, phrases such as *the sum of all actual (possible) utterances.*

For the sake of clarity, where other terms are used in the following quotations, I will replace them with either [langue] or [parole] – in square brackets so that the substitution is marked.

According to Saussure

> If we could embrace the sum of word-images stored in the minds of all individuals, we could identify the social bond that constitutes [langue]. It is a storehouse filled by members of a given community through their active use of [parole], a grammatical system that has a potential existence in each brain, or, more specifically, in the brains of a group of individuals. For [langue] is not complete in any speaker; it exists perfectly only within a collectivity.
>
> (1974, 13–14)

A number of points need to be stressed here. First, that as the reference to 'a given community' makes clear, Saussure's mention of the minds of 'all individuals' should be taken to refer to all individuals within a particular language community. Second, that langue is supra-individual: were Martians to kidnap a single English speaker they could not extract the langue of English from him or her alone. Third, that langue is a *system*, and one that has generative power ('potential existence'). Thus, if those same Martians were able to gather every example of English speech and feed them into a super computer they still could not end up with our langue, for langue is that set of rules, that system, that is able not just to generate all those acts of English speech, but also all the *potential but as yet unuttered acts of speech* that *could* be generated by it. (However, Saussure argues [1974, 15] that although we no longer speak dead languages, we can gain access to their linguistic systems [langues]; this suggests that langue *can* be said to be accessible even to those without the ability to *generate* paroles, so long as they can understand all previously generated paroles.) Fourth, it is also the system that allows native speakers to *understand* all the acts of speech correctly generated (in other individuals) by itself.

Saussure stresses that langue is not a function of the individual speaker: it is passively assimilated by the individual and does not require premeditation (contrast speaking in a *foreign* language). Parole, on the other hand, he insists is 'an individual act' which is wilful and intellectual (1974, 14).

During the early years of the current revival of interest in the work of Saussure both Roland Barthes (1967a) and Jonathan Culler (1975) pointed out that assigning different elements to either langue or to parole was not unproblematic, but the over-arching distinction between rule and behaviour has proved extremely fertile in a range of different contexts. It may well be that the more recent growth of interest in PRAGMATICS marks the end of a rather uncritical use of the distinction: in our post-pragmatics age there are rather fewer who are prepared unreservedly to accept Saussure's contention that the 'science of language is possible only if the other elements [of parole] are excluded' (1974, 15). Culler assumes the possibility of a relatively unproblematic relating of langue and parole to Chomsky's COMPETENCE AND PERFORMANCE (1975, 9), and he seems to use these terms (here and elsewhere) relatively interchangeably.

In literary criticism this distinction has been most influential as a model. The use of the LINGUISTIC PARADIGM by STRUCTURALIST critics has led to a succession of attempts to find parallels to langue and parole in the 'system of literature'. In an essay entitled 'Structuralism and Literary Criticism' (first published in French in 1964), Gérard Genette suggested that

> literary 'production' is a *parole*, in the Saussurian sense, a series of partially autonomous and unpredictable individual acts; but the 'consumption' of this literature by society is a *langue*, that is to say, a whole the parts of which, whatever their number and nature, tend to be ordered into a coherent system. (1982, 18–19)

One of the more interesting attempts to develop this analogy is to be found in a number of successive attempts by Jonathan Culler to distinguish between a general LITERARINESS and the specific acts of literary READING this enables. Culler does not always refer directly to Saussure but sometimes to the distinction between competence and performance. However, given the comments made above this should not be too significant.

Culler argues that just as Linguistics has changed its focus with the realization that description of a finite set of sentences is no longer enough, and that 'linguistics must instead describe the ability of native speakers, what they know when they know a language', so too the study of literature must 'become a poetics, a study of the conditions of meaning' (1980, 49), and abandon the attempt merely to 'analyse a corpus of works' (1980, 50). This argument is linked to a view of literature as INSTITUTION:

> Just as sequences of sound have meaning only in relation to the grammar of a language, so literary works may be quite baffling to those with no knowledge of the special conventions of literary discourse, no knowledge of literature as an institution. (1980, 49)

According to Culler, 'the conventions which make literature possible, are the same whether one adopts the reader's or the writer's point of view', and he suggests that 'as a reader oneself, one can perform all the experiments one needs' (1980, 50, 51).

Here some caveats become necessary. We seem to have moved a long way from Saussure's supra-personal system (langue) to a competence to which anyone can obtain access by means of a process of introspection that would hardly have been challenged by the New Critics. Moreover, a clear difference between linguistic and literary competence would appear to be that whereas the former normally involves *both* the generation *and* the understanding of all grammatical sentences within one's native language, literary competence for most people is limited to understanding rather than production of literary works. Furthermore, whereas langue (as Saussure pointed out – see above) is passively assimilated by the individual and does not require premeditation, literary 'competence' seems on the evidence to require an educational system to raise it to a certain level. Certainly the lowest common denominator of literary competence would appear to be a good deal lower than that of linguistic competence in our CULTURE.

Genette and Culler are by no means the only theorists to attempt to apply the langue/parole distinction to literature. In his *Introduction to Poetics* Tzvetan Todorov clearly defines poetics as the study of the literary equivalent of langue.

> It is not the literary work itself that is the object of poetics: what poetics questions are the properties of that particular discourse that is literary discourse. Each work is therefore regarded only as the manifestation of an abstract and general structure, of which it is but one of the possible realizations. Whereby this science is no longer concerned with actual literature, but with a possible literature in other words, with that abstract property that constitutes the singularity of the literary phenomenon: *literariness*. (1981, 6–7)

It is worth noting that whereas Culler sees the literary equivalent of parole to be the *analysis* of individual texts, Todorov sees these texts (he actually refers to works rather than texts) *themselves* as if they were acts of literary parole – while Genette has suggested that it was the *production* of literature that constituted the literary parole (see above). The difference – and the fact that there can be such a difference – suggests that the literary assimilation of the langue/parole distinction may be a little less straightforward than has sometimes been suggested.

Lexia/lexie See FUNCTION

Linguistic paradigm Ferdinand de Saussure established a number of extremely influential analytical distinctions in his work which, while originally applied by him to the study of language, have subsequently been applied to other things. Concepts such as SYNTAGMATIC AND PARADIGMATIC relations, LANGUE AND

PAROLE, and SIGNIFIER AND SIGNIFIED have all been pressed into service by theorists concerned with a range of non-linguistic phenomena.

Jonathan Culler gives an extended account of two such uses of the linguistic paradigm in his *Structuralist Poetics*: Claude Lévi-Strauss's structural analysis of MYTHOLOGY and Roland Barthes's of fashion (Culler 1975, 32–54). But once one has grasped the essential idea, the method has a potentially unending set of applications. Thus for example one can treat a meal with several courses like a sentence composed of several words: in a given culture there are all sorts of different dishes that can be chosen as the first course, but once chosen these constrain what is chosen as the second course – and so on.

Within the field of literary criticism one can refer to the way in which terminology and distinctions taken from the grammar of verbs have been applied to the study of NARRATIVE by Gérard Genette. Hence he uses *tense* to designate temporal relations between narrative and story; MOOD to designate forms and degrees of narrative 'representation'; and *voice* to designate the narrative situation or its instance (1980, 30–1).

All of these extensions of linguistic distinctions involve treating other SIGN-systems as if they were fundamentally similar to language: language, in other words, is taken as a *paradigm* for the study and analysis of other sign-systems.

Jacques Lacan's claim that the UNCONSCIOUS is structured like a language represents a more global use of language as explanatory paradigm; other theorists have taken Noam Chomsky's distinction between COMPETENCE AND PERFORMANCE and applied it to literature: readers of literature are said to possess (perhaps to different degrees) a fundamental competence *vis-à-vis* the READING of literary WORKS, a competence which results in certain specific performances – that is, specific readings of literary works.

In addition to applying particular distinctions originating in the study of language to non-linguistic sign-systems, those influenced by Saussure and other linguisticians have tended to place great significance on the fact of binary opposition itself: a fondness for binary distinctions is one of the marks of those using, or influenced by, the linguistic paradigm.

See also BRICOLEUR; HOMOLOGY; SEMIOTIC.

Lisible See READERLY AND WRITERLY TEXTS

Literariness In his essay 'The Theory of the Formal Method' Boris Eichenbaum quotes tellingly from Roman Jakobson's 'Recent Russian Poetry, Sketch 1', first published in Prague in 1921. In the extract quoted, Jakobson makes the polemical claim that

> The object of study in literary science is not literature but literariness – that is, that which makes a given work a work of literature. Until now literary historians have preferred to act like the policeman who, intending to arrest a certain person, would, at any opportunity, seize any and all persons who chanced into the apartment, as well as those who passed along the street. The literary historians

used everything – anthropology, psychology, politics, philosophy. Instead of a science of literature, they created a conglomeration of home-spun disciplines. (Eichenbaum 1965, 107; for an alternative translation see Èjxenbaum 1971a, 8)

Eichenbaum comes back to this point in his essay 'Literary Environment':

Literary-historical fact is a complex construct in which the fundamental role belongs to *literariness* – an element of such specificity that its study can be productive only in immanent-evolutionary terms. (Èjxenbaum 1971b, 62)

It is arguable that it is this insistence upon the specificity of literature and, thus, of the *study* of literature, which is one of the key reasons why Russian Formalism is formalist.

The insistence served to distinguish the study of literature not just from such other disciplines as those listed by Jakobson, but also from the study of other art-forms. This insistence upon the *specificity* and distinctiveness of literature, and of the need for it to be studied in a specific and distinctive manner, not occasionally tipped over into an insistence upon the *autonomy* of literature and of the irrelevance to Literary Studies of all references to, as Jakobson put it, environment, psychology, politics, and philosophy. It should be stressed that such developments were criticized by leading Russian Formalists. Thus Jakobson himself stated that neither he, nor Tynyanov, Shklovsky or Mukařovský ever declared that art was a closed sphere, that they had emphasized not the separation of art but 'the autonomy of the aesthetic function' (Tynyanov *et al.* 1977, 19).

At its best a concern for literariness certainly served to prevent neglect of certain crucial aspects of the literary WORK: its aesthetic dimension, the complexity of its relation to the life of its time, the complexity of the way(s) in which it is read, and the highly MEDIATED nature of what can – rather unsatisfactorily – be termed literary communication.

See also codes of reading (entry for CODE); LANGUE AND PAROLE.

Literary mode of production (LMP) A term proposed by Terry Eagleton in his *Criticism and Ideology* (1976). Eagleton here attempts to apply and refine the orthodox MARXIST concept of 'Mode of Production'. In the orthodox view each major period of world history is characterized by a dominant mode of production such as the feudal mode or the capitalist mode (Marx also mentioned the Asiatic mode of production, and of course looks forward to the socialist one). A mode of production is defined – again in the orthodox view – in terms of its *forces of production*, and of its *relations of production* (otherwise referred to as the control or ownership of the *means of production*). Thus the capitalist mode of production would involve the revolutionizing of the forces of production through industrialization, alongside the private ownership of the means of production – meaning that the relations of production are between two main groups: the owners of capital, and those who own nothing but their labour power.

Traditional Marxist literary criticism attempted to relate literature (seen as part of the SUPERSTRUCTURE) to society's economic BASE, understood in terms of its mode of production. What Eagleton attempts to do is to make this process more receptive to local 'relative autonomies', STRUCTURES which MEDIATE between base and superstructure. According to him, a number of distinct modes of literary production will exist and co-exist in any literate society, and some of these may be 'survivals', that is to say they may have arisen in one society (with its own distinctive general mode of production), and have survived so as to be found in a subsequent society possessed of a different general mode of production. He notes that

> A classical instance of such survivals is typically to be found in the historical mutation from 'oral' to 'written' LMPs, where the social relations and kinds of literary product appropriate to the 'oral' LMP normally persist as significant constituents of the 'written' LMP itself, both interactive with and relatively autonomous of it. (1976, 45)

Locutionary act See SPEECH ACT THEORY

Logic of the same A term which has entered into FEMINIST discourse in English from the writings of the French writer Luce Irigaray. It describes a process of argumentation whereby x is treated as equivalent to y and thus effectively subsumed into the value-scheme of y. The foremost example of this is the PATRIARCHAL assumption that the male represents a standard, and that the female is thus necessarily less than this standard, or formed in response to it. In her *Speculum of the Other Woman* (publication in English 1985), she argues that woman is forced into a subjectless position by this patriarchal logic of the same: Freud models his account of the little girl's development on his account of the little boy's development, thus presenting female sexuality as 'the negative response to the male's desire' (Millard 1989, 159).

More widely, the logic of the same is typically seen in the sort of argument that runs 'x is like y, let us consider x as if it were y, x is y'. Discussions of literary influence are particular prone to this variant form of SLIPPAGE.

Logocentrism A coinage of Jacques Derrida's, (and sometimes used interchangeably with *phonocentrism*), logocentrism refers to systems of thought or habits of mind which are reliant upon what Derrida, following Heidegger, terms the metaphysics of PRESENCE – that is, a belief in an extra-systemic validating presence or CENTRE which underwrites and fixes linguistic meaning but is itself beyond scrutiny or challenge. For Derrida, such a position is fundamentally idealist, and he argues that the dismantling of logocentrism is simultaneously the deconstruction of idealism or spiritualism 'in all their variants' (1981b, 51).

In 'Writing Before the Letter' (with which *Of Grammatology* opens), Derrida says of the *history of metaphysics* that it has

> always assigned the origin of truth in general to the logos: the history of truth, of the truth of truth, has always been . . . the debasement of writing, and its repression outside 'full' speech. (1976, 3)

Logocentrism, then, is associated by Derrida with the making of ÉCRITURE subject to speech (the English translation of écriture as writing may be misleading: see the entry for écriture).

Derrida's much-quoted assertion that '*there is nothing outside of the text*' (1976, 158), which can also be rendered in English as 'there is no outside-text', has to be read in the light of his attack on logocentrism: the TEXT cannot be assigned a meaning that is underwritten by an origin, a PRESENCE, which resides in self-validating isolation beyond the confines of the text.

See also DIFFÉRANCE.

Logos Richard Harland provides the following useful gloss on Jacques Derrida's use of this term:

> a Greek word that illuminatingly brings together in a single concept the inward rational principle of verbal texts, the inward rational principle of human beings, and the inward rational principle of the natural universe. Even more illuminating, 'logos' combines all these meanings with a further meaning: 'the Law'. For 'logos' as an inward rational principle serves to control and take charge of outward material things. (1987, 146)

It should be added that in Derrida's view the sense of security provided by a belief in logos is illusory: there are, from his perspective, no such inward rational principles.

See also PRESENCE.

Ludism From a Latin root meaning to play, *ludism* and *ludic* are used interchangeably in English with *play* and *playful* in DECONSTRUCTIONIST writing or by writers influenced by deconstructionist ideas. More recently play and playful have perhaps been more favoured, probably because their use allows reference to a wider range of meanings.

The central idea behind all these usages is that once the illusion of PRESENCE has been dispensed with, READING and interpretation no longer involve a decoding that is subject to the firm discipline of some CENTRE of authority that has access to the CODE book; instead the READER can observe and participate in the free play of signifiers endlessly generating a succession of MEANINGS none of which can claim superiority or authority. The main senses of 'play' involved here are: play as in 'to play a game', and play as in 'to play a fish' or 'to play a hose'. In other words there is a combined sense of the absence of discipline alongside the almost aestheticized experiencing of interrelated tensions and forces. Vicki Mistacco expresses it as follows:

> 'Ludism' may be simply defined as the open play of signification, as the free and productive interaction of forms, of signifiers and signifieds, without regard for an original or an ultimate meaning. In literature, ludism signifies textual play; the text is viewed as a game affording both author and reader the possibility of producing endless meanings and relationships. (1980, 375)

This view is closely related to a belief in the (metaphorical) death of the AUTHOR, the stern parent who would restrict the child's play.

Recent discussions of POSTMODERNISM have suggested that one important way in which it can be distinguished from MODERNISM is by reference to its more playful and unserious tone. Instead of a view of the loss of CENTRE in the contemporary world as tragic, the postmodernist views this as a justification of playfulness – exploring the potentialities of SIGNIFICATIONS without an irritable searching after final truths or unified meanings.

It should be noted that in such uses the fact that games often have *rules*, and that playing among both animals and humans is often the way in which the player is prepared for life in the non-ludic world, is not generally accorded much importance.

M

Manner (maxims of) See SPEECH ACT THEORY

Marginality Literary criticism from the earlier part of the present century focused a certain amount of attention on to the way in which AUTHORS occupying marginal or ambiguous positions *vis-à-vis* social or national identity were often able to see beyond the accepted or conventional attitudes and beliefs of their time, as their marginality made it difficult for them to be – or feel – fully incorporated in any dominant system of values. MODERNIST literature in particular is characterized by its relation not only to authors who occupied various forms of marginal position, but also by its overt concern with marginality as representative of something central to modern existence. Thus we can point to the large number of major early twentieth-century authors who were (to quote the title of a book by Terry Eagleton) exiles or emigrés – caught on the margins between different CULTURES. More recently, FEMINIST writers have focused attention on to the way in which PATRIARCHY marginalizes female experience and thus makes male experience the determining and dominating norm.

Subaltern is sometimes used is a sense very similar to marginal or marginalize: it implies that individuals may be recruited to serve in subordinate positions under a determining and defining established authority.

Jacques Derrida's concept of *supplementarity* is sometimes associated with marginality. The logic behind such an association appears to be that if all representation and interpretation requires a supplementary element – can never feed merely upon that which is to be represented or interpreted – then attention is necessarily drawn to the margins of that which is to be interpreted or represented, to the borderline between the thing itself and that which is brought to supplement it. Derrida makes the point with regard to writing:

> Writing is dangerous from the moment that representation there claims to be presence and the sign of the thing itself. And there is a fatal necessity, inscribed in the very functioning of the sign, that the substitute make one forget the vicariousness of its own function and make itself pass for the plentitude of a speech whose deficiency and infirmity it nevertheless only supplements.
>
> . . .
>
> 'The sign is always the supplement of the thing itself' (1976, 144, 145).

See also PRESENCE.

Marvellous See FANTASTIC

Marxist literary theory and criticism The singular term is perhaps misleading: there have been a number of variants of Marxist literary theory, and even today not all who call themselves Marxist literary theorists (or critics) would be able to reach more than a very general agreement concerning their fundamental beliefs. We can perhaps dispense with the clumsy 'Marxist literary theory and criticism': one thing that does distinguish Marxist literary criticism (unlike, say, the criticism of F. R. Leavis), is that it is and sees itself to be theory-dependent. Marxism constitutes a general philosophical outlook, one which differs from other such outlooks in important ways but which is characterized by its monist view of reality. Like all such monist beliefs, therefore, its adherents feel that it has something to say about everything: even if the details of particular fields of study may have to be worked out in the course of applied study, the direction of this study is in part laid down by pre-existing fundamental principles.

Marxism is a materialist philosophy, one which insists upon the primacy of material living conditions rather than ideas or beliefs in the life of human beings. It sees history as, in Marx's words, 'the history of class struggle' – the history of struggle for control of the material conditions upon which life rests. It is on the basis of these material conditions, and in response to the struggle for them, that ideas, philosophies, mental pictures of the world, develop – as secondary phenomena. These secondary phenomena may provide human beings with an accurate picture of reality, including themselves and their situation, but they may not. Ideologies are all related to class positions and thus, in turn, to material conditions and the struggle for their control, but this is not to say that they provide a reliable picture of these. Traditional Marxists have laid great stress upon the distinction between BASE (or basis) and SUPERSTRUCTURE, seeing the social base as essentially economic in nature, and the superstructure as constituting the world of mental activities – ideas, beliefs, philosophies, and (in the opinion of some but not all Marxists, art and literature).

For Marxists, all is in movement, and because there is no separate or pure realm of ideas, or values, or spiritual phenomena – all is interconnected, however complex and MEDIATED the interconnections turn out to be. The complexity of these interconnections takes, according to Marx, a characteristic form: a dialectical rather than a mechanical and purely hierarchical one. And this opens up the possibility for human beings to gain at least partial control over their life-circumstances: Marxism has traditionally been an active and interventionist philosophy, not a spectatorial or passive one, although this may be changing with a growing suspicion of the dangers of too partisan an attitude to theory.

Marxist ideas about literature have a long history. Marx himself was extremely well-read in classical and contemporary literature, and literary allusions and references abound in his work. A number of early Marxists sought to apply Marx's ideas to literature: both in terms of the interpretation and evaluation of existing literary works, and also in terms of advice to writers and those with (or seeking) political power about what sort of literature should be encouraged. The active and interventionist nature of Marxism has recurrently led to such attempts to *use* literature for social or political ends: some of these have gained a bad press in the reviews of history – as in the case of Soviet Socialist Realism – others have received a more positive response, as in the case of Brecht's attempt to use his political theatre in the interests of social revolution. It should be noted that Marxism did not introduce the political use of art and literature to the world; there is a long tradition of such attempts – one which it is fair to say the modern academic study of literature consistently underplays and undervalues.

Early Marxist writings on literature and art tended to be of a generalizing nature, seeking to explain why large bodies of writing took the form that they did by relating them to the social and economic conditions of their emergence. Thus G. V. Plekhanov's essay *Art and Society* (1912) has a long opening section on 'French Drama and Painting of the Eighteenth Century' which attempts to relate the class structure of eighteenth-century France with the more general characteristics of the drama and painting of the period. To a large extent this sort of impulse has remained central to Marxist literary criticism, although it can take a crude 'vulgar Marxist' form in which art is seen directly and unproblematically to mirror or reflect a society's class structure or economic base, or it can take a more sophisticated form in which increased attention is paid to complex processes of mediation between a society and its art and literature. A good example of the latter would be the work of the Romanian-

French critic Lucien Goldmann – sometimes referred to as a 'genetic STRUCTU-
RALIST' – whose attempt to relate the literature of seventeenth century France
to the society from which it emerged makes use of a number of important
concepts which see this relationship in terms of forms of complex mediation,
such as 'mental structure' and 'world-view'.

Marxist literary criticism has had two periods of significant influence: in
the 1930s, and in the 1960s. In both periods this influence has been related to
a more general interest in and commitment to Marxist ideas. Undoubtedly the
most influential and important Marxist literary critic of the 1930s (and after)
was the Hungarian Georg Lukács, associated in particular with a strong defence
of the REALISM to which he believed his Marxism committed him, alongside a
concomitant hostility on the artistic and the political level to all forms of
MODERNISM. Lukács's relationship to Stalinism is complex: on the one hand,
his general position *vis-à-vis* realism and modernism was in tune with the 'line'
of Stalin and Socialist Realism, although this line tended to be played down as
the period of the Popular Front developed. But Lukács's own position was a lot
more sophisticated than that of Stalin or his henchman Zhdanov, and Lukács's
very positive view of the high art of the bourgeoisie was not really equatable
with Zhdanov's belief that the greatest literature in the world was then being
written in the Soviet Union. In Lukács's defence it has too to be pointed out
that his criticism, although generalizing in many ways, attempts to grapple with
the particularities of individual works of literature in a way that was not
common at this time amongst Marxist critics – although it is also true of the
British critic Alick West, whose *Crisis and Criticism* was published in 1937.

Since 1960 Marxist literary criticism has reflected the diversities of
Marxism in the modern world. As a generalization we can say that the less
contentious it has become to see literary works in the context of their
emergence and subsequent life, the more Marxist ideas have penetrated literary
criticism in general. Committed modern Marxist critics are more likely than
their predecessors to be engaged in the study of mediating processes: ideology,
the 'political unconscious' of the American Marxist Fredric Jameson, the
LITERARY MODES OF PRODUCTION of the British Marxist Terry Eagleton, and
the STRUCTURES OF FEELING of Raymond Williams (who is more difficult to
situate with regard to Marxism). They are also less likely to be happy with a
straightforward relegation of literature to the realm of the superstructure. The
influential French Marxist Pierre Macherey's *A Theory of Literary Production*
(first published in French in 1974), for instance, by seeing the writing of
literature as a form of production necessarily sees it as more than the simple
reflection of economic facts that vulgar Marxism attributed to literature.

A group of Russian theorists and critics centred around the figure of
Mikhail Bakhtin has been particularly influential over the past two decades,
during which time their writings from the inter-war period have reached
Western European and American readers in translation for the first time. In
addition to Bakhtin himself the names of P. N. Medvedev and V. N. Vološinov
should be mentioned: whether Bakhtin was responsible for works published

under their names is still under discussion. The extent to which these writers were Marxist is also a matter for discussion: given their situation in the Soviet Union of the 1920s and the 1930s they had to pay at least lip-service to Marxist ideas, and Bakhtin appears to have retained a Christian belief all of his life. But their writings unquestionably engage productively with Marxist ideas, seeing literature and art in its genetic socio-historical context, but paying close attention to matters of linguistic, cultural and aesthetic detail and often applying Marxist principles more rigorously than the official watchdogs of Soviet art and culture were doing. They were anti-formalists (c.f. Medvedev's and Bakhtin's *The Formal Method in Literary Scholarship*, first published in 1928), but did not confuse this with a belief that formal issues were unimportant.

Since the 1970s one is likely to find literary critics or theorists describing themselves as 'Marxist-FEMINISTS', or 'STRUCTURALIST-Marxists', or seeking to combine or relate Marxism and POST-STRUCTURALISM. What we can call monolithic Marxism is much less common, and if events in eastern Europe are anything to go by, will become even less so.

Meaning and significance Use of the word *meaning* has been associated with literary-critical discussion for a very long time, although certain theoretical arguments have made it a rather more contentious term today than it has been in the past (see below). The pairing of *meaning* with *significance*, however, is very much associated with one particular theorist: the American critic E. D. Hirsch. In his book *Validity in Interpretation* Hirsch defines these two terms in ways that are matched and complementary:

> *Meaning* is that which is represented by a text; it is what the author meant by his use of a particular sign sequence; it is what the signs represent. *Significance*, on the other hand, names a relationship between that meaning and a person, or a conception, or a situation, or indeed anything imaginable. (1967, 8)

The definition has to be seen in the light of increasing debate about the respective rôles and authority of AUTHOR and READER in the interpretation of literary WORKS, for it proposes a clear separation of powers: the author is responsible for meaning while significance comes from the interaction of this meaning with that which lies outside the work. Thus if Milton was telling the truth when he claimed that by his use of the 'particular sign sequence' that is 'Paradise Lost' he meant to justify the ways of God to man (interpreting this as a shorthand expression of a larger and more complex intention), then this is what the meaning of 'Paradise Lost' *is*. But if a particular reader is reminded of his or her own religious conversion when reading the poem, because an earlier reading was instrumental in effecting that conversion, then that is (part of) the work's *significance* for him or her.

Significance for Hirsch does not have to be this personal and idiosyncratic, but it is important to stress that it is not completely unconstrained either: if the paper of the first edition in which I read 'Paradise Lost' was yellow, such that every time I read the poem I think of bananas, this would *not* constitute significance on Hirsch's definition, because it is not a relationship between authorial *meaning* (as he defines it) and something else. So that for Hirsch the author exerts control over both meaning and significance, it is just that this control is more MEDIATED and less complete with regard to the latter.

The distinction certainly has the great virtue that it provides something for the individual who believes that the death of the author has not yet taken place, but who also believes that personal elements enter into a literary work's reading and that readers – individually or collectively – donate something to the artistic and aesthetic experiences associated with the work, which are not all placed in the work by the author like CODES placed in a computer program by its designer.

Hirsch's distinction has not escaped criticism, however. It is clearly unacceptable to those who accept the arguments of 'The Intentional Fallacy' and believe that the literary work is cut off from its author at birth and contains its meaning in itself and not in terms of what its author intended. It is also unacceptable to those who believe that the author is dead, and who see Hirsch's argument as still in thrall to the METAPHYSICS OF PRESENCE, wanting a fixed CENTRE to arrest the free play of the SIGNIFIERS in the work.

But it has also come under attack from other directions. In spite of Hirsch's subsequent attempts to modify his position so as to take into account the *implications* of authorial intention that were not – and perhaps could not be – apparent to the author at the time of writing, Hirsch's reliance upon authorial intention has worried some commentators. Others have felt that his concentration upon meaning is itself fundamentally misplaced, for literary works (the argument runs) do not have meanings in the way that UTTERANCES do: they are objects for interpretation or for APPRECIATION. From this perspective it is as misleading to ask what a literary work means as it is to ask what a Grecian urn or a dip in the sea means: literary works are not utterances but aesthetic objects. (See the arguments in Stein Haugom Olsen's essay, 'The "Meaning" of a Literary Work', [1987, 53–72].)

See also DEFERRED/POSTPONED SIGNIFICANCE.

Méconnaissance In Lacan, applied to Freud's apparent *misrecognition* of 'everything that the ego neglects' (1977, 22). The term carries with it a suggestion of ideologically derived blindness perhaps bordering on bad faith.

Media Studies The rise of the academic study of radio, and – in particular – television and film, has been especially marked in the last two decades in Britain, although this area of studies has a longer history in the USA. This development has been of particular importance for the academic study of literature in perhaps two ways. First, because the academic study of media content, especially with regard to motion pictures, used theories and traditions from Literary Studies which were thus tested out and scrutinized in a different context from that in which they had been developed. Second, because new theories and traditions arising in Media Studies have been exported back to Literary Studies, and have often been of significant influence there.

As a generalization, we can say that two academic disciplines in particular contributed to the establishment and development of Media Studies: Literary Studies (especially in ENGLISH departments, so far as Britain was concerned), and Sociology. Historically, again so far as Britain is concerned, the academic study of film often borrowed more extensively from Literary Studies in its early years: *Auteur* theory, to take a striking example, came to Film Studies in Britain from the attempt of a group of French theorists to treat the Director of a film as if he or she were like the AUTHOR of a literary work, and to see all his or her films as having something in common in much the same way as all the novels by – say – Henry James can be seen to share common features and elements. The academic study of television, in contrast, very often owed its greatest academic debt to Sociology, and in its early years often concentrated less on what was seen as the impressionistic content analysis or interpretation of the literary critic, and much more on the study of *institutions* and *audiences*: who owned or controlled the organizations that produced TV programmes; what effects did these programmes have on those who followed them. Where TV content was analysed – again in the early years of the development of an academic subject – the analysis was likely to draw on traditions taken from American behaviourist Psychology: testing viewers' attitudes before and after watching a particular TV show, for example.

This outline history is of course an oversimplification, and numerous specific cases could be adduced to demonstrate that it is. But it is certainly the case that one of the crucial functions performed by Media Studies in the 1960s and after was as a SITE on which traditions emanating from Literary Studies and Sociology could engage in mutual criticism. The results of this process of interdisciplinary discussion and cross-fertilization has been extremely valuable for both Literary Studies and for Sociology. If literary critics were able to suggest that sociological analyses of programme content and audience responses were often crude and unreliable, and failed to confront complex processes of MEDIATION, response and interpretation; sociologists were able to counter by suggesting that a failure on the part of literary critics to engage with the wider issues of social control beyond that of the author him or herself meant that an aesthetic force or motive was often attributed to TEXTUAL features which needed to be understood and explained in a completely different way.

Beyond this, the rise of Media Studies undoubtedly contributed to students of literature taking a far more critical attitude to the notion of the CANON. Study of film or television inevitably confronted academics with the issue of the POPULAR, an issue that had been of concern to MARXIST literary critics in an earlier period, but which in the 1940s and 1950s was a matter for relatively little critical concern in Britain and the USA. If students following Media Studies courses could engage in serious study of soap operas, then why could not students taking degrees in, say, English not study popular fiction? And such questions inevitably raised issues connected with ideology: not just the ideology contained in the texts studied, but the ideology or ideologies which lay behind choices about what was to be studied and how it was to be studied.

Other examples of cross-fertilization are more specific. The study of NARRATIVE, for example, can today hardly be confined to literary narrative. So much that is important in narrative theory involves analysis of film that the literary student ignores it at his or her peril.

Mediation A stress on the highly mediated nature of human interaction and communication is common to many recent theories. Such a stress militates against simple (or simplistic) views of direct transference or copying such as are attributed by their critics to so-called *reductive* or *mechanistic* views. Central to processes of mediation are systems of *transformation*, and this means that a point at one end of a chain of complex mediations can never be accurately recaptured by an unproblematic 'reading-off' at the other.

This is clearly relevant to efforts to reach social or historical insights through the READING of literary WORKS (or to the attempt to understand literary works by means of social or historical investigations), as all sorts of mediating factors such as ideology or literary CONVENTION have to be taken into account if these efforts and investigations are to bear fruit.

In his *The Political Unconscious* Fredric Jameson draws attention to the two-sidedness of mediation, which is both something the investigator *does*, by a process of *transcoding* or inventing a set of terms 'such that the same terminology can be used to analyze and articulate two quite distinct types of objects or "texts", or two very different structural levels of reality' (1981, 40), and it is also the *uncovering* of relationships independent of the investigator:

> What is crucial is that, by being able to use the same language about each of these quite distinct objects or levels of an object, we can restore, at least methodologically, the lost unity of social life, and demonstrate that widely distant elements of the social totality are ultimately part of the same global historical process. (1981, 226)

In summary: the investigator both mediates between different levels or instances, and also uncovers mediations between these same levels or instances. *Both* of these elements should be borne in mind with reference to the following comment by Jameson:

> Mediation is the classical dialectical term for the establishment of relationships between, say, the formal analysis of a work of art and its social ground, or between the internal dynamics of the political state and its economic base.
> (1981, 39)

'Establishing of relationships' should perhaps be understood both as 'establishing that there are relationships' and also as 'creating relationships'.

See also HOMOLOGY.

Message See FUNCTIONS OF LANGUAGE

Metacriticism 'Criticism of criticism': in other words, critical theory which has as its subject literary (or other) criticism, and which attempts to analyse and categorize examples of critical practice and to establish generally applicable principles for it. In contemporary usage the term is often replaced by *literary theory*, although this can have a rather wider meaning.

Metafiction See METALANGUAGE

Metalanguage Technically, any language used to describe or refer to another language: 'a language about a language'. One of the characteristics of human word language is that it can function as its own language; we can discuss our language in that same language (as I am doing now). This is a characteristic not shared by animal communication systems: dogs cannot bark about barking.

This has a bearing on literature and literary criticism precisely because both exploit this resource. Gérard Genette suggests a version of the LINGUISTIC PARADIGM in which the literary WORK is compared to a language and literary criticism to a metalanguage (1982, 29). However, literature can itself serve as its own metalanguage, as in *metafiction*. One consequence of this is that the play of *levels* in a literary work can be very complex, and recent study of NARRATIVE in particular has performed an important function in making our awareness of the specificity and interrelations of different narrative levels much sharper.

A *metanarrative* can thus be either a narrative which talks about other, embedded narratives, or a narrative which refers to itself and to its own narrative procedures. Metanarratives can play an extremely important rôle *vis-à-vis* the establishment of a particular ideological position in a work of fiction: Anne Cranny-Francis has pointed out, for example, how recent FEMINIST rewritings of fairy-tales can problematize the READER's relationship to familiar tales by means of metanarratives which change this relationship from a passive to an active one (1990, 89).

Metafiction is, literally, fiction about fiction. To a certain extent the term overlaps with *metanarrative* because any work of fiction which contains a metanarrative will contain a metafictional element. It is generally used to indicate fiction including any *self-referential element*, (not necessarily resulting from a metanarrative: thematic patternings can also contribute to the formation of a metafictional effect in a work). Metafiction typically involves games in which levels of narrative reality (and the reader's perception of them) are confused, or in which traditional REALIST conventions governing the separation of MIMETIC and DIEGETIC elements are flouted and thwarted.

See also the entries for diegesis and mimesis (in which some variations in Genette's definition of a number of the terms mentioned here are discussed), and the entry for FRAME.

Metalepsis According to Gérard Genette, any transgressing of NARRATIVE levels, such as when Sterne implores the reader of *Tristram Shandy* to help Mr Shandy get back to his bed (1980, 234).

Metalingual See FUNCTIONS OF LANGUAGE

Metanarrative See DIEGESIS AND MIMESIS; METALANGUAGE

Metaphor See SYNTAGMATIC AND PARADIGMATIC

Metaphysics (of presence) See PRESENCE

Metonymy See SYNTAGMATIC AND PARADIGMATIC

Microdialogue See INTERIOR DIALOGUE

Mimesis See DIEGESIS AND MIMESIS

Mirror text See *MISE-EN-ABYME*

Mise-en-abyme. From the French meaning, literally, to throw into the abyss. The term is adapted from heraldry, and in its adapted form generally involves the recurring internal duplication of images of an artistic whole, such that an infinite series of images disappearing into invisibility is produced – similar to what one witnesses if one looks at one's reflection between two facing mirrors. Mieke Bal recommends the term *mirror-text* for literary examples of *mise-en-abyme*, as in verbal examples it is not the whole of the WORK which is mirrored but only a part. For Bal, when the primary FABULA and the embedded fabula can be paraphrased in such a manner that both paraphrases have one or more elements in common, 'the subtext is a *sign* of the primary text' (1985, 146). The possibilities for reflexivity and self-reference opened up by such repetitions are not limited to MODERNIST art and literature, but have been utilized by artists and writers over many centuries.

For a detailed study of *mise-en-abyme* which covers both the fine arts and literature, see Lucien Dallenbach (1989).

The term is sometimes used by DECONSTRUCTIONIST writers to invoke the sense of vertigo produced by that instability of MEANING resulting from the endless play of SIGNIFIERS in a TEXT.

Misprision/misreading See REVISIONISM

Mode Apart from serving as a general synonym for 'type', mode enters into recent critical vocabulary mainly in connection with NARRATIVE theory. A usage associated with the linguistician M. A. K. Halliday equates mode with what can be termed the 'medium' of a text or 'channel of communication'. Thus a telephoned message is in a different mode from a written one.

Alternatively, alterations in narrative DISTANCE can be said to produce different modes; thus a sudden shift into irony on the part of a NARRATOR involves a change of mode.

In Gerald Prince's definition MOOD (see also the entry for PERSPECTIVE AND VOICE) consists of two sub-categories: *perspective* (or point of view) and *distance* (or mode) (1988, 54). In other words: one determines the mood of a narrative by finding out (i) what perspective on characters and events the narrative has and (ii) how close to or distanced from these characters and events the narrative is.

It is fair to say that none of these usages is sufficiently well-established to be dominant or authoritative, so care needs to be taken in using or interpreting this word in critical writing.

Modernism and Postmodernism Both of these terms reach beyond national-cultural and generic boundaries; they describe artistic and cultural artifacts and attitudes of (mainly) the present century which possess certain family resemblances. The term *postmodernism* can, further, be used to refer not just to art and CULTURE but also more comprehensively to aspects of modern society.

It is not easy to define modernism and postmodernism independently because the boundaries between the two terms vary according to different usages – as Andreas Huyssen, for example, points out.

> the amorphous and politically volatile nature of postmodernism makes the phenomenon itself remarkably elusive, and the definition of its boundaries exceedingly difficult, if not per se impossible. Furthermore, one critic's postmodernism is another critic's modernism (or variant thereof), while certain vigorously new forms of contemporary culture (such as the emergence into a broader public's view of distinct minority cultures and of a wide variety of feminist work in literature and the arts) have so far rarely been discussed *as* postmodern . . . (1988, 58–9)

Indeed, as Ihab Hassan points out, this indeterminacy can draw in other terms such as *avant-garde*:

> Like other categorical terms – say poststructuralism, or modernism, or romanticism for that matter – postmodernism suffers from a certain *semantic* instability. That is, no clear consensus about its meaning exists among scholars. . . . Thus some critics mean by postmodernism what others call avant-gardism or even neo-avant-gardism, while still others would call the same phenomenon simply modernism. (1985, 121)

In like vein, David Harvey has suggested that there is more continuity than difference in the movement from modernism to postmodernism, and that the latter represents a crisis within the former in which fragmentation and ephemerality are confirmed while the possibility of the eternal and the immutable is treated with far greater scepticism (1989, 116). Similarly, Alex Callinicos (1989) has argued that there is no sharp distinction between modernism and postmodernism, and that the belief that there is can be explained by reference to the particular political and cultural disappointments of the generation of 1968 in Western Europe and the USA.

Of the terms so far mentioned, perhaps the least problematic is *avant-garde*. The term comes from military terminology, and refers to the (normally small) advance guard which prepares the way for a larger, following army – what later became known as shock-troops. In the context of cultural politics the term was used in the early part of the present century to refer to movements which had the aim of assaulting CONVENTIONAL standards and attitudes – particularly but not exclusively in the field of culture and the arts. Thus Cubism, Futurism, Dadaism, Surrealism and Constructivism are all conventionally described as avant-gardist in essence. It is striking that the avant-garde is normally discussed in terms of *movements*, whereas modernism is normally discussed in terms of individual artists and WORKS. This may be at least partly because avant-garde movements typically saw their cultural task as a part of a larger cultural-political campaign dedicated to the destruction of bourgeois standards, and it is the overtly political and activist element in many avant-garde movements which is frequently used as one of the criteria for distinguishing between avant-gardism and modernism. The very name *avant-garde* implies a concern for what will follow after, whereas many modernist artists were often profoundly pessimistic or resigned about the likelihood that their work might inspire any form of wider social or cultural change. The standard works on the avant-garde are Poggioli (1971) and Bürger (1984).

The term *modernism* has achieved a more stable meaning during the past decade, although the attempt to, as it were, 'backdate' postmodernism to apply to works of art previously described as modernist has shaken this stability somewhat. (Thus works such as Virginia Woolf's *The Waves* and James Joyce's *Finnegans Wake* have been confidently described as *modernist* for some years, but during the last decade or so the term *postmodernist* has begun to be applied to them by many critics.) In general usage, though, modernism describes that art (not just literature) which sought to break with what had become the dominant and dominating conventions of nineteenth-century art and culture. The most important of these conventions is probably that of REALISM: the modernist artist no longer saw the highest test of his or her art as that of verisimilitude. This does not mean that all modernist art gave up the attempt to understand or represent the extra-literary world, but that it rejected those nineteenth-century standards of realism which had hardened into unquestioned conventions. Instead, the modernist art-work is possessed, typically, of a *self-reflexive* element: we may lose ourselves in the fictional 'world' of, say, *Pride and Prejudice* when reading Jane Austen's novel, but when reading James Joyce's *Ulysses* or Virginia Woolf's *The Waves* we are made conscious that we are reading a novel. (Just as we might look at a painting by Turner and lose ourselves in the scene depicted, while a painting by Picasso thrusts its 'paintingness' upon our attention.)

We can compare the attack on perspective in the visual arts and on tonality in music with the attempt of various modernist writers to escape the constraints of traditional views of 'character' and 'plot'. Thus modernism announces itself as a break with the past similar, in some ways, to the assault on traditional values associated with romanticism. One of the qualities which distinguishes modernism from romanticism, however, is a generally more pessimistic, even tragic view of the world. Generalization is dangerous here, and it seems that British literary modernism (which, revealingly, was contributed to by many non-Britons) is perhaps more pessimistic than Continental modernism. But the work of T. S. Eliot, Ezra Pound, D. H. Lawrence, Franz Kafka, Knut Hamsun – to take some representative names – is typically characterized by a pessimistic view of the modern world, a world seen as fragmented and decayed, in which communication between human beings is difficult or impossible, and in which commercial and cheapening forces present an insuperable barrier to human or cultural betterment.

In general, modernists are hostile towards, or at least suspicious of, developments in contemporary science and technology. This is not universally the case: it is not true, for example of Vladimir Mayakovsky or of the Italian Futurists. But it is revealing that the latter have often been described as avant-garde rather than modernist. This suspicion of science and technology, in many cases directly attributable to revulsion from the use of technology to slaughter millions in the First World War, and often associated with a disgust at commercialism, is one of the clearest ways of distinguishing modernism from much postmodernism.

Here one needs to point out that an involvement in a cultural and artistic revolution does not necessarily imply political progressiveness: the work of Knut Hamsun, T. S. Eliot, Ezra Pound, Luigi Pirandello, D. H. Lawrence, and W. B. Yeats is central to modernism, but the social and political vision which can be extracted from it is more backward- than forward-looking, more conservative than progressive in political terms. This is not true of all modernism, but it serves to demonstrate that artistic and cultural experimentation, innovation, and anti-traditionalism could well go along with political traditionalism, conservatism, or even fascism: Pound's and Hamsun's fascist commitment was of long duration, and (at least according to some accounts) unshaken by the revelations of Nazi atrocities which followed the Second World War. In contrast, an important modernist writer such as Virginia Woolf maintained a consistent liberalism which shaded into support for the Labour Party during the 1930s, and, like many other important modernist writers, Woolf had no truck with fascism at any time.

Mention of Woolf prompts the observation that the development of modernism seems to be associated with a certain 'masculinization' of art: in contrast to the dominant position of women novelists in the nineteenth century, women take a long time to reattain this supremacy subsequent to the modernist revolution. Part of the explanation of this may relate to the association of modernism with social and geographical mobility, and the adoption of a bohemian life-style – much more difficult for women than for men, as Woolf pointed out (in the course of a different argument) in her *A Room of One's Own*.

Behind much modernist pessimism lies not just the empirical discovery that full communication between human beings is difficult in the modern age, but a more philosophical belief that although the world may be single and knowable, it is knowable only in small pieces at once. David Harvey has argued that modernism took on multiple perspectivism and relativism as its epistemology for revealing 'what it still took to be the true nature of a unified, though complex, underlying reality (1989, 30). (Postmodernism, in contrast, tends to retain the relativism while abandoning the belief in the unified underlying reality, and David Harvey quotes François Lyotard's definition of the postmodern as 'incredulity towards metanarratives' [1989, 45] – a definition which is itself, paradoxically, something of a metanarrative; the resemblance between postmodernism and DECONSTRUCTION is strongly apparent at this point.) For the modernist, therefore, human beings are doomed to exist in a state of social – and even existential – fragmentation, while yearning (unlike the postmodernist) to escape from this situation. Here the influence of Freud is probably important, for Freud turned the attention of many writers inward, towards subjective experience rather than the objective world. On the one hand, this led to the development or refinement of important new techniques: Joyce's and Woolf's development of internal monologue and stream-of-consciousness, Eliot's refinement of the dramatic monologue. But it also tied in with a pessimistic belief in the unbridgeability of the gap between subjective experience and an objective world, the belief that 'It is impossible to say just what I mean!'.

Furthermore, this alienation has the effect – or is associated with – a problematizing of human individuality and identity. 'Who am I?' asks Virginia Woolf's Bernard, in her experimental novel *The Waves*, and his question is emblematic of a recurrent problem for modernist artists. Thus one of the conventions attacked by modernist novelists is that of 'character', where this is taken to represent a unified, stable and coherent person, knowable both to him or herself as well as to others. Just as Bernard is not sure who he is, so in Kafka's *The Castle*, K. finds that he can obtain no stable description of Klamm, who is seen in different ways by different people, or by the same people at different times. This dependence of identity upon the observer is pursued to perhaps its farthest extreme in modernist literature in some of the plays of Luigi Pirandello, and clearly ends up in varieties of solipsism. It should be added that in this respect a work such as James Joyce's *Ulysses* seems relatively conventional.

Ihab Hassan has traced the term *postmodernism* back to Frederico de Onis's use of the term *postmodernismo* in his *Antología de la Poesía Espanola e Hispanoamericana* (1934), but the term only enters Anglo-American critical discourse in the 1950s, and only in a significant way in the 1960s. At first the term seems to indicate a new periodization: postmodern art or culture is that art or culture which, in the years after the Second World War, extends or even

109

breaks with modernist techniques and conventions without reverting to realist or pre-modernist positions. But before long critics start to use the term to refer to particular cultural, artistic – or even social – characteristics irrespective of when they manifested themselves. The use of the word 'social' is significant: *postmodernism* is typically used in a rather wider sense than is *modernism*, referring to a general human condition, or society at large, as much as to art or culture (a usage which was encouraged by Jean-François Lyotard's book *The Postmodern Condition: a Report on Knowledge* [English translation, 1984]). *Postmodernism*, then, can be used today in a number of different ways: (i) to refer to the non-realist and non-traditional literature and art of the post-Second World War period; (ii) to refer to literature and art which takes certain modernist characteristics to an extreme stage; and (iii) to refer to aspects of a more general human condition in the 'late capitalist' world of the post 1950s which have an all-embracing effect on life, culture, ideology and art, as well as (in some but not all usages) to a generally welcoming, celebrative attitude towards these aspects.

Thus those modernist characteristics which may produce postmodernism when taken to their most extreme forms, would include the rejection of representation in favour of self-reference – especially of a 'playful' and non-serious, non-constructive sort; the willing, even relieved, rejection of artistic AURA and of the sense of the work of art as organic whole (although David Harvey has argued that modernist (unlike postmodernist) art is essentially auratic [1989, 22]); the substitution of confrontation and teasing of the reader for collaboration with him or her; the rejection of 'character' and 'plot' as meaningful or artistically defensible concepts or conventions; even the rejection of MEANING itself as a hopeless delusion, a general belief that it is not worth trying to understand the world – or to believe that there is such as thing as 'the world' to be understood. Postmodernism takes the subjective idealism of modernism to the point of solipsism, but rejects the tragic and pessimistic elements in modernism in the conclusion that if one cannot prevent Rome burning then one might as well enjoy the fiddling that is left open to one. This and other broad definitions of postmodernism allow for the possibility of dubbing many literary and artistic works of the early part of the present century, or even of previous centuries, as to a greater or lesser extent postmodernist: the fiction of Franz Kafka, Knut Hamsun's *Hunger*, Ezra Pound's 'Cantos', and even Laurence Sterne's *Tristram Shandy*. They also open the way to seeing post-modernist elements in the work of various POST-STRUCTURALIST and deconstructive critics such as Jacques Derrida, Michel Foucault, and Jacques Lacan.

Postmodernism is characterized in many accounts by a more welcoming, celebrative attitude towards the modern world. That this world is one of increasing fragmentation, of the dominance of commercial pressures, and of human powerlessness in the face of a blind technology, is not a point of dispute with modernism. But whereas the major modernists reacted with horror or despair to their perception of these facts, in one view of the issue it is typical of postmodernism to react in a far more accepting manner. David Harvey argues that postmodernism is mimetic of social, economic, and political practices in the societies in which it appears, and he compares the superimposition of different but uncommunicating worlds in many a postmodern novel with 'the increasing ghettoization, disempowerment, and isolation of poverty and minority populations in the inner cities of both Britain and the Unites States' (1989, 113). Harvey also makes some very suggestive comparisons between the new organizational structures of post-Fordist capitalism (productive dispersal alongside capital concentration) and postmodernist ideology.

In our third possible usage of the term there is also a perception that the world has changed since the early years of this century. In the developed ('late capitalist') countries the advances of the communications and electronics industries have (it is argued) revolutionized human society. Instead of reacting to these changes in what is characterized as a Luddite manner, the post-modernist may instead counsel celebration of the present: celebration of the loss of artistic aura that follows what Benjamin (one of the most important prophets of postmodernism) calls 'mechanical reproduction'. Thus the paintings of an Andy Warhol or a Roy Lichstenstein (often categorized as Pop Art but arguably also postmodernist) force us to look more carefully and less dismissively at aspects of the commercial culture of our age, arguably carrying on the earlier work of Marcel Duchamp who, in 1919, could exhibit a mass-produced urinal as if it were a sculpture. In common with some much earlier avant-gardists, many postmodernists are fascinated with rather than repelled by technology, do not reject 'the POPULAR' as being beneath them, and are very much concerned with the immediate effect of their works: publication is more a strategic act than a bid for immortality. Alex Callinicos has, however, pointed out that such accounts tend to under-represent the relations between many of the 'high modernists' and popular culture, and he instances T. S. Eliot's interest in Music Hall and Stravinsky's indebtedness to Ragtime (1989, 15).

In the field of literature it is perhaps most uncontroversial to call the following writers and their works postmodernist: Samuel Beckett, Eugene Ionescu, John Barth, John Ashberry, Thomas Pynchon, Donald Barthelme, William Burroughs, Walter Abish, Alain Robbe-Grillet, Peter Handke, Carlos Fuentes, and Jorge Luis Borges. Two related terms describing postmodernist fiction are *fabulation* and *surfiction*. Both terms imply an aggressive and playful luxuriation in the nonrepresentational, in which the writer takes delight in the artifice of writing rather than in using writing to describe or make contact with a perceived extra-fictional reality.

Moment During the 1920s and 1930s the word *moment* was given a particular meaning in Virginia Woolf's writing, one similar to James Joyce's *epiphany*. A Woolfian moment typically involved the sensation of time pausing, of a number of human and/or non-human factors coming together in a unity which was both unique but which also had the power to 'speak' an inner truth or set of inner truths, both of the participants and components and to the observer. During the past two decades a rather different meaning of *moment* has emerged, one which shares an emphasis upon the self-speaking intensity that may suddenly flash out from the coming-together of a number of separate elements, but which focuses upon social-cultural and historical as well as individual and subjective forces. The 'moment' of *Left Review*, then, is that particular concatenation of forces – social, political, cultural – which provides both the impetus to found the journal and also the audience and context to appreciate and form it.

Used thus the term shares much with the rather more technical *conjuncture*, which latter has a somewhat more mechanical sense of social and political forces coming together like railway-lines to a junction. *Conjuncture* seems to have risen and fallen in concord with the changing authority of Louis Althusser, and although it is still encountered, the mechanistic connotations of its rigorously Latinate etymology have something of a 1970s flavour to them. (This was a time when the human SUBJECT had to be excluded from the heady realms of theory.)

Moment has suffered less of decline, perhaps partly because this term seems to allow more space for the human and the experiential than does *conjuncture*.

Compare PROBLEMATIC.

Monoglossia/monologic See DIALOGIC

Monovalent discourse See REGISTER

Mood According to Gérard Genette, 'one can tell *more* or tell *less* what one tells, and can tell it *according to one point of view or another*; and this capacity, and the modalities of its use, are precisely what our category of *narrative mood* aims at' (1980, 161–2). The term is borrowed from grammatical mood, and its adoption by Genette is a good example of the reliance by NARRATOLOGISTS upon the LINGUISTIC PARADIGM.

See also MODE; PERSPECTIVE AND VOICE.

Motivated See ARBITRARINESS; FUNCTION

Multivalent In Chemistry, the valency of a substance represents its ability to combine with or displace a standard hydrogen atom. Used metaphorically, the term thus indicates an ability to combine with or displace other elements so as to create something new. In literary-critical DISCOURSE the term multivalent normally indicates that a TEXTUAL element assumes a variety of different sorts of significance as it combines with other textual or extra-textual elements (e.g. interpretative techniques or READINGS).

Muted In current usage applied particularly to non-dominant groups in a given society who are denied the right of and the means to expression – especially self-expression. FEMINISTS have drawn attention to the way in which women typically constitute a muted group, unable to express their real situation and thus experiencing it as an individual deviation from a proclaimed norm rather than as the common experience which it in fact is.

Elaine Showalter credits two essays by the Oxford anthropologist Edwin Ardener, with the establishment of this term. According to him, she reports, muted groups must 'mediate their beliefs through the allowable forms of dominant structures' (1986, 261). Particularly important is Edwin Ardener's belief that women's beliefs and expression find expression through ritual and art, and can be deciphered by the ethnographer. Muting, in other words, is not silencing; it involves the partial silencing and suppression of valid expression, but not to the extent that this cannot be brought to the surface by the right investigator. Not surprisingly the concept has been used by feminist literary critics as an indication of the sort of READING that should be given to literary WORKS written by women in male-dominated societies.

Myth Two of the most influential of contemporary thinkers – Claude Lévi-Strauss and Roland Barthes – have helped to revivify the concept of myth in recent times. Lévi-Strauss's discussion of myth in *The Savage Mind* helped to establish the idea of myth as *a kind of thought*, one, as he puts it, based on elements that are 'half-way between percepts and concepts' (1972, 18). This is very different from the traditional view of myth, conveniently defined by Robert Scholes and Robert Kellogg as 'a traditional plot which can be transmitted' (1966, 12).

This shift of emphasis from myth as a sort of PLOT to myth as a way of thinking with close resemblances to (along with some differences from) ideology, can also be found in Roland Barthes's highly original *Mythologies*. Barthes's great achievement was to bring myths home to contemporary life, to make present-day European readers aware that myths were not just something that other people (remote African tribes, Russian peasants, the ancient Greeks) believed in and created – but were part of the stuff and fabric of everyday modern life in the West. *Mythologies* includes brief studies of such diverse topics as wrestling, soap powders, the face of Greta Garbo, steak and chips, and striptease. Barthes explained that for him the notion of myth explained a particular process whereby historically determined circumstances were presented as somehow 'natural', and that it allowed for the uncovering of 'the ideological abuse' hidden 'in the display of *what goes without saying*' (1973, 11). Myth, for Barthes, thus performs a NATURALIZING function, one which can be likened to an inversion of DEFAMILIARIZATION. *Mythologies* was a very influential book, leading directly to a British book entitled *Television Mythologies* in 1984 and indirectly to a rather different usage of the word 'myth'.

If Lévi-Strauss sees myth as a kind of thought, for Barthes it is 'a type of speech', and his emphasis is very similar to that of Lévi-Strauss's: 'Myth is not defined by the object of its message, but by the way in which it utters this message' (1973, 109), it is 'depoliticized speech' (1973, 142).

In recent usage, then, the concepts of myth and of ideology are interlinked: myths perform an ideological function while ideologies function by means of myths. This shift away from more traditional meanings is perhaps what led the poet Basil Bunting, responding to a questionnaire for a special issue on myth of the journal *Agenda* in 1977, to claim that arguments about what the devil myth meant were unprofitable, because the word does not seem to mean anything in particular.

Clemens Lugowski's *Form, Individuality and the Novel*, first published in German in 1932 and only recently published in English, makes use of the concept of the *mythic analogue* in a way reminiscent of, though predating, the work of Barthes and Lévi-Strauss. Introducing the modern reissue of Lugowski's work, Heinz Schaffler notes that 'Lugowski's inquiry implies that while the original vitality of myth has faded, the remnants of mythic thought have gone over into aesthetic structures', and this remnant Lugowski dubs the mythic analogue (1990, xiii). (Although Lugowski is unlikely to have been influenced by Marx, this argument has much in common with Marx's comments on myth in what has become known as the Introduction to the *Critique of Political Economy*, in which Marx relates the achievement of Greek art to Greek mythology.) As with Barthes and Lévi-Strauss, myth for Lugowski involves a way of representing reality. By reference to the *Decameron* he suggests that the mythic analogue involves a 'view of the world as a form of timeless, static existence' (1990, 42) – which reminds us of Barthes's view of myth as a transformation of history to a sort of common sense.

N

Narrated monologue See FREE INDIRECT DISCOURSE

Narratee The 'target' at whom a NARRATIVE is directed. A narratee is not just the individual by whom a narrative is received; there has to be some evidence that the narrative is actually intended for a particular goal for it to count as the (or a) narratee. This leads Prince (1988) to argue that the narratee must be inscribed in the TEXT. He argues that there is a difference between a narratee and both the READER and the IMPLIED READER. In the final section of James Joyce's *Ulysses* therefore, if we follow Prince on this matter, the narratee is Molly Bloom herself, but the implied reader is rather a person who can, for example, pick up the classical analogies contained within the text of *Ulysses* as a whole, with the real reader being anyone who actually reads the novel.

Narratees may be single or multiple, personified or non-personified. Thus in a complex WORK such as Joseph Conrad's *Heart of Darkness*, those sitting and listening to Marlow's account are the narratees of his narrative, but they are not the narratees of the FRAME narrative. Translating all this into a less technical form, we can say that whereas Marlow talks to certain personified individuals who are characters within the novel, the anonymous frame narrator directs his (or her) comments to an unpersonified, non-specific narratee who exists within the novel as narratee and nothing else.

One should add that of course a well-defined narratee exerts considerable influence on the formation of the implied reader as well as on the attitudes and behaviour of the real reader.

Narration This is a rather slippery term in contemporary NARRATIVE theory, and is given different weight by different theorists. By some it is used as a synonym for narrative, by others as the act or process whereby a narrative is produced. The second of these is the definition chosen by Rimmon-Kenan, for whom narration is both (i) the *communication* process in which the narrative as message is transmitted and (ii) the *verbal* nature of the medium used to transmit the message (1983, 2). For Rimmon-Kenan the communication process involved in narration is a double one, both contained in the TEXT (Marlow narrates his STORY to those listening to him in *Heart of Darkness*) as well as involving the text (Joseph Conrad is engaged in narration when writing *Heart of Darkness* for READERS to read) – although for her the former of these processes is the more important (1983, 3).

Michael J. Toolan discusses a number of alternative usages, and suggests his own: narration is 'the individual or "position" we judge to be the immediate source and authority for whatever words are used in the telling' (1988, 76).

Compare the distinctions listed in the entry for ENUNCIATION and its cognates.

Narrative Gerald Prince defines this term as 'the recounting of one or more real or fictitious events' but as 'product and process, object and act, structure and structuration' (1988, 58). So far as other theorists are concerned, however, it almost seems a case of perm any two from this list of six.

Thus Gérard Genette points out that the word *narrative* (in French, récit) can refer to three separate things: either the oral or written narrative statement that undertakes to tell of an EVENT or events; or the succession of real or fictitious events that are the subject of the DISCOURSE, with their varied relations; or, finally, the act of narrating (1980, 25–6). In his own usage he reserves the word narrative for the first of these three, while the second he refers to as STORY or DIEGESIS and the third as *narrating*. This makes good sense, but others have suggested alternative usages and one should be prepared for the possibility that the term may be used in any one or more of the three alternatives suggested by Genette.

On two points there is, however, agreement. First that a narrative must involve the recounting of an event or events, otherwise it is not a narrative but a description. And second that these events can be either real or fictitious. The person telling the TV News what happened in an accident in which she was involved is as much delivering a narrative as is the person telling a joke or the Marlow of *Heart of Darkness*.

See also REGISTER.

Narrative movements See DURATION

Narrative situation Used by Mieke Bal in a technical sense, and fixed according to the answers evinced by a set of typical questions. Is the NARRATOR a character or not? Does the narrator exist within the world of the STORY? Is the NARRATIVE FOCALIZED through the narrator? (1985, 126). In other words, narrative situation has nothing to do with whether the narrative is ostensibly delivered in Paris or Rome, or whether the narrator narrates in a sitting or standing position, but is defined according to the narrator's relationship to the narrative and the story. From this perspective the narrative situations in Joseph Conrad's *Heart of Darkness* and Woody Allen's film *Broadway Danny Rose* have certain striking similarities, even though the setting, story, and action of the two WORKS have precious little in common.

Narratology According to Mieke Bal, 'narratology studies narrative texts only in so far as they are narrative' (1985, 126). In other words, a TEXT such as *The Catcher in the Rye* can be studied in a number of ways, but not all of these belong to narratology. It should be noted that a literary-critical study of a text is not necessarily the same as a narratological study of it. If the text is studied as a source for information about the problems of adolescence then that is not primarily a literary-critical approach to the text – although a literary-critical approach could involve a concern with its treatment of adolescent problems – nor is it a narratological approach. Narratology is concerned only with the issue of how the EVENTS which make up this particular STORY are narrated.

Gerald Prince suggests variant definitions of this term, and in addition to one similar to that advanced by Bal, he suggests that narratology can refer to the STRUCTURALIST-inspired theory which studies the functioning of NARRATIVE in a medium-independent manner, and he attempts to define both narrative COMPETENCE as well as what narratives have in common and what enables them to differ from one another (1988, 65).

Narrator Whereas Gerald Prince describes the narrator as 'the one who narrates' (1988, 65), and Katie Wales as 'a person who narrates' (1989, 316), Mieke Bal stresses that for her the narrator is the narrative agent, 'the linguistic subject, a function and not a person, which expresses itself in the language that constitutes the text' (1985, 119). The tension between these two approaches pin-points a problem: whereas the term evokes a sense of a human individual for most people, many NARRATIVES do not stem from recognizably human or personified sources, but from a SUBJECT position within the text.

This point becomes clearer when we remember that the narrator must be distinguished not just from the real AUTHOR, but also from the implied author.

This is obvious in the case of a *personified narrator*: Charles Marlow, who we meet with in four of Joseph Conrad's fictions, is neither Joseph Conrad nor that authorial presence and CENTRE that we sense (according to some commentators) in each complete fiction of Conrad's, and which some prefer to name the implied author. But the same point can be made about the narrator of George Eliot's *Middlemarch*, who is neither George Eliot (or Marian Evans!) nor the 'sense of an author' we get when reading *Middlemarch*. (Although narrator and implied author are more difficult to distinguish in *Middlemarch* than they are in, say, Conrad's *Lord Jim*.) But if the narrator of *Middlemarch* is not a real or implied author, it does not follow that he/she is (as Wales has it) 'a person' – otherwise I would not be driven to the awkwardness of a formulation like 'he/she'. That unwillingness to refer to the narrator of *Middlemarch* as 'he' or 'she' – or, come to that, as 'it' – reveals that although many narrators assume certain human characteristics, they must sometimes be distinguished from human individuals. Indeed, it may be argued that (like literary characters) they need to be distinguished from human individuals even when they are personified and appear most human – as with, for example, Charles Marlow. Moreover, even if a narrator may be personified, he or she may still be relatively anonymous. The FRAME narrator of Henry James's *The Turn of the Screw* is so anonymous that there is no firm evidence as to whether we are dealing with a male or a female.

Level of personification is thus one important element in distinguishing between narrators, but it is not the only one. Other important elements are: *narrative level* (does the narrator belong to the same 'reality' as the characters, or is he/she *extradiegetic*? (See the entry for DIEGESIS AND MIMESIS.) Does the narrator *participate in the story* fully, partially, or not at all? (The narrator may be fully personified and portrayed on a REALISTIC level, but merely recounting a STORY in which he/she observed without personal involvement.) Is the narrator *perceptive or obtuse*? *Wuthering Heights* has one (relatively) perceptive narrator and one obtuse one; *Huckleberry Finn* and *Gulliver's Travels* have narrators who are at times perceptive, at times obtuse. Is the narrator *overt or covert*? In other words, are we aware of a narrating subject or does the text seem transparent, giving us a view of character and action which so occupies our attention that we are not conscious of any narrator? Is the narrator *reliable or unreliable*? Do we believe everything that the narrator tells us, or suspect that either deceit or obtuseness on his/her part requires us to see more than he or she does?

Naturalization See DEFAMILIARIZATION

Négritude A neologism coined by the Martinique writer Aimé Césaire in his *Cahier d'un Retour au Pays Natal* (*Notes on a Return to the Land of My Birth*) in 1939. One of the definitions of the term provided by Césaire is simple and all-embracing: '*Négritude* is the simple recognition of the fact that one is black, the acceptance of this fact and of our black destiny, our history, and our culture' (Kesteloot 1968, 80). Following Césaire, the term was applied to a movement of Black (mainly African) writers resident in Paris, and was in conscious opposition to the French colonial policy of integrating colonial peoples and their cultures into French CULTURE. The Senegalese writer Léopold Sédar Senghor was an influential figure in the movement.

The term was taken up by some Black American writers in the 1960s, for whom it became a shorthand way of celebrating Blackness and Black culture. During this time its use generally betokened an anti-rational, anti-colonialist standpoint, the associations its use by Black writers in Paris had gathered by the time that visiting Black American writers encountered it. It suggested the anti-rational in as much as its use went hand in hand with a rejection of the rational in favour of more mystical, collective and emotional forms of understanding; anti-colonialist in as much as Black Americans identified their own situation as oppressed group in the United States with that of Black Africans fighting against European domination. Much Black American writing of the 1960s and 1970s used these associations to label and legitimize a sort of writing that broke with what were seen as culturally alien forms of expression. It had its critics, however, who argued that many negative STEREOTYPES of Black people were perpetuated by the term.

New Historicism A term applied to a loose grouping of critics and theorists whose approach to the study of the past bases itself upon READINGS both of literary and of non-literary TEXTS. The writings of Michel Foucault and Raymond Williams constitute a major influence on its members, and the New Historicists have succeeded in defining (or suggesting) new objects of historical study, with a particular emphasis upon the way in which causal influences are mediated through discursive practices (see the entry for DISCOURSE).

A key figure in the rise of the New Historicism is the Renaissance critic Stephen Greenblatt, and in his recent collection of essays *Learning to Curse* (1990) he admits that for him the term describes not so much a set of beliefs as

> a trajectory that led from American literary formalism through the political and theoretical ferment of the 1970s to a fascination with what one of the best new historicist critics [Louis A. Montrose] calls 'the historicity of texts and the textuality of history'. (1990, 3)

Elsewhere he describes the New Historicism as a practice rather than a doctrine (1990, 146). Greenblatt sees the New Historicism's creation of 'an intensified willingness to read all of the textual traces of the past with the attention traditionally conferred only on literary texts' (1990, 14) to be central to its value. Thus in a study of a design by Dürer for a monument to commemorate the defeat of peasants involved in protest and rebellion, Greenblatt notes that intention, genre and historical situation all have to be taken into account, as all are social and ideological and must be involved in any 'reading' of the design (1990, 112). He continues:

> The production and consumption of such works are not unitary to begin with; they always involve a multiplicity of interests, however well organized, for the crucial reason that art is social and hence presumes more than one consciousness. And in response to the art of the past, we inevitably register, whether we wish to or not, the shifts in value and interest that are produced in the struggles of social and political life. (1990, 112)

The New Historicist, in other words, has as much to say about the reading of texts as about their composition.

For those who like negative definitions, Greenblatt cites three definitions of the word 'historicism' from *The American Heritage Dictionary*, all of which he sees to be counter to the practice of New Historicists:

1. The belief that processes are at work in history that man can do little to alter.
2. The theory that the historian must avoid all value judgments in his study of past periods or former cultures.
3. Veneration of the past or of tradition. (cited in Greenblatt 1990, 164)

Although Greenblatt and other New Historicists pay tribute to the work of various POST-STRUCTURALISTS, the anti-formalist element in their work clearly distances them from important aspects of post-structuralism.

See also CIRCULATION; RESONANCE.

New Readers A coinage of M. H. Abrams, used during the earlier days of debate about POST-STRUCTURALISM and DECONSTRUCTION to refer to such individuals as Jacques Derrida, Stanley Fish, and Harold Bloom – and their followers.

Norm. According to Jan Mukařovský, the basic prerequisite for an aesthetic norm is not its statability, 'but the general consensus, the spontaneous agreement, of the members of a certain community that a given esthetic procedure is desirable and not another' (1964, 44). Clearly this can be generalized: *any* norm and not just aesthetic ones, are characterized, in their own sphere, by general consensus and spontaneous agreement rather than by an agreed statement or formulation. Members of the prague school such as Mukařovský thus use *norm* in a manner which is very close to CONVENTION; certainly Mukařovský's account of the way in which breaking norms involves DEFAMILIARIZATION, is very close to Roman Jakobson's (1971) account of the way in which too rigidified a system of conventions leads to AUTOMATIZATION of response.

Felix Vodička suggests that the literary critic needs to reconstruct the relevant literary norms in order to read a work of literature written in a context in which norms different from those of his or her own culture flourish. He argues that the norms are contained

> in the literature itself, that is, in the works that are being read and liked, and by which are measured and evaluated new, or additional, literary works (1964, 74)

adding that normative poetics or literary theories allow us to know only the rules which a period believes *should* guide literary composition. Thus for him, the richest source of evidence for literary norms is to be found in evaluative statements about contemporary literature. Vodička does not consider literary norms to be totally isolated from contemporaneous, non-literary norms, but sees these two fields in interactive relationship (1964, 75).

The *normative fallacy*, according to Pierre Macherey, is apparent when criticism attempts to modify a literary work in order that it may be more thoroughly assimilated, 'denying its factual reality as being merely the provisional version of an unfulfilled intention'. For Macherey, the normative fallacy is a variety of a more fundamental fallacy, the *empiricist fallacy*, which we witness whenever criticism 'asks only how to *receive* a given object' (1978, 19).

Normative fallacy See NORM

Nucleus See EVENT

Opalescence See FLICKER

Opaque and transparent criticism Terms coined by A. D. Nuttall in his *A New Mimesis* to distinguish what he terms two languages of criticism: 'the first "opaque", external, formalist, operating outside the mechanisms of art and taking those mechanisms as object, the second "transparent", internal, realist, operating within the "world" presented in the work' (1983, 80). Thus a statement such as 'In the opening of *King Lear* folk-tale elements proper to narrative are infiltrated by a finer-grained dramatic mode' involves the use of opaque critical language, whereas 'Cordelia cannot bear to have her love for her father made the subject of a partly mercenary game' involves the use of transparent critical language (Nuttall's own examples).

Open texts See OPEN AND CLOSED TEXTS

Open and closed texts The theorist who has done most to popularize the idea that TEXTS can be either open or closed is Umberto Eco. His formulation is, however, rather complex and he defines 'open' and 'closed' in rather unexpected ways. As a result, the terms are often used in a sense that is rather the reverse of what he recommends.

The problem is very clear in the following discussion by Eco of texts such as Superman comic strips and novels by Ian Fleming (the creator of 'James Bond'). For Eco, such texts are closed precisely because they are open to any sort of READING:

> Those texts that obsessively aim at arousing a precise response on the part of more or less precise empirical readers . . . are in fact open to any possible 'aberrant' decoding. A text so immoderately 'open' to every possible interpretation will be called a *closed* one. (1981, 8)

In contrast, where the AUTHOR of the text has envisaged the rôle of the READER at the moment of generation, according to Eco the text is, paradoxically, open to successive interpretations. These interpretations and reinterpretations, according to Eco, echo one another, and operate within certainly textually imposed constraints (unlike responses to what he calls closed texts).

> You cannot use the [open] text as you want, but only as the text wants you to use it. An open text, however 'open' it be, cannot afford whatever interpretation. (1981, 19)

At the root of Eco's argument here lies a relatively traditional belief in the possibility of distinguishing between correct and incorrect interpretations of a certain sort of valued text.

> [I]t is possible to distinguish between the free interpretative choices elicited by a purposeful strategy of openness and the freedom taken by a reader with a text assumed as a mere stimulus. (1981, 40)

The theory thus depends upon two sorts of distinction: between different sorts of texts, and between different sorts of response to, or interpretation of, texts. As I have said, there are strongly traditional elements here in spite of the new terminology, and indeed, at one point in his essay 'The Poetics of the Open Work' Eco stops talking about *texts* and refers to *works of art*:

> A work of art, therefore, is a complete and *closed* form in its uniqueness as a balanced organic whole, while at the same time constituting an *open* product on account of its susceptibility to countless different interpretations which do not impinge on its unadulterable specificity. Hence every reception of a work of art is both an *interpretation* and a *performance* of it, because in every reception the work takes on a fresh perspective for itself. (1981, 49)

Oppositional reading

For Eco, open texts, works of art, are thus *in movement*, another coinage of his by which he seeks to describe their power to generate a never-ending series of new but valid reading experiences and interpretations.

Eco's discussion is thought-provoking and fruitful, but the complexities of a terminology that requires us to remember that a closed text is open to any sort of response and that an open text constrains what the reader does to it, have ensured that his suggested definitions have not obtained wider popularity – even though the terms *open* and *closed* are regularly and loosely used in discussions of literary and other texts.

Beyond this, it may be that the suggested distinction between these two sorts of text is perhaps too absolute, that *all* texts attempt to constrain how the reader makes use of them, and that all readings may choose to accept such constraints to a greater or a lesser extent.

See also READERLY AND WRITERLY TEXTS.

Opponent See ACT/ACTOR

Oppositional reading A reading which rejects and seeks to undermine the terms overtly or implicitly proposed by a given TEXT for acceptance by the READER prior to and during its own reading. Thus an oppositional reading of Henry James's *The Turn of the Screw* might view this text as reflective of STEREO-TYPED views of women as hysterical, unreliable, mysterious, corrupted by repressed passion, and so on.

Optimal reader See READERS AND READING

Orality A term used to denote an extended complex of elements associated with oral CULTURES – that is, cultures either unaffected by literacy and the written word or only marginally affected by them. One of the most influential (and accessible) theoretical contributions to the study of orality is Walter J. Ong's *Orality and Literacy* (1982), in which Ong argues that in a predominantly oral culture thought differs from the thought typical of a culture characterized by universal or near-universal literacy. The thought and expression of an oral culture, according to Ong, are *additive rather than subordinative, aggregative rather than analytic, redundant or 'copious', conservative or traditionalist, close to the human lifeworld, agonistically toned* (that is, polemical and emotive), *empathetic and participatory rather than objectively distanced, homeostatic,* and *situational rather than abstract* (1982, 37–57).

Ong's arguments have not gone unchallenged, and there is a growing literature concerned with debates around the concept of orality. These are of relevance to Literary Studies in a number of ways. For example: it seems clear that poetry emerged in an oral culture, and that some of its inherited characteristics owe something to the thought-patterns of an oral culture. Understanding more about an oral culture may help us to understand more about both the poetry of the distant past and also of more recent periods.

Orchestration In the work of Mikhail Bakhtin, part of an analogy between musical and novelistic structure (see also POLYPHONY). The different voices active in a given CULTURE at a given time can be orchestrated so as to reveal different aspects alone and in harmony/disharmony with one another.

Order Both the temporal succession of events in a STORY and also the placing in linear succession of EVENTS in a NARRATIVE.

See also ACHRONY; ANACHRONY; ANALEPSIS; PROLEPSIS.

Organicism In literary criticism, particularly during the heyday of the New Critics, it came to be an item of faith that the work of literature (or art) had to be treated as an *organic* structure – that is, having the qualities of a living unit with its parts organically rather than mechanically related.

During the same time F. R. Leavis extended the analogy from the individual literary work to literature as a whole; in his essay 'Literature and Society' he argues that

> A literature . . . must be thought of as essentially something more than a separation of separate works: it has an organic form, or constitutes an organic order, in relation to which the individual writer has his significance and his being. (1962a, 184)

Leavis goes on to argue that this approach is to be distinguished from that of the MARXIST, in that it stresses not economic and material determinants but intellectual and spiritual ones, and that although it accepts that material conditions have an enormous importance, 'there is a certain measure of spiritual autonomy in human affairs' (1962a, 184). Leavis also made much of the concept of 'the organic community', most notably in *Culture and Environment* which was written with Denys Thompson and first published in 1932, although directly comparable ideas can be found in the essay 'Literature and Society' (and in many other places in Leavis's writing) as well. The conservative-nostalgic concept of the organic community in Leavis's work owes much to T. S. Eliot. It represented a lost unity in sharp contrast to the alleged disintegration and divisions of modern urban society, a unity both among human beings and between human beings and their environment, in which a CULTURE shared by all the community's members and interwoven with the realities of their daily lives could be found.

It is necessary to fill in this historical sketch of earlier usages of *organic* because it is in reaction to these that a more recent usage is based. Representative is a discussion by Christopher Hampton of the passage quoted above from Leavis's 'Literature and Society'. Hampton's objection to Leavis's position centres upon the fact that as a result of the terms he uses 'history vanishes; and with it the influence of the changing conditions of material existence which determine not only the ways in which people's lives are shaped but also the cultural products of their thinking, including literature (1990, 50). Hampton's critique is sharper and less conciliatory than that of others – notably Raymond Williams in a number of his studies – but it sums up a particular sort of reaction against certain of Leavis's ideas. And in so doing it sums up what is meant by the current, pejorative use of the term *organicist*: viewing either literature, or art, or culture, or social life as organic unities superior to material or economic determinants and untroubled by inner fissures, dissent, or tension.

Ostranenie See DEFAMILIARIZATION

Other To characterize a person, group, or institution as 'other' is to place them outside the system of normality or convention to which one belongs oneself. Such processes of exclusion by categorization are thus central to certain ideological mechanisms. If woman is other, then that which is particular to the experience of being a woman is irrelevant to 'how things are', to the defining conventions by which one lives. If members of a given racial group are collectively seen as other, then how they are treated is irrelevant to what humanity demands – because they are other and not human.

What lies behind use of this term is the perception that when we divide reality up into separate components these are typically seen in an sort of FIGURE-GROUND manner, with one component representing a norm and other components representing divergences from this norm.

When granted a capital letter the term invokes Jacques Lacan's theory of the way in which the SUBJECT seeks confirmation of itself in the response of the Other. As he puts it one of his less opaque pronouncements in 'The Agency of the Letter in the Unconscious or Reason Since Freud',

> If I have said that the unconscious is the discourse of the Other (with a capital O), it is in order to indicate the beyond in which the recognition of desire is bound up with the desire for recognition.
>
> In other words this other is the Other that even my lie invokes as a guarantor of the truth in which it subsists. (1977, 172)

Also illuminating is Lacan's comment in 'On a Question Preliminary to any Possible Treatment of Psychosis', that the Other is, 'the locus from which the question of [the subject's] existence may be presented to him' (1977, 194).

According to Anthony Wilden,

> Lacan's Other represents the patrocentric ideology of our culture. The Other is only theoretically *ne-uter*, for it is not pure 'Otherness'. It is the principle of the locus of language and of the signifier, which for Lacan, is naturally the phallus . . . (1972, 261)

See also STEREOTYPE.

Overcoding See CODE

Overdetermination From the work of Sigmund Freud: if a symbol is the result of several separate or related causes then it is described as overdetermined. Freud saw the dream symbol as overdetermined because its full explanation could not involve merely one source or MEANING but had to take account of several interrelated sources and meanings. Writing of one of his own dreams, Freud suggests that certain elements are to be seen as 'nodal points' 'upon which a great number of dream-thoughts converged, and [which] had several meanings in connection with the interpretation of the dream' (1976, 388).

It is with the former sense of 'many determining forces fused into one resultant symbol (or event, or state of affairs)' that the term has entered into more general currency, however. A clear implication is that if something is overdetermined, then its analysis and explication will involve a sort of exploding into component parts or sources: the commentary will be much longer than the symbol because the symbol is so concentrated. Both dream analyses and analyses of poetic symbols are invariably much more extensive than the symbols themselves.

The term achieved some fashionability in the 1960s following its use by the French MARXIST philosopher Louis Althusser in his essay 'Contradiction and Overdetermination' (in Althusser 1969, 87–128). The use ushered in by Althusser was more historico-political: a range of different social forces could result in a single, overdetermined event such as a political revolution.

Thus overdetermination as concept served to warn against simplistic cause-and-effect views in a range of disciplines. It reminded the investigator that just as it was unlikely that the analysis of symbol or event could be completed by reference to a single cause, so too a single cause would be unlikely to lead unproblematically to an isolated event. And, moreover, that as overdetermination involved a play of interrelated and opposed forces, the result of this play could be very different from what might be predicted because of the diversions imposed by successive and complex MEDIATIONS.

P

Parabolic text A coinage of Barbara Herrnstein Smith which draws on the two meanings of *parabolic*: 'displaying the infinitely open curve of a parabola, and forming parables for an infinite number of propositions' (1978, 144). A parabolic text, then is *open* rather than *closed*, receiving and transforming varied approaches to it as a parabolic dish antenna 'captures' a range of different signals, but it also has the quality of a parable, supporting a succession of never-ending applications.

See also OPEN AND CLOSED TEXTS.

Paradigm shift A term introduced by Thomas S. Kuhn in his *The Structure of Scientific Revolutions* (first published 1962). Kuhn suggested that particular learned communities or specialities rested upon acceptance of 'a set of recurrent and quasi-standard illustrations of various theories in their conceptual, observational, and instrumental applications'. These, he proposed, are the community's *paradigms*, which can be found revealed in its 'textbooks, lectures, and laboratory exercises' (1970, 43). Kuhn (as his title suggests) was particularly interested in how changes take place in scientific thinking, and his concept of the paradigm plays a central rôle in his explanation. Kuhn's paradigms are not just the illustrations he mentions but also the assumptions which are to be found behind, and constituted by, these illustrations. In other words, a paradigm is constituted by a set of beliefs which both enables and constrains research: a framework or scaffold which can underpin or support further work but which of necessity also excludes a range of possibilities.

Readers of Kuhn's book from the Humanities were much struck by his accounts of cases of scientific evidence which was not recognized as such because it did not fit into known and accepted paradigms: for instance the scientist who actually isolated oxygen but was unable to recognize what he had done because it did not fit into the phlogiston theory within the confines of which he was working. This had more than a passing resemblance to then-influential theories of ideology, and Kuhn's ideas attracted much attention outside the realms of the philosophy of science.

In particular, Kuhn's view of the necessity for a *paradigm shift* to enable major advances in scientific theory to take place seemed to have something (but only something) in common with what Louis Althusser was saying concerning the need for the theorist to move from ideology to science. The difference is that for Kuhn there is no promised land of science; paradigm succeeds paradigm like the succession of blinkered generational views with which Philip Larkin's poem 'High Windows' presents us, each seeming as if it represents an advance but each with its own inevitable limitations.

Kuhn's concept of the paradigm shift attracted criticism, however, because of its 'inwardness': the shift was engendered and triggered by the pressure of internal contradictions rather than by (as in traditional Marxist views) the pressure of external forces which, in Darwinian mode, excluded theories which could not adapt to new external needs. The term has entered into literary-critical vocabulary in relation, very often, to arguments about the CANON (a WORK is only recognized as major when new literary paradigms allow it to be understood or appreciated), and in relation to arguments about interpretation (we interpret the evidence of a TEXT differently when our literary paradigms change, just as the scientist interprets the evidence provided by an experiment when his or her scientific paradigms change).

See also COPERNICAN REVOLUTION; *ÉPISTÈME*; PROBLEMATIC, for comparable concepts.

Paradigmatic See SYNTAGMATIC AND PARADIGMATIC

Paralipsis Gérald Genette suggests this term for an ELLIPSIS which is created not by missing out a temporal unit in the NARRATIVE succession, but by omitting a constituent element or elements in a period of STORY time that is covered in the narrative.

Paraliterature See CANON

Parergon See FRAME

Patriarchy Technically, government by men – either within the family or in society at large – with authority descending through the father. In recent usage the term has been used to point both to the actual exercise of power and also to the ideological system – the ideas and attitudes – used to bolster, justify, and protect this power. Patriarchy thus has political, economic, social and ideological dimensions.

Much recent FEMINIST literary criticism has aimed to uncover patriarchal ideas in WORKS of literature as well as in the systems surrounding these works: education, publishing, journalism, reviewing, and the general 'systems of literary production' specific to different CULTURES and societies.

Pause See DURATION

Performatives See SPEECH ACT THEORY

Perlocutionary act See SPEECH ACT THEORY

Perspective and Voice The distinction made by Gérard Genette between MOOD and voice is perhaps the best way into the topic which was once conceptualized in relatively unproblematic terms under the rubric of *point of view*, but which with the advances in NARRATIVE theory in recent years has become much a more complex topic known by a range of terms, the most accepted of which is probably *perspective*.

Genette has drawn attention to the importance of a long-neglected distinction between *who sees?* and *who speaks?* – in his terminology expressed in terms of the opposition between mood and voice (1980, 30). According to Genette, the category of mood gathers together the problems of DISTANCE which American critics have traditionally discussed in terms of the opposition between *telling and showing*, and he suggests that these terms represent a resurgence of the Platonic terms DIEGESIS and MIMESIS. *Voice*, in contrast, he reserves to describe the way the narrative situation, along with the NARRATOR and his or her audience, are implicated in the narrative (1980, 29–31). To summarize: *mood* operates at the level of connections between STORY and narrative, while voice designates connections both between narrating and narrative, and narrating and story (1980, 32).

Thus, for example, although the narrative voice in Joseph Conrad's *Under Western Eyes* is that of the personified narrator, the English teacher of languages, what is observed (in both senses of the word) frequently goes beyond that of this character, and the reader is told things which he could not possibly know if he were a living human being rather than a fictional character/narrator. Those following Genette have often preferred to replace *mood* by *perspective*, as the pair 'perspective and voice' matches up rather more neatly with 'who sees/who speaks'. In what follows I will adopt this terminology, and use 'perspective' to indicate 'who sees' and 'voice' to indicate 'who speaks'.

In Mieke Bal's terminology, perspective covers both the physical and psychological points of perception in a narrative, but it does not involve the actual *agent* performing the act of narration (1985, 101). Perspective can be further specified in terms of another of Genette's terms: FOCALIZATION. A narrative which has zero focalization is one in which it is impossible to fix the perspective in terms of which the narrated characters, events and situations are being observed and presented. Many works of fiction which were traditionally described as characterized by an *omniscient* point of view are described by modern narratologists as having a zero focalization. One could suggest that a novel such as George Eliot's *Middlemarch* was characterized by zero-focalization – which does not of course mean that the reader associates no set of values or attitudes, or even traces of personification – to the narrating of the work. The term *focalized narrative*, in contrast, can also be rendered as *internal perspective*: the story is told from the perspective of a point (normally a consciousness) which is internal to the story, or intra-diegetic. Such focalized narratives can be *fixed*, as in Jean Rhys's *After Leaving Mr Mackenzie* where everything we learn comes from the heroine/narrator Julia Martin, *variable*, as in Emily Brontë's *Wuthering Heights* in which some events are presented from the perspective of Mr Lockwood, some from that of Mrs Dean, and some from that of Isabella (in the long letter she writes), or *multiple* as in Tobias Smollett's *Humphry Clinker* in which the epistolary technique allows the same events to be presented more than once from different and contrasting perspectives. It will be clear that the distinction between variable and multiple perspective is not always so very easy to establish.

External focalization denotes a focalization that is limited to what, were the story true, the observer could actually have observed 'from the outside'; in other words, it involves no accounts of characters' thoughts, feelings, and emotions unless these are revealed in external behaviour or admitted to by the characters. According to Genette, external focalization involves a perspective which is intra-diegetic but outside that of the characters. In his Introduction to Genette's *Narrative Discourse*, Jonathan Culler has referred to the criticism made by Mieke Bal of Genette's distinction between *internal focalization* and *external focalization*. Culler notes that Bal claims that the two terms refer to rather different cases, for whereas

> In what Genette calls *internal focalization* the narrative is focused *through* the consciousness of a character, . . . *external focalization* is something altogether different: the narrative is focused *on* a character, not through him.
>
> (Genette 1980, 10)

An alternative way of referring to types of focalization is by means of reference to varieties of narrative *vision*.

Because of these variations in usage care needs to be exercised in the use of these terms.

See also ENUNCIATION; FRAME; NARRATIVE SITUATION.

Phallocentrism A term dating from recent FEMINIST theory and used to refer to interlocking social and ideological systems which accept and advance a PATRIARCHAL power symbolically represented by the phallus. 'Phallus' has to be understood as a *cultural* construction attributing symbolic power to the *biological* penis. The concept clearly builds upon artistic and CULTURAL representations of the penis which, in both ancient and modern societies, have been incorporated into ideological justifications of male power. The transformation of penis to phallus has a clear ideological colouring: a penis is one of a pair of matched sexual organs both of which are necessary for reproduction, while a phallus is seen as *prime* source of biological fruitfulness and thus can be used to underwrite the domination of one GENDER by the other. (Jacques Derrida, incidentally, sees such a view of the phallus as an example of a transcendental signifier: see the entry for TRANSCENDENTAL SIGNIFIED.)

In contemporary feminist usage, phallocentric patterns of thought consciously or unconsciously assume and advance a view of the masculine as natural source of power and authority, and of the feminine as naturally subject to this. Thus man is PRESENCE, woman ABSENCE, and this absence is symbolically underwritten by overt or concealed reference to the absent phallus. For some feminists, the phallus has an even more all-embracing set of symbolic meanings; Madeleine Gagnon, for example, writes that

> The phallus, for me at this time, represents repressive capitalist ownership, the exploiting bourgeoisie, the higher knowledge that must be gotten over; it represents an erected France that watches, analyzes, sanctions. The phallus means everything that sets itself up as a mirror. Everything that erects itself as perfection. Everything that wants regimentation and representation. That which does not erase/efface but covets. That which lines things up in history museums. That which constantly pits itself against the power of immortality. (1980, 180)

The term seems to have entered contemporary feminism through the Lacanian critique of Freud. Lacan's essay 'The Signification of the Phallus', based upon a lecture delivered in 1958 and first published in French in 1966, is by no means feminist in orientation. But in exploring the phallus as signifier in this and other writings, Lacan opened the way to a feminist appropriation of the term using, initially, a STRUCTURALIST conceptual framework.

Phallocratic denotes, literally, rule by the phallus – on the model of democratic, autocratic, and so on. Used in feminist DISCOURSE to indicate a system of power and authority which is based upon phallocentric values.

Phallic criticism is criticism which not only abides by and furthers phallocentric values, but which also uses methods associated with the exercise of phallocentric power and is backed by the institutional resources of phallocentrism.

Phallogocentrism A portmanteau term combining PHALLOCENTRISM and LOGO-CENTRISM, coined by Jacques Derrida in his critique of Jacques Lacan in 'The Purveyor of Truth' (1975). For Derrida, Lacan's reading of Edgar Alan Poe's 'The Purloined Letter' is guilty of phallogocentrism because Lacan sees the letter unproblematically as phallus, rather than recognizing that meaning cannot exist in such unproblematic one-to-one relationships.

Although the term was intended to imply criticism it has appealed to feminists and others eager to imply a connection between male, PATRIARCHAL authority, and systems of thought which legitimize themselves by reference to some PRESENCE or point of authority prior to and outside of themselves. The hidden, legitimizing presence, in other words, is always, at root, that of the Father, whose authority is a starting point or unconsidered assumption rather than something that can be justified or admitted.

David Lehman's explanatory note to a short poem by himself, published in the *Times Literary Supplement* for May 18–24, 1990, attributes to Benjamin Krull the following definition of phallogocentrism: 'what happens when you eliminate the space between the second and third words of the sentence *the pen is mightier than the sword*' (1990, 524). This suggests that the term's meaning has undergone a shift from that which Derrida originally intended (which would, presumably, neither surprise nor dismay Derrida).

Phatic See FUNCTIONS OF LANGUAGE

Phenomenology Phenomenology originates in the writing of the German Edmund Husserl, whose philosophy takes as its starting point the world as experienced in our consciousness. It thus rejects the possibility of considering the world independently of human consciousness, but seeks rather to get back to concrete reality through our experience of it. For Husserl, consciousness is always consciousness of something: it is directed outwards rather than inwards – even if it is directed on to something imagined. It is thus too simple to describe phenomenology as idealist, for although it posits the impossibility of our gaining a knowledge of the world which is untouched by our perception of that world, it does suggest that through an eidetic method we can build up a successively more and more accurate understanding of the objects of our consciousness by filtering off accidental and personal elements in our perception of them. In order so to analyse our consciousness we must suspend all preconceptions about the objects with which it is concerned (see the entry for *EPOCHÉ*). As Terry Eagleton comments,

> But if Husserl rejected empiricism, psychologism and the positivism of the natural sciences, he also considered himself to be breaking with the classical idealism of a thinker like Kant. Kant had been unable to solve the problem of how the mind can really know objects outside it at all; phenomenology, in claiming that what is given in pure perception is the very essence of things, hoped to surmount this scepticism. (1983, 56–7)

It is not hard to understand the interest that such ideas aroused amongst students of art and literature, for whom the pseudo-objectivity of positivism seemed no more applicable to the study and appreciation of art-works than did variants of Kantianism which too soon could end up in solipsism and an abandonment to unfettered personal 'taste'. A range of literary theorists and aestheticians found something in Husserl's ideas upon which they felt they could build. One of the earliest was the Polish aesthetician Roman Ingarden, who argued that a READING of a WORK of literature CONCRETIZES it (much as the performance of a play concretizes the written TEXT).

The Geneva School of criticism owes its largest debt to Husserl and phenomenological ideas. Its members were mostly associated with the University of Geneva, and have on occasions been referred to collectively as the 'Critics of Consciousness'. (Founder-members include Marcel Raymond and Albert Beguin, but more recently the best-known member is Georges Poulet. J. Hillis Miller was also associated with the school, although he has since moved to pastures new.)

READER-RESPONSE CRITICISM owes an important debt to phenomenology and the Geneva School, particularly in the person of the German critic Wolfgang Iser. Iser's essay 'The Reading Process: a Phenomenological Approach' (reprinted in Iser 1974) is a good example of the creative development of a number of aspects of phenomenology – and, too, of the way in which phenomenology leads naturally to some of the preoccupations of reader-response critics. Take, for example, the first sentence of the essay:

> The phenomenological theory of art lays full stress on the idea that, in considering a literary work, one must take into account not only the actual text but also, and in equal measure, the actions involved in responding to that text. (1974, 274)

Iser then moves on to discuss Ingarden's theory of artistic concretization, and concludes that the literary work has two poles: the artistic pole (the text created by the AUTHOR), and the aesthetic pole (the realization accomplished by the READER) (1974, 274). The argument is an interesting one, although the proposed nomenclature is perhaps odd, suggesting as it does that there is nothing aesthetic about the author's created text and nothing artistic about the reader's realization.

Pleasure

Iser stresses in particular the work's *virtuality*: like the text of a play which can be produced in innumerable ways, a literary work can lead to innumerable reading experiences. (Compare Derrida's argument that 'reading is transformational' [1981b, 63].) He also makes use of Husserl's argument that consciousness is *intentional*, that it is directed and goal-seeking rather than random and all-absorbing. So far as the reading of literature is concerned, this allows Iser to place a high premium not just upon the reader's 'pre-intentions' – what he or she goes to the text with – but also upon the intentions awakened by the reading process itself (and, indirectly, by the text). One of the best-known of Iser's arguments involves the literary work's 'gaps'. According to him, no literary work is complete: all have gaps which have to be filled in by the reader, and all readers and readings will fill these in differently (1974, 280; Iser makes similar points in a number of other essays). Iser's gaps bear a close relationship to Roman Ingarden's 'spots of indeterminacy': see the entry for CONCRETIZATION.

It will be seen that such a position offered a good base for the mounting of a counter-offensive against the New Critical anathematizing of the Affective Fallacy: it showed how readers' responses could be taken account of without giving the individual reader absolute freedom to do with the text as he or she wished: the reader has licence to fill in only the gaps. Whether 'filling in the gaps' is an adequate metaphor for what readers do to texts is, however, open to question.

See also SUB-TEXT.

Phonocentrism See LOGOCENTRISM

Play See LUDISM

Pleasure The attitude of literary critics towards pleasure can perhaps be compared to that of MARXISTS towards fashion: during the present century they seem never to have been quite sure whether or not they approve of it, but on balance they do not. Freud's *pleasure principle* dominated the new-born infant, but in the maturing or mature individual was placed under the sway of the *reality principle*, regaining its sway only in fantasy or day-dreaming (see the discussion in Mitchell 1974, 13). Pleasure was thus infantile, temporary, not to be confused with the adult experiences offered by literary WORKS – although to the extent that the READING of literature was seen to be regressive and comparable to dream-experiences then pleasure might enter into it.

In the 1930s and 1940s the premium placed upon a stern moral experience and evaluation of literature by F. R. Leavis and his followers seemed on occasions to consign words such as *pleasure* to the vocabulary of the literary dilettante.

However much common readers may have gone on using terms such as *pleasure* and *enjoyment* with reference to their reading of literary works, within modern movements in literary criticism during the present century these have generally had something of a thin time. In 1975, however, Roland Barthes's *Le Plaisir du Texte* was published (translated as *The Pleasure of the Text* in 1976), and pleasure suddenly became much more respectable amongst literary critics and theorists. Barthes's *plaisir* is difficult to translate into English, and has a generally more indulgent and more specifically sexual/sensual force than its more staid English counterpart. Barthes distinguishes between *pleasure of the text* and *texts of pleasure*: the former can be spoken, whereas the latter are perverse and are outside any imaginable finality (1976, 51–2). *The Pleasure of the Text* is, however, not an easy work to summarize or describe, and perhaps its most important effect was to bring the issue of reader-gratification through the reading experience back into the forefront of critical attention.

The issue of pleasure has also been taken up by recent FEMINIST theorists, some of whom have argued convincingly that pleasure has been NATURALIZED in particular ways within PATRIARCHAL societies, ways which devalue, MARGINALIZE or ignore specifically female forms of pleasure. Thus not only are descriptions or definitions of pleasure at the content-level of literary works to be held up to renewed scrutiny, but also the pleasures to be obtained by women from the writing and reading of literary works have to be reconsidered from non-patriarchal perspectives.

Poetic See FUNCTIONS OF LANGUAGE

Point of view See PERSPECTIVE AND VOICE

Politeness In a useful recent article entitled 'The Politeness of Literary Texts' Roger Sell traces the application of this term from 'the zenith of its lofty meaning' in the eighteenth century when it 'embraced intellectual enlightenment and civilization as prized by the Augustans', through to the way in which the term has been redefined by anthropological linguists (1991, 208). It is this most recent usage that has established the term's current process of redefinition: 'the strategies, linguistically realized, by which human beings hold their own or grasp for more' (Sell 1991, 211, after Brown & Levinson 1978 and 1987).

Sell details a number of recent attempts on the part of scholars interested in a *rapprochement* of linguistic and Literary Studies to connect the concept of politeness with literary TEXTS, particularly with regard to the way in which these – or their AUTHORS – handle face-threatening acts (FTAs) in the language of authorial personae and characters. His own approach, however, is wider: he sees all interaction, and all language, as operating within politeness parameters (1991, 215), a position that he associates with Mikhail Bakhtin's view that all language use is DIALOGIC, and thus to some extent engages with those others who hear or read it. For Sell politeness is 'a matter of choice and co-operativeness in interpersonal relations' (1991, 221), more a form of helpfulness than the purely selfish manoeuvring for personal advantage some other theorists view it as. He distinguishes between *selectional* and *presentational* politeness, the former involving the avoidance of anything 'threatening the readers' positive or negative face' and the latter observing 'the co-operative principle at all costs, so that his readers would never be in the slightest doubt as to what was happening, what he meant, or why he was saying what he was saying' (1991, 221, 222).

As this makes clear, the concept owes a lot to, or has much in common with, aspects of both SPEECH ACT THEORY and PRAGMATICS. It can be added that once one starts to talk about the politeness of literary texts the way is open to talk about their impoliteness. Just as impoliteness can be a technique for getting one's own way in interpersonal relations, so too an author may challenge and manipulate a reader's expectations and responses through, for example, making it very difficult for him or her understand what is happening, what is meant, or why what is being said is being said. Clearly much early MODERNIST literature can be said to make recourse to impoliteness of this sort.

Polyglossia See HETEROGLOSSIA

Polyphonic Literally, many-voiced. The term is associated with the theories of Mikhail Bakhtin, especially with his idea of the *polyphonic novel*. In his study of Dostoevsky Bakhtin argues that Dostoevsky was the creator of the polyphonic novel:

> *A plurality of independent and unmerged voices and consciousnesses, a genuine polyphony of fully valid voices is in fact the chief characteristic of Dostoevsky's novels.* What unfolds in his works is not a multitude of characters and fates in a single objective world, illuminated by a single authorial consciousness; rather a *plurality of consciousnesses, with equal rights and each with its own world*, combine but are not merged in the unity of the event. (1984, 6)

Bakhtin uses the word *voice* in a rather special way, to include not just matters linguistic but also matters relating to ideology and power in society. A voice for Dostoevsky refers the listener not just to an originating person, but to a network of beliefs and power-relationships which attempt to place and situate the listener in certain ways. As he puts it,

> Language is not a neutral medium that passes freely and easily into the private property of the speaker's intentions; it is populated – overpopulated – with the intentions of others. Expropriating it, forcing it to submit to one's own intentions and accents, is a difficult and complicated process. (1981, 294)

That process is the means whereby *language* is transformed into a *voice*.

Bakhtin's view that the polyphonic novel was born with Dostoevsky has been challenged, and he himself seems sometimes to have accepted that polyphonic elements can be found in many novels in many CULTURES and times. But his work on Dostoevsky has drawn attention to a representative lack of a single CENTRE of authority in the modern (or MODERNIST) literary WORK.

And this can be said to relate to arguments about the death of the AUTHOR, for if there is no authorial presence in a novel, no centre of authority established by the author, but the author's is only one voice (or several voices), then clearly in a certain traditional sense of the term the author is no more.

Bakhtin's views here take up and extend a number of more traditional views relating to the literary use of personae.

Brian McHale points out that a rather different use of the concept can be found in the work of the Polish PHENOMENOLOGIST Roman Ingarden. According to Ingarden,

> the literary artwork is not ontologically uniform or monolithic, but *polyphonic*, stratified. Each of its layers has a somewhat different ontological status, and functions somewhat differently in the ontological make-up of the whole.
>
> (McHale 1987, 30)

For Ingarden there are four such strata: that of word-sounds, that of meaning-units, that of 'presented objects' (which are distinguished from 'real-world objects'), and that of 'schematized aspects' ('presented objects' do not have the same determinacy as 'real-world objects', and they are inevitably schematic – which is why it bespeaks a failure to approach the artwork as artwork if one asks questions such as 'How many children had Lady Macbeth?') (based on McHale 1987, 33).

See also DIALOGIC; HETEROGLOSSIA.

Polyvalent discourse See REGISTER

Polyvocality See POLYGLOSSIA

Popular Dissatisfactions with the literary CANON, along with the impact of interdisciplinary ventures involving not just literature but also other art-forms and the products of the mass media, have led to a renewed interest in the issues raised by the word *popular*. Raymond Williams points out that the word stems from a legal and political term meaning 'belonging to the people', but that in the historical shifts towards the widespread modern usage of 'well-liked' there has been a strong pejorative streak relating to the implication the word carries of 'setting out to gain favour' (1976, 198).

In current critical usage terms such as *popular culture*, *popular literature* and *popular art* typically cover the senses both of '*for* the people' and '*of* the people'. Williams suggests that this is a relatively recent development, as previously a term such as 'folk culture' was reserved for usages involving the culture produced by people for themselves. We can suggest, however, that the etymological relation between *popular* and *people* inevitably leads the former word to respond to shifts of attitudes and meaning attached to the latter one – especially of a socio-political nature. Thus during 1938 Bertolt Brecht's polemics against the anti-MODERNIST positions of Georg Lukács included interesting proposed definitions (working definitions in the sense that they were proposed to be put to work in specific cultural practices) of both popular and CULTURE. The link between views of 'the people' (both the term and the reality to which the term refers) and views of the *popular* are clear in Brecht's comments:

> Our concept of what is popular refers to a people who not only play a full part in historical development but actively usurp it, force its pace, determine its direction. We have a people in mind who make history, change the world and themselves. We have in mind a fighting people and therefore an aggressive concept of what is *popular*.
>
> Popular means: intelligible to the broad masses, adopting and enriching their forms of expression / assuming their standpoint, confirming and correcting it / representing the most progressive section of the people so that it can assume leadership, and therefore intelligible to other sections of the people as well / relating to traditions and developing them / communicating to that portion of the people which strives for leadership the achievements of the section that at present rules the nation. (Bloch *et al*. 1977, 81)

Brecht's comments only reached English-speaking readers in any significant way in 1977, and they chimed in with a more general move against assigning purely pejorative associations to the term *popular* within the context of literary or artistic discussion. Even with regard to pulp literature – that which previously had been seen as the most blatant example of material foisted on the people by others for financial or *ideological* reasons – attempts were made to discover elements of the 'genuine', that is to say, elements which expressed something valid about their lives and experiences to the consumers of this material themselves.

The very considerable influence of the work of Mikhail Bakhtin during the 1980s also involved a renewal of interest in the concept of the popular, directing attention towards traditions of expression and resistance both within and outside canonical literature and art.

See also CULTURE, DIALOGUE.

Popular culture See CULTURE; POPULAR

Pornoglossia According to Deborah Cameron, since the word *pornography* means 'pictures of prostitutes', perhaps *pornoglossia* would be a good name for the language which reduces all women to men's sexual servants' (1985, 77). Pornoglossia, then, is a use of language to describe women purely in terms of their sexual usefulness, availability, or attractiveness to men.

Position/ality See READING POSITION

Postmodernism See MODERNISM AND POSTMODERNISM

Post-structuralism A term that is sometimes used almost interchangeably with DECONSTRUCTION, while at other times being seen as a more general, umbrella term which describes a movement one important element in which is deconstruction. Thus Richard Harland (1987), for example, suggests that the post-structuralists fall into three main groups: the *Tel Quel* (a French journal) group of Jacques Derrida, Julia Kristeva and the later Roland Barthes; Gilles Deleuze and Félix Guattari (authors of the influential *Anti-Oedipus: Capitalism and Schizophrenia* [published in French in 1972]) and the later Michel Foucault; and (on his own) Jean Baudrillard (Harland 1987, 2). Whether Jacques Lacan is a structuralist or a post-structuralist (or both) is a matter for continuing debate.

The degree of uncertainty that surrounds the use of this term can, however, be suggested by noting that Alex Callinicos proposes a rather different division of post-structuralism into two main strands of thought. The first of these is what Richard Rorty has dubbed TEXTUALISM, while the second is one in which the master category is Michel Foucault's 'power-knowledge'. This 'worldly post-structuralism', as Callinicos calls it using a term of Edward Said's, involves an 'articulation of "the said and the unsaid", of the discursive and the non-discursive' (Callinicos 1989, 68). Callinicos argues that whereas the textualists see us as imprisoned in TEXTS, unable to escape the discursive (or unable to see any reality unmediated by DISCOURSES), 'worldly post-structuralism' leaves open the possibility of contact with a reality unmediated by or through discourses.

If one accepts this division it has to be said that post-structuralism in its textualist version has had a far more significant impact upon Literary Studies than has the Foucaultian variant, although many of Foucault's ideas have been taken up for criticism and development by FEMINIST critics.

'Textualist' post-structuralism represents at the same time both a development and a deconstruction of STRUCTURALISM – a demonstration of its argued inner contradictions. A classic example of this is to be found in an early (1968) interview of Derrida by Julia Kristeva, published in *Positions*. Derrida here takes issue with what he claims is Saussure's maintenance of a rigorous distinction between 'the *signans* and the *signatum*, [and] the equation of the *signatum* and the concept', which, he argues,

> inherently leaves open the possibility of thinking a *concept signified in and of itself*, a concept simply present for thought, independent of a relationship to language, that is of a relationship to a system of signifiers . . . (1981b, 19)

Within Saussure's revolutionary view of language as a system of DIFFERENCES with no positive forms, that is, Derrida argues that one can discover (by deconstructing Saussure's argument) a relic of the old ideas, an extra-systemic entity, a TRANSCENDENTAL SIGNIFIED. By pursuing the implications of Saussure's arguments as far as possible one is able to go beyond them: the rigorous structuralist thus stands like Keats's Cortez, staring at the Pacific of post-structuralism (although his wild surmise is hardly silent).

Derrida's own position is best followed through certain key terms such as deconstruction, LOGOCENTRISM, DIFFÉRANCE, transcendental signified, META-PHYSICS OF PRESENCE, and so on – which to avoid repetition I will not reconsider here. Suffice to say that central to his endeavour (as he himself admits) has been a commitment to the rooting out of a belief in absolute and extra-systemic determinants of meaning. Thus central to the post-structuralist impact on literary theory and criticism has been its argument that the play of SIGNIFIERS cannot be stopped or made subject to the sway of any extra-textual authority: there is, as Derrida infamously puts it, nothing outside the text. Post-structuralism is therefore implicated in the death of the AUTHOR, and in con-sistently opposing any textual interpretation claiming either finality or un-deconstructable authority. It has also contributed to a suspicion of any argument or position which grants the individual human SUBJECT powers of self-determination or of historical causation: Louis Althusser's long-lasting attack on humanism can be seen to prefigure many later post-structuralist attempts to see the subject as SITE rather than CENTRE.

Power In NARRATIVE theory, that which either allows or prevents a SUBJECT from reaching its object. A power can be an individual character, or it can be an abstraction such as fate, age, nature, and so on (see Bal 1985, 28).

The issue of power has entered into recent discussion of literature mainly in connection with issues loosely related to ideology. Literature is often subject to control (through censorship, restrictions on literacy, use of powers associated with the ownership of libraries, publishing houses, reviewing media) precisely because it can challenge existing authorities – or because these at least believe that it can.

Pragmatics From two important early theorists of SEMIOTICS, Charles Morris and Charles Peirce, has come a useful tripartite distinction between *syntactics* (SIGNS and their relations to other signs), *semantics* (signs and their relations to the 'outside world'), and *pragmatics* (signs and their relations to users). The distinction has been most fruitful within the realm of Linguistics, where it has enabled theorists such as Ferdinand de Saussure and those who followed his example to isolate different systems of formal rules (syntactic and semantic) from language in its actual, day-to-day use (its pragmatic existence). Saussure and his disciples argued that language at the pragmatic level was subject to too many random and unquantifiable pressures to constitute a proper object of study. To be studied it had to be reduced to an ideal state untouched by the accidents and casual pressures of everyday usage.

Ignoring the pragmatic aspect of language use in this way was very useful to linguisticians, and during the time of Saussure's greatest influence was seen by some to be a precondition for the formal study of language. At the same time, during the 1960s and 1970s, the theories of the American linguist Noam

Chomsky also argued for a linguistic object of study which could be isolated apart from the pragmatic use of language.

But in recent years more and more disquiet has been expressed at the banishing of the realm of the pragmatic from the concern of the theorist of language, and the recent growth of concern with pragmatics, which has its primary origin within the discipline of Linguistics, involves a certain reaction against the ideas and practices of Saussure and Chomsky. Thus Stephen Levinson, in his *Pragmatics*, suggests that the recent growth of interest in pragmatics owes much to a reaction against Chomsky's treatment of language as an abstract device or mental ability which is dissociable from the uses, users, and functions of language (1983, 35). He adds, however, that this is not the whole story:

> Another powerful and general motivation for the interest in pragmatics is the growing realization that there is a very substantial gap between current linguistic theories of language and accounts of linguistic communication. . . . For it is becoming increasingly clear that a semantic theory alone can give us only a proportion, and perhaps only a small if essential proportion, of a general account of language understanding. (1983, 38)

This development in Linguistics has its parallels in other disciplines, including Literary Criticism. A recent collection of essays edited by Roger Sell and entitled *Literary Pragmatics* contains a number of attempts to transpose some of the more general principles of pragmatics to a literary context. Central to such a project is a commitment to moving away from the study of literary WORKS as closed or purely formal structures of TEXT to a recognition of them as MEDIATING elements in chains of communication.

> Literary pragmatics takes for granted that no account of communication in general will be complete without an account of literature and its contextualization, and that no account of literature will be complete without an account of its use of the communicative resources generally available. In effect, it reinstates the ancient linkage between rhetoric and poetics . . . (1991, xiv)

Perhaps paradoxically such emphases can take us back to formal systems. It is well-known that ancient rhetoric tended to generate these: in its modern variants attempts to isolate the sets of rules and CONVENTIONS that bind writers to READERS, and which can be seen as the forces which choreograph actual READINGS of works of literature, can lead straight into SYSTEMS as formal and formalized as grammars.

Literary pragmatics typically tries to bring together centrifugal and centripetal movements: moving into the text and isolating pragmatic techniques (implicature, presupposition, persuasion), and relating these to forces outside the text in the worlds of writer and reader such as power relations, CULTURAL traditions, systems of publishing and distribution, censorship, and so on, with a stress throughout on *particular* pragmatic conjunctions and interactions.

139

Even in abridged form this begins to look like an ambitious project, and literary pragmatics seems to enjoy greatest success in attempts to isolate relatively isolated pragmatic mechanisms, often in highly localized studies.

See also DISCOURSE.

Prefiguring See PROLEPSIS

Presence According to Jacques Derrida in the early and influential article 'Structure, Sign and Play in the Discourse of the Human Sciences', 'all the names related to fundamentals, to principles, or to the center have always designated an invariable presence – *eidos, archē, telos, energeia, ousia* (essence, existence, substance, subject) *alētheia*, transcendentality, consciousness, God, man, and so forth' (1978, 279–81). All of these represent extra-systemic entities, points of reference or CENTRES of authority which escape from that play of DIFFERENCE which, following Saussure, Derrida believes to be the sole source of MEANING. The *metaphysics of presence*, then, is a LOGOCENTRIC belief in and reliance upon some such extra-systemic point of authority.

See also COPERNICAN REVOLUTION.

Privilege The verb *to privilege* and cognate noun and adjective forms are frequently used by recent theorists to indicate a hierarchical structuring of causal factors. To privilege gender in a consideration of class and gender in historical change, then, is to suggest that gender is more influential than class in historical causality.

When NARRATIVE theorists talk of privilege, however, they generally refer to the possession of information which is either exclusive to a particular narrator or to some form of understanding which is not shared by the characters (or other characters) in the narrative.

Proairetic code See CODE

Problematic Problematic as noun came into the vocabulary of Anglo-Saxon theorists through Louis Althusser's *For Marx*, first published in English translation in 1969. According to Althusser he borrowed the concept (in French, of course) from Jacques Martin, 'to designate the particular unity of a theoretical formation and hence the location to be assigned to this specific difference' (1969, 32).

Although Althusser assigned the term to *theoretical* formations it is often used to designate ideological ones as well; any complex of beliefs which (whatever their implicit or explicit contradictions) hang together in a self-supporting unity may be referred to as a problematic by recent theorists. It is probably too late to alter this drift of meaning, but Althusser's usage does have the virtue of fitting in with his concept of epistemological break, that is, of a shift from one problematic to another such as he claimed to discover in the writings of Karl Marx.

The term can be used in a way that makes it appear similar to Foucault's concept of the *ÉPISTÈME*, in as much as it may be believed that a particular problematic represents what is 'thinkable' for those in its grip, and beyond which thought cannot venture.

See also PARADIGM SHIFT for another comparable concept.

Projection characters Characters into whom an author projects (often contradictory) aspects of him or herself.

Prolepsis Also, following Prince (1988), *anticipation*, *flashforward* or *prospection*. Any narrating of a narrative EVENT before the time in the STORY at which it will take place has been reached in the NARRATIVE. Some theorists, including Genette, have argued that the term be extended to the *evocation* (as well as the narrating) of such 'future' events. If this is accepted, it will follow that many prolepses cannot be recognized as such on first reading of a narrative: the story of the 'gringos' who disappear looking for silver at the opening of Joseph Conrad's *Nostromo* is proleptic of the final fate of many other characters in the novel, but the evocation of these fates by this early account can take place only in the READER's memory or upon a second READING of the novel. Prolepses would thus be either overt or implied. As I have argued with reference to ANALEPSIS, there is perhaps a case for restricting the term prolepsis to more overt cases, while examples such as the scene cited above can be described as 'proleptic of' later events rather than as clear examples of prolepsis. An alternative solution is to use terms such as *prefiguring* and *foreshadowing* for the evocation of future events, and to reserve prolepsis for more overt narrative references to such events.

It should be added that even overt prolepses may be difficult to recognize as such on first reading of a narrative; they may initially be read as examples of ACHRONICITY.

A *completing prolepsis* is one which is needed to achieve a full chronological coverage because of a later omission in the narrative; a *repeating prolepsis* or *advance notice* supplies information that will be provided afresh later on in the narrative.

Gérard Genette distinguishes between *internal prolepses*, which are sited within the time-span of the story, and *external prolepses*, which are sited outside of the story's temporal limits (1980, 68–71).

Prospection See PROLEPSIS

Psycho-narration See FREE INDIRECT DISCOURSE

Punctual anachrony See ANACHRONY

Punctuation Punctuation in its traditional sense has been of considerable concern to literary scholars and critics; the task of establishing a reliable TEXT has always included a responsibility with regard to its punctuation – often no easy job, as writing and publishing conventions regarding punctuation are not stable. The imposition of modern punctuation conventions on literature originally published with very sparse and free punctuation is a difficult and controversial matter, and an anecdote of I. A. Richards's has suggested that William Empson's interest in ambiguity in literature stemmed from his reading of a discussion of the unpunctuated form of Shakespeare's 'The Expense of Spirit in a Waste of Shame' by Laura Riding and Robert Graves.

More recent theorists in a range of different disciplines have given a metaphorical meaning to this term, extending its coverage to include more than just the insertion stops or divisions in written (or spoken) language for the purpose of refining MEANING and limiting ambiguity. Social psychologists, for example, have drawn attention to the way in which conflicting views of the same process of interpersonal process can be explained by reference to the manner in which the participants involved punctuate the interaction differently. (In a classic version: 'I drink because she nags me'; 'I nag him because he drinks'.)

Punctuation, in other words, involves the imposition of order and causality on a set of otherwise discrete facts by means of boundary-setting and grouping. It is not just the syntax of sentences that can be established by punctuation, but the syntax of relationships – and of literary WORKS. AUTHORS can impose a certain amount of punctuation on their works by means of chapter and other divisions: anyone who feels that this is not the case should read a work such as Joseph Conrad's *The Shadow-Line* both in its manuscript form (in which there are no divisions) and in its published version (in which the work is divided into numbered sections).

In an original essay on James Joyce's *A Portrait of the Artist as a Young Man*, Maud Ellmann has devoted considerable attention to the issue of punctuation in the work, showing how the growth and maturing of the hero, Stephen, involves experimentation with punctuation activities, and that these are to be seen both as attempts to master the world and as the unwitting imposition of intermittency upon himself (1981, 197–8).

In the work of Jacques Derrida the term *espacement*, normally translated as *spacing*, seems to mean something very similar to punctuation in its broader sense.

The term *segmentation* carries a comparable force within Linguistics, where it refers to the way in which language is 'chunked' or divided into segments. Segmentation is most frequently discussed at the level of intonation, and it is well-known that a change in intonation can alter the meaning of an utterance. (Some of the humour in Peter Sellers's parodic version of the Beatles' *A Hard Day's Night*, which imitates Sir Laurence Olivier's 'Richard the Third' delivery, depends upon re-segmentation of the well-known lyrics.) Segmentation can also, however, be applied to written language. Where written language is concerned it is clear that segmentation and punctuation (in the traditional sense) are not necessarily synonymous. Punctuation marks may be taken as the visual indicators of a sort of internal or ideal intonation, but they are not just that nor do they exert complete control over such sense-determining 'intonation'. According to Geoffrey Leech and Michael Short, segmentation is, along with sequence and salience, one of the three main factors of textual organization (1981, 217). (Salience involves 'significant prominence' – for example, as caused by 'end focus', or the principle that we notice that which comes last in a sequence.) For sequence, see the entry for FUNCTION.

Q

Quality and quantity (maxims of) See SPEECH ACT THEORY

R

Radical alterity A term used by Jacques Derrida to indicate the essential self-alienation of the SIGNIFIER from itself.

> The *representamen* [which we can render as *signifier*] functions only by giving rise to an *interpretant* that itself becomes a sign and so on to infinity. The self-identity of the signified conceals itself unceasingly and is always on the move. The property of the *representamen* is to be itself and another, to be produced as a structure of reference, to be separated from itself (1976, 49–50).

In other words, signifiers are never themselves alone: to function they need to be interpreted, and this involves the creation of a new SIGN which consists, according to Saussure, of a signifier and a SIGNIFIED, thus producing a new signifier which needs to be interpreted – and so on *ad infinitum*.

It will be noted that the posited process is completely internal to language; it allows for no way in which the signifier can function other than by means of interaction with other signifiers. It is possible to argue that it is through praxis that the signifier functions, and that one avoids the infinite regress described by Derrida only by rejecting a view of language as a totally closed system and allowing for a linguistic engagement with non-linguistic reality. (It is only from within the relatively closed systems of certain contemporary theories that such a proposition appears questionable and proof that one is trapped within the metaphysics of PRESENCE.)

This argument has important consequences for theories relating to literary interpretation, for the influence of the LINGUISTIC PARADIGM in recent years has meant that when once it has been decided that *language* is a closed system, it takes very little time before this decision is extended to other fields, and we find ourselves with 'literature' (in general) seen as a comparably closed system, or back with the closed individual literary WORK that previous formalisms such as that of the New Critics have argued for.

Radical feminism See FEMINISM

Reach See ANALEPSIS

Readerly and writerly texts Translated from Roland Barthes's coinages *lisible* and *scriptible* in his *S/Z* (1990, 4–5). Barthes uses the terms to distinguish between traditional literary WORKS such as the classical novel, with their reliance upon CONVENTIONS shared by writer and READER and their resultant (partial) fixity or CLOSURE of meaning, and those works produced especially in the present century which violate such conventions and thus force the reader to work to produce a meaning or meanings which are inevitably other than final or 'correct'. Thus

> The writerly text is a perpetual present, upon which no *consequent* language (which would inevitably make it past) can be superimposed; the writerly text is *ourselves writing*, before the infinite play of the world (the world as function) is traversed, intersected, stopped, plasticized by some singular system (Ideology, Genus, Criticism) which reduces the plurality of entrances, the opening of networks, the infinity of languages. (1990, 5)

Readerly texts, in contrast, are products rather than productions, and they make up the enormous mass of our literature (1990, 5).

Behind these comments lies a polemical element: Barthes, as he himself admits, wishes to challenge the conventional division of labour between producers and consumers, between writers and readers. The writerly text involves such a challenge, for it forces the reader to engage in the process of writing – that is, it forces him or her to be creative in the manner traditionally limited to the writer-function. '[T]he goal of literary work (of literature as work) is to make the reader no longer a consumer, but a producer of the text' (1990, 4). This of course ties in with Barthes's comments on the death of the author – see the entry for AUTHOR.

A comparable distinction is that provided by Umberto Eco in his *The Role of the Reader* (1981) between OPEN AND CLOSED TEXTS.

Reader-response criticism See READERS AND READING

Readers and reading According to the American critic Stanley Fish, in a book published in 1980:

Twenty years ago one of the things that literary critics didn't do was talk about the reader, at least in a way that made his experience the focus of the critical act. (1980, 344)

Writing the present entry in 1991, one can note in passing that ten years ago, one of the things that literary critics had not fully stopped doing, was talking about 'literary critics' as if they were all male.

Since the time about which Fish is writing, however, more and more attention has been devoted to the identity, rôle and function of readers of literature, and this has led to the coining of a range of new terms. Some of this attention has stemmed from a number of different critical theories and approaches which are often collectively described as *reader-response criticism*, but some of it can best be seen in relation to the loosening of New Critical dogmas. Once appeal to the intentional and affective fallacies lost its force, curiosity about the reader faced no interdiction. A sure indication of this sense of new-found freedom is the gradual movement away from talk of 'the reader' towards reference to 'readers' – a movement accompanied by the willingness of critics to say 'I' rather than 'we', which in its turn has to be related to a growing awareness of the dangers of ethnocentricity and parallel GENDER and class biases. For this reason it may be a little misleading to think of reader-response criticism as a school: the term gathers together a range of attempts to theorize about readers and to study them and the reading process, and Terry Eagleton's joke description 'The Reader's Liberation Front' catches some of the diversity in the reality described. Indeed, not all criticism categorized as reader-response criticism is actually concerned with readers' response(s); much of it is concerned with other issues: readers' COMPETENCE, the reading process *in toto*, the TEXT's formation of the reader, and so on.

Perhaps not surprisingly, much of the criticism described as reader-response criticism is concerned with the novel. We are much more conscious of reading as a process when reading a novel than when reading a poem – especially a lyric poem which can be held as a finished unit more easily in the memory. Wayne Booth's 1961 book *Rhetoric of Fiction* popularized the notion of the *implied author*, and by extension the term *implied reader* was coined to describe the reader which the text (or the author through the text) suggests that it expects (Booth himself talks of the *postulated* or *mock* reader). It should be noted that this term, like all other terms with the form 'the X reader', although singular, actually has the purpose of describing a group or category of reade*rs*. Jacques Derrida argued in 1971 that all reading is transformational, and in the same comment warned against reading (in this case the classic texts of MARXISM) 'according to a hermeneutical or exegetical method which would seek out a finished signified beneath a textual surface' (1981b, 63). Although Derrida is not normally thought of as a reader-response critic, the same insistence upon those transformational and creative aspects of reading which we associate with this group of critics can be found in his work.

The characteristics of the *inscribed reader*, in contrast, are actually there to be discovered in the text itself, waiting for the actual reader to slip on like a suit of clothes. Umberto Eco has introduced the similar concept of the *model reader*; he argues that

> To make his text communicative, the author has to assume that the ensemble of codes he relies upon is the same as that shared by his possible reader (hereafter Model Reader) supposedly able to deal interpretatively with the expressions in the same way as the author deals generatively with them. (1981, 7)

This may be taken to imply that the model reader is external to the text, but later in the same chapter of his book Eco makes it clear that for him the concept is more intra-textual in nature and that the model reader is thus also to be understood to be inscribed in the text:

> In other words, the Model Reader is a textually established set of felicity conditions . . . to be met in order to have a macro-speech act (such as a text is) fully actualized. (1981, 11)

Rather different is the *intended reader*, because here the evidence may be either intra- or extra-textual: an author's comment in a letter that a WORK of literature was written to be read by a particular person or group of people can be used as evidence substantiating a case for a particular intended reader, but clearly not for a particular inscribed reader. Again related but slightly different are the *average* and the *optimal* or *ideal reader*. The former term comes from Michael Riffaterre (he later replaces it with *archi-lecteur* or composite reader), and describes (paradoxically) as much readings as readers, in other words, the responses engendered in different readers by particular textual elements. Riffaterre has also coined the term *retroactive reading* to describe a second-stage, hermeneutic reading which comes subsequent to an initial, *heuristic reading* or reading-for-the-meaning process (1978, 5).

Rather different is *symptomatic reading*: if we define a symptom as a non-intentional SIGN then it follows that a symptomatic reading treats a work much as a doctor examines a patient for symptoms. The doctor (in the exemplary situation) does not ask the patient what is wrong with him or her, but looks for clues the meaning of which the patient is ignorant. A symptomatic reading, then, seeks to use such clues in a work as a way into the secrets of the author, or of his or her society or CULTURE, or whatever.

The optimal/ideal reader is a term used to refer to that collection of abilities, attitudes, experience, and knowledge which will allow a reader to extract the maximum value from a reading of a particular text. (For some commentators, the maximum *legitimate* value.) It should be noted that whereas for some critics the optimal/ideal reader is a universal figure, for most he or she is particular to given texts: the ideal reader for *Humphry Clinker* may not be the ideal reader for 'My Last Duchess'. Closely related again is the *informed reader*, a term given currency by Stanley Fish. According to Fish

> The informed reader is someone who (1) is a competent speaker of the language out of which the text is built up; (2) is in full possession of 'the semantic knowledge that a mature . . . listener brings to his task of comprehension,' including the knowledge (that is, the experience, both as a producer and comprehender) of lexical sets, collocation probabilities, idioms, professional and other dialects, and so on; and (3) has *literary* competence. That is, he is sufficiently experienced as a reader to have internalized the properties of local discourses, including everything from the most local of devices (figures of speech, and so on) to whole genres. (1980, 48)

In spite of the fact that all of these terms have sprouted on the grave (or the sick-bed) of the New Critics, it can be argued that all of them except the intended reader retain a certain text-centredness. Rather different is the *empirical reader*, used to describe those actual human beings who read a given literary work in varied ways and get varied things out of their readings. This concept arises perhaps more from the sociology of literature than from literary criticism as such, but study of the empirical reader and of empirical readings can have important implications for literary criticism. In particular, confirmation that one literary work can generate a range of different reading experiences, over time, between cultures or groups (or within them), and even for the same individual, leads necessarily to the question of the status and authority of these different reading experiences. If there is an optimal reader is there also an optimal reading, or is it a characteristic of major literature that it can generate a succession of new reading experiences as the individual reader or his or her culture changes? It has to be said that study of empirical readings is at a very early stage; Norman N. Holland's *5 Readers Reading* (1975) contained interesting material, but it could more accurately have been entitled *5 Readers Remembering What they Read*.

It is important to distinguish the reader or readers from the NARRATEE or NARRATEES, although in very special circumstances (a lyric poem addressed to and read only by a given person) the two rôles may be filled by one and the same person.

See also COMPETENCE AND PERFORMANCE; NEW READERS; READERLY AND WRITERLY TEXTS: RECEPTION THEORY.

Reading community See INTERPRET[AT]IVE COMMUNITY

Reading position According to Anne Cranny-Francis, the concept of reading position helps us to understand how an audience is constructed by a literary TEXT. For her, a reading position is 'the position assumed by a reader from which the text seems to be coherent and intelligible' (1990, 25). Put another way: the text *situates* the READER in certain ways. Just as we have to get into a certain position to see certain physical objects, so too in order to read Jane Austen's *Pride and Prejudice* the reader has to adopt a stance with regard to the values and procedures of the NARRATIVE, unless a decision is made to give the WORK an OPPOSITIONAL READING.

Realism Debates around the concept of realism go back a long way, and recent arguments need to be seen as the latest attempts to grapple with certain perennial problems. (There is an excellent historical account of the development of this term – not limiting itself to literary or artistic usages – in Raymond Williams's *Key Words*.) The most important elements in recent discussion of realism seem to stem from two sources: first the influence of what has become known as the Brecht–Lukács debate, and second what we can call the realist-imperative in FEMINIST theory.

The Brecht–Lukács debate dates from the 1930s, but Brecht's contributions were not made known to Lukács at that time nor were they published until much later. In his published writings the Hungarian MARXIST Georg Lukács had, by the mid-1930s, arrived at a definition of realism which placed a high premium upon the artist's (i) portraying the *totality* of reality in some form or other, and (ii) *penetrating beneath* the surface appearance of reality so as to be able to grasp the underlying laws of historical *change*. For Lukács, then, the artist's task is similar to that set for himself by Marx: to understand world history as a complex and dynamic totality through the uncovering of certain underlying laws. In practice this led Lukács to place a supreme value upon certain works of classical realism in the novel – the names of Tolstoy, Balzac and Thomas Mann are frequently on his lips or at the tip of his pen – and to wage an unceasing campaign against different aspects of what he classified as MODERNISM. At the end of his *The Historical Novel* (written 1936–7) Lukács refers to the 'misunderstanding' of his position that 'we intended a formal revival, an artistic imitation of the classical historical novel' (1969, 422), but even so many commentators have seen his opposition to modernism to be so all-embracing that this is actually what would have been needed to satisfy his requirement that a literary WORK be 'realistic'.

So that when Brecht, writing about the concept of realism, stated that we 'must not derive realism as such from particular existing works' (Bloch *et al.* 1977, 81), the unstated target is clearly Lukács (especially as he goes on to refer to Balzac and Tolstoy). Brecht's argument is, in a nutshell, an anti-ESSENTIALIST one. In other words, realism for him is not intrinsic to a literary work, coded into it for all time like the name in a stick of rock, but a function of the rôle the work plays or can play in a given society at a particular historical moment. To simplify, we can say that whereas for Lukács a work is realistic or not depending upon whether it portrays a socio-historical totality in terms of its underlying laws of transformation, for Brecht a work is realistic not once and for all, but by reference to its ability at a particular time and place to allow individuals to understand and to change the conditions of their existence.

Not surprisingly, then, Brecht's view of the formal experimentation associated with modernism is far more favourable than is that of Lukács's.

Interestingly, too, Brecht's views on this issue have something in common with those expressed by Roman Jakobson in his 1921 essay 'On Realism in Art'. Both stress the need for continuous formal regeneration and transformation in order to prevent AUTOMATIZATION, although it has to be said that Brecht's position has a practical-political element which Jakobson's lacks.

If the crudities of some theories of socialist realism inherited from the Soviet Union of the 1930s and 1940s led to a movement away from any concern with realism on the part of more recent theorists, the women's movement and associated feminist theories have placed it back on the agenda even when the term itself is not used. Recent feminist literary criticism and theory tends to be sharply distinguished from a range of other contemporary theories which either deny that the literary work reflects and reflects upon non-literary reality, or which express uninterest in such processes if indeed they take place. The essential point in this context was made in an article dating from the early years of contemporary feminist literary criticism by Cheri Register: 'Feminist criticism is ultimately cultural criticism' (1975, 10). Feminist literary critics are interested in literary works not 'in themselves' but in relation to a reality they reflect, distort, form and change. Thus even if the term realism itself is not too frequently encountered in feminist criticism, realism in a broad sense as an assumption lies behind much of it.

See also SYNTAGMATIC AND PARADIGMATIC

Recall See ANALEPSIS

Receiver See SHANNON & WEAVER MODEL OF COMMUNICATION

Reception theory A term generally used in a relatively narrow sense to describe a particular group of (mainly German) theorists concerned with the way in which literary WORKS are 'received' by their READERS over time, but also sometimes used in a looser sense to describe any attempt to theorize the ways in which art works are received, individually and collectively, by their 'consumers'. The names most frequently mentioned as core members of the particular group of theorists are Hans Robert Jauss, Wolfgang Iser, Karl-Heinz Stierle and Harald Weinrich.

The translators of an article by Karlheinz Stierle entitled 'The Reading of Fictional Texts' suggest that the German term *Rezeption* as used by those known as 'reception theorists', 'refers to the activity of reading, the construction of meaning, and the reader's response to what he is reading' (Stierle 1980, 83, n1). In analysing the activity of reading, reception theorists make considerable use of a concept defined by Hans Robert Jauss – along with Wolfgang Iser the most important founder-member of the group. In an early and highly influential essay entitled 'Literary History as a Challenge to Literary Theory', Jauss singles out three ways in which a writer can anticipate a reader's response, and these seem to represent his view of the component parts of the reader's *horizon of expectations*:

> first, by the familiar standards or the inherent poetry of the genre; second, by the implicit relationships to familiar works of the literary-historical context; and third, by the contrast between history and reality ... The third factor includes the possibility that the reader of a new work has to perceive it not only within the narrow horizon of his literary expectations but also within the wider horizon of his experience of life. (1974, 18)

All of these elements may fuse into a single if complex tradition which a TEXT accumulates as it becomes well-known, a tradition with which its reader has to contend or grapple as he or she reads and responds to it. A well-known text, in other words, raises more specific expectations for the reader than one that has accrued no such tradition. (The implication of the last-quoted sentence above is that the reader of an *old* work does *not* have to perceive it within the wider horizon of his or her experience of life, and this implication perhaps reveals a certain formalist element in the theory.)

An important part of the theory as it has developed and matured involves a view of literary texts as partially open, and as the responses engendered by them to be (again partly) the creation of their readers. Thus in a much-quoted example, Wolfgang Iser sees the sense a reader actively *makes* of a literary text to be contained within certain limits imposed by the text itself.

> In the same way, two people gazing at the night sky may both be looking at the same collection of stars, but one will see the image of a plough, and the other will make out a dipper. The 'stars' in a literary text are fixed; the lines that join them are variable. (1974, 282)

This argued element of textual containment has, incidentally, led the American critic Stanley Fish to distinguish his own concept of the INTERPRET[AT]IVE COMMUNITY from the reception theorists' horizon of expectations: for Fish the text is itself constituted by the pre-existing CONVENTIONS of the interpretive community.

Reception theory is distinguished by a certain interdisciplinarity, and its exponents make use of elements from aesthetics, Philosophy, Psychology, and (particularly), from PHENOMENOLOGY.

Referential See FUNCTIONS OF LANGUAGE

Referential code See CODE

Refraction In the writings of Mikhail Bakhtin, according to the editor of *The Dialogic Imagination*, the intentions of the writer of prose are subject to refraction through 'already claimed territory' (Bakhtin 1981, 432). As the written word proceeds from writer to READER its direction is changed as a light-ray changes direction when it hits a prism. The metaphorical prisms in question exist both within the WORK (the other voices that the AUTHOR inhabits as the TEXT unfolds), and also outside the work: usages and associations in the reader's or critic's CULTURE through which the author's words have to struggle before making contact with the reader – in whose consciousness yet other refractions may take place.

Perhaps the least convincing aspect of Bakhtin's case here involves his distinction between poetry and prose, which is surely difficult to justify.

Register The concept of register comes originally from the study of music, where it refers to the compass of a musical instrument or of a human voice. From here a succession of metaphorical adaptations take it to Phonetics where it is used to refer to the pitch of speech utterances, and to Linguistics in general in which it is used (with variations) to refer to context-dependent linguistic characteristics – either spoken or written, and encompassing any set of choices which are made according to a conscious or unconscious notion of appropriateness-to-context (vocabulary, syntax, grammar, sound, pitch, and so on). There are, similarly, accepted (if changing) registers for church sermons, academic lectures, political speeches, declarations of undying love, and so on. An 'A-level' examination answer on Thomas Hardy's novel *Jude the Obscure*, marked by a friend of mine, which started 'What a miserable bugger Jude Fawley was', albeit undeniably accurate and dramatic, does not conform to the register to which such answers are normally expected to conform.

From Linguistics the concept has, by a further metaphorical leap, been adopted within literary criticism and NARRATOLOGY. Tzvetan Todorov, for example, in his *Introduction to Poetics*, lists a number of categories by which different *registers of DISCOURSE* may be recognized. These include the discourse's *concrete or abstract* nature, the absence or presence of *rhetorical figures*, the presence or absence of *reference to an anterior discourse* (giving, respectively, *polyvalent* and *monovalent* discourse), and, finally, the extent to which the language involved is characterized by 'subjectivity' or 'objectivity' (1981, 20–7).

It seems clear that the work done by the concept of register in Literary Studies to some extent duplicates that done by the concept of genre.

Relation (maxim of) See SPEECH ACT THEORY

Repetition The use of repetition is obviously central to a number of literary effects, and in consort with other elements such as metre, stress and rhythm in poetry it is a key means whereby the technical rate of redundancy is increased in a WORK. So far as poetry is concerned this can be related to ORALITY and the origins of poetry in oral performance: we repeat things more in spoken than in written communication to guard against mistakes. It would be a mistake to stop here, however, for repetition in literature has crucial aesthetic significance, and performs far more important functions than that of guarding against errors in transmission. The use of repetition can contribute to the formation of *patterns* in a literary work – thematic, symbolic, and STRUCTURAL.

An influential study of the importance of repetition to fiction is J. Hillis Miller's *Fiction and Repetition*, which includes studies of seven central fiction texts from *Wuthering Heights* to *Between the Acts*. Hillis Miller distinguishes between two types of repetition, a distinction which he bases on Gilles Deleuze's opposition of Nietzsche's concept of repetition to that of Plato. Deleuze summarizes the distinction in two formulations: 'only that which resembles itself differs', and 'only differences resemble one another' (Hillis Miller 1982, 5). This may seem confusing, but in the following comment Mieke Bal pinpoints a distinction similar to that indicated in Deleuze's contrast:

> The phenomenon of *repetition*, . . . has always had a dubious side. Two events are never exactly the same. The first event of a series differs from the one that follows it, if only because it is the first and the other is not. Strictly speaking, the same goes for verbal repetition in a text: only one can be the first. . . . Obviously, it is the onlooker . . . who remembers the similarities between the events of a series and ignores the differences. (1985, 77)

Bal places repetition under the general heading of FREQUENCY, and the entry for this item should be consulted for information about types of repetition in NARRATIVE.

Representatives See SPEECH ACT THEORY

Represented speech and thought See FREE INDIRECT DISCOURSE

Resonance A term used by the NEW HISTORICIST writer Stephen J. Greenblatt in preference, he explains, to 'allusion'– a term which he finds inadequate because it seems to imply a 'bloodless, bodiless thing' in contrast to the 'active charge' suggested by 'resonance' (1990, 163). What is being alluded to is the complex set or sequence of living meanings that a cultural artifact, or activity, (for example) can release when introduced into the right situation. We are close here to some of the issues discussed by Raymond Williams in connection with his use of the term STRUCTURES OF FEELING, and Greenblatt's acknowledged indebtedness to Williams may be relevant in discussion of his metaphorical use of the term 'resonance'.

According to Greenblatt, the New Historicism

> obviously has distinct affinities with resonance; that is, its concern with literary texts has been to recover as far as possible the historical circumstances of their

original production and consumption and to analyze the relationship between these circumstances and our own. (1990, 170)

See also CIRCULATION.

Retroactive reading See READERS AND READING

Retrospection See ANALEPSIS

Retroversion See ANALEPSIS

Revisionary ratios See REVISIONISM

Revisionism In current literary-critical usage this term is mainly associated with the theories of the American critic Harold Bloom, although it is still possible to find some more traditional MARXIST literary critics using it in the pejorative sense established in the writings of Lenin, where it refers to attempts to revise Marxism in such a way as to dilute or negate its revolutionary impetus.

In Harold Bloom's writings *revisionism* is used in a non-pejorative sense to indicate a general theory or set of theories concerning the manner in which the poet (Bloom uses this word in a wide sense) revises the work of his (Bloom's use of the female gender is very sparing) precursors. Thus, for Bloom, poetic influence 'is part of the larger phenomenon of intellectual revisionism' (1973, 28). Bloom sees this 'larger phenomenon' in terms of concepts much influenced by Freud; thus the poet's relation to these precursors is highly oedipal in character: the struggle against them is the struggle of the son against the father (or, to stress PATRIARCHAL authority, the Father). The aspirant poet has somehow to destroy the power of his precursors, and, normally, of one especially potent patriarchal precursor, while simultaneously absorbing and transforming his strength and authority. The *strong* poet is the poet who succeeds in this task, and in his *The Anxiety of Influence* Bloom restricts himself to the strong poets, those who have the persistence to wrestle with their major precursors, 'even to the death' (1973, 5). Bloom's insistence upon the *anxiety* associated with influence is consistent with this view: the poet's attitude to his precursors is characterized by the same anxious mixture of love and rivalry to which the Freudian term *Oedipus complex* has been assigned. Bloom's use of Freud here thus shifts the literary-critical use of the oedipal theme from the level of literary content in the narrower sense to a more all-embracing biographical-content level. For Bloom, the poet suffers always from a sense of *belatedness*, a sense that he or she has come after important things have been said, and after they have been said in ways which constrain the poet and against which he or she has to struggle.

Restricting himself initially to the question of how the strong poet reads his precursor, Bloom asserts that poetic influence *'always proceeds by a misreading of the prior poet, an act of creative correction that is actually and necessarily a misinterpretation'* (1973, 30; Bloom's italics). But having argued for this position, Bloom is soon ready to extend it to the READINGS of the common READER and the literary critic, which he requires to be no less oedipal than those of the strong poet. He argues that most 'so-called "accurate"' interpretations of poetry are worse than mistakes, and suggests that 'perhaps there are only more or less creative or interesting mis-readings', because every reading is necessarily a *clinamen* – Bloom's term for a poetic misreading or misprision 'proper', and the first of six 'revisionary ratios' outlined in *The Anxiety of Influence* (1973, 14–16). The others are as follows.

Tessera, or completion and antithesis, 'A poet antithetically "completes" his precursor, by so reading the parent-poem as to retain its terms but to mean them in another sense, as though the precursor had failed to go far enough.'

Kenosis, or a breaking with the precursor, in which the poet's humbling of himself also empties out his precursor.

Daemonization, in which

> The later poet opens himself to what he believes to be a power in the parent-poem that does not belong to the parent proper, but to a range of being just beyond that precursor. He does this, in his poem, by so stationing its relation to the parent-poem as to generalize away the uniqueness of the earlier work.

Askesis, or a movement of self-purgation in which the poet yields up part of his own self-endowment so as to separate himself from others, including the precursor.

Apophrades, or the return of the dead, in which the poet holds his work so open to that of the precursor that the impression is given that the work of the precursor was actually written by the poet (1973, 14–16).

The extent to which these categories are available to use by critics other than Bloom is probably limited, but in more general terms *The Anxiety of Influence* has been Bloom's most influential work, and terms such as *revisionism*, *misprision*, and, especially, *misreading* have entered into current critical usage.

See also AGON.

S

Salience See PUNCTUATION

Satellite event See EVENT

Scare-quotes See ERASURE

Scene See DURATION

Scriptible See READERLY AND WRITERLY TEXTS

Segmentation See PUNCTUATION

Self See SUBJECT

Self-consuming artifact From a book entitled *Self-consuming Artifacts* by Stanley Fish (1972). Literary TEXTS are self-consuming in the sense that affects produced in the course of a READING of them are destroyed as the reading proceeds. As Fish puts it in a later work,

> To read the *Phaedrus*, then, is to use it up; for the value of any point in it is that it gets *you* (not any sustained argument) to the next point, which is not so much a point (in logical-demonstrative terms) as a level of insight. It is thus a *self-consuming artifact*, a mimetic enactment in the reader's experience of the Platonic ladder in which each rung, as it is negotiated, is kicked away. (1980, 40)

Semantic axis A term coined by Mieke Bal in connection with her proposal for a method to determine which of a character's characteristics are of NARRATIVE relevance and which are of only secondary importance. According to Bal, semantic axes are pairs of contrary meanings such as *large* and *small* or *rich* and *poor*. To determine which axes are productive of the most fruitful analytical results one has, Bal suggests, to concentrate upon 'those axes that determine the image of the largest possible number of characters, positively or negatively' (1985, 86).

To a certain extent this proposal formalizes what has long been a stock-in-trade of literary criticism – the recognition that although characters from a literary WORK may be individually very different, they may nonetheless all represent different options along a linear continuum (or on many such continua). Thus the very different characters in Joseph Conrad's *Heart of Darkness* may be grouped along a continuum ranging from 'restraint' at one end to 'abandon or moral collapse' at the other. Whether Bal's proposed formalization of such insights is useful is debateable; the main danger inherent in it would appear to be that of over-simplification or reductionism. To group the characters of *Heart of Darkness* as I have (not originally) suggested may be illuminating, but it might be dangerous to see this as an in some way *dominant* or even *exclusive* ordering principle, and although Bal cannot be blamed for misapplications of her proposal it must be said that the diagrammatic example which she gives does lead this reader to fear that the concept may encourage reductionism.

As is the case with other concepts and techniques, this particular one may be more productive and less dangerous when applied to FORMULAIC literature than when applied to more classic or CANONICAL works.

155

Semantic position. A term associated with translations of Mikhail Bakhtin's work, which seeks to convey the fact that a *voice* is not just a mark of specific human individuality but a commitment (recognized or unrecognized) to a given ideological persuasion or persuasions. 'Position' here is of course a metaphor, and just as a physical position determines not just what we can see but also how we see what we can see, how we *situate ourselves in relation to the object of our view*, so too our adoption of a certain voice has (the argument runs) comparable implications on the ideological level. ('Voice' here must be given the wider meaning which Bakhtin habitually attributes to it: it is not just that people with, say, a middle-class accent tend to have middle-class views, but that the totality of a person's voice will reflect, imply and entail a set of ways or orienting oneself amongst other people in a particular context or contexts.)

A person's semantic position is supra-individual for another reason: it assumes and expects certain things of other people, and in turn places a certain pressure upon them either to conform or to resist this placing.

The concept has been found to offer certain fruitful approaches to the analysis of literary dialogue (in the non-Bakhtinian sense of the word).

Seme See SEMEME

Sememe A term coined by Umberto Eco to indicate a basic semiotic unit, by analogy with, for example, *phoneme* as the smallest intelligible unit of significant sound in a language. Thus a sememe would represent the smallest independent unit on the semiotic plane, although the significance of an individual sememe – as with the phoneme – can be refined, altered or dis-ambiguated by processes of selection and combination.

Eco suggests, further, that '*a sememe is in itself an inchoative text whereas a text is an expanded sememe*' (1981, 18).

Eco's use of the term *styleme* represents a similar sort of coinage: a styleme is the smallest independent unit on the *stylistic* plane.

Such terms, and others, represent a good example of the way in which use of the LINGUISTIC PARADIGM generates terms analogous to those in use within the discipline of Linguistics.

The term *seme* is to be found in the English translation of Roland Barthes's *S/Z*, where it is described by Barthes as being more or less interchangeable with the term *signifier* (see the entry for SIGN) on the semantic plane: 'semantically, the seme is the unit of the signifier' (1990, 17).

Compare IDEOLOGEME.

Semic code See CODE

Semiology/semiotics The term *semiotic* was coined at the close of the nineteenth century by the American philosopher Charles Sanders Peirce to describe a new field of study of which he was the founder, and *semiotics* traces its descent from this point. *Semiology* was coined by the Swiss linguistician Ferdinand de

Saussure, and in his posthumously edited and published *Course in General Linguistics* he defended the coinage as necessary for the naming of that new science which would form part of social psychology and would study 'the life of signs within society' (1974, 16). (This placing of semiology in social psychology, incidentally, was subsequently to incur the wrath of Jacques Derrida, who suggests that it is only by making the phonetic SIGN the pattern of all other signs [as he does], that Saussure can inscribe general semiology in a psychology – a step Derrida believes to be ill-conceived [1981b, 22].)

Today semiology and semiotics are generally used interchangeably, although attempts have been made to give each a distinct meaning; at one time *semiology* seemed generally preferred in Britain (perhaps because French theorists preferred the term *sémiologie*) while *semiotics* was more common in the USA. The latter term now appears to be rather more common, and I will thus adopt it in what follows. (Both terms are based upon adaptations of the Greek word *sēmeion*, meaning 'sign', and the spelling semeiology is sometimes encountered in older texts.)

Saussure's comments are general and predictive, whereas Peirce's are more detailed and comprehensive in scope, and attempt to present a more integrated and formalized system. (It is Peirce we have to thank for the distinction between icon, index and symbol: see the entry for SIGN.) W. T. Scott has suggested that it was precisely the 'abstractness, density and range' of Peirce's proposal that militated against its being developed by later scholars who were neither philosophers nor logicians, nor others with an interest in abstract universals of mind and meaning. In contrast, Scott continues, 'the sketchiness and concreteness of de Saussure's work makes it more approachable', and its association with Linguistics helped to attach semiology to what has been perhaps the most theoretically prestigious of the human sciences during recent decades (1990, 71). Central to this association has been the use by semioticians of the LINGUISTIC PARADIGM.

What is certain is that between the 1960s and the 1980s attempts to establish a unified science of signs known as *semiotics* flourished, and that this threw up an extended terminology and set of concepts that have been pressed into use in a very wide range of fields of study – including that of literary criticism. Although Saussure was certainly no narrow formalist, semiotics has often been characterized by a formal-technical approach to the study of signs which, although it may have a place for terms such as *context*, has not emphasized social and CULTURAL determinants. On occasions many of Saussure's terms – SIGNIFIER and SIGNIFIED, LANGUE and PAROLE – have been recruited into the service of more or less acultural and asocial variants of semiotics, often under the aegis of STRUCTURALISM.

In contrast, other versions of semiotics have seen themselves, following Saussure's own suggestion, as a part of the Social Sciences rather than as an abstract, formal and technical discipline, and have seen their work to be closely related to Cultural Studies. It is significant, for example, that the English translation of Umberto Eco's essay 'Towards a Semiotic Inquiry into the

157

Television Message' was first published in *Working Papers in Cultural Studies* in Britain, and that although this essay states a initial concern to consider television outputs as 'a system of signs', it also commits itself to a belief in the importance of empirical investigations into how viewers actually 'read' and understand what they see – what they actually 'get' (1972, 104).

For Jonathan Culler, semiotics is not primarily concerned to produce inter-pretations, but rather to show how interpretations, or meanings, are generated.

> Semiotics, which defines itself as the science of signs, posits a zoological pursuit: the semiotician wants to discover what are the species of signs, how they differ from one another, how they function in their native habitat, how they interact with other species. Confronted with a plethora of texts that communicate various meanings to their readers, the analyst does not pursue a meaning; he seeks to identify signs and describe their functioning. (1981, vii–viii)

Semiotics is less fashionable today than it was a decade ago, and work which would have been described as belonging to semiotics in the 1970s and 1980s generally receives a rather looser categorization today. Those who do describe themselves as semioticians today are very likely to attach a much greater ideological significance to the sign than was the case in the 1970s and 1980s. One source of this shift of emphasis is probably the work of Mikhail Bakhtin and his circle, work which has reached the English-speaking world only in the last two decades even though much of it was written and/or published in the 1920s and 1930s. V. N. Vološinov's *Marxism and the Philo-sophy of Language*, for instance, which was first published in Russian in 1929, appeared in English only in 1973. The first chapter of Vološinov's book is entitled 'The Study of Ideologies and Philosophy of Language', and it devotes particular attention to the nature of the *sign*.

> The domain of ideology coincides with the domain of signs. They equate with one another. Wherever a sign is present, ideology is present, too. *Everything ideological possesses semiotic value*. (1986, 10)

The work of Roland Barthes has been influential in both the more formalist and the more culturally oriented variants of semiotics during different stages of his intellectual career. Structuralist semiotics need not necessarily be formalist: the Cultural Anthropology of Claude Lévi-Strauss is structuralist, but can be accused of formalism only to a limited degree.

As suggested above, a use of the linguistic paradigm has often been crucial to semiotic analyses: widely different systems such as complete CULTURES (Lévi-Strauss), striptease (Roland Barthes), or the UNCONSCIOUS (Jacques Lacan) are examined as sign-systems operating like a language, and what a component of the system *is* is subordinated to, or explained in terms of, what semiotic function it performs. Not surprisingly, this can take semiotic analysis close to aspects of traditional literary analysis. Thus Robert Scholes's 'semiotic analysis' of 'Eveline', one of the stories in James Joyce's collection *Dubliners*, (Scholes 1982, 87–104) relies heavily on the codes of reading defined by Roland Barthes in his *S/Z* (see the entry for CODE).

Perhaps because modern literary criticism has been dominated by the need to generate interpretations, semioticians have been less interested in literature than one might have expected, although Jonathan Culler has argued that literature is the most interesting form of semiosis, as it is cut off from the immediate PRAGMATIC purposes which simplify other sign situations, and thus allows the 'potential complexities of signifying processes [to] work freely in literature'. Moreover, Culler claims, literature presents us with a difficulty in saying exactly what is communicated at the same time as we are aware that 'signification is indubitably taking place' (1981, 35).

Literary semiotics, like semiotics in general, comes in both formalist and cultural editions (to oversimplify somewhat). Robert Scholes points out that Yuri Lotman's *Analysis of the Poetic Text* (1976) and Michael Riffaterre's *Semiotics of Poetry* (1978) (two influential studies) both 'approach poems through conventions and codes but share with the New Critics a sense of the poetic text as largely self-referential rather than oriented to a worldly context', whereas Barbara Herrnstein Smith's *Poetic Closure* (1968), although it also concentrates upon codes and CONVENTIONS as a way into the interpretation of texts, reveals her 'willingness to speak of a poem's "sense of truth"' that links her to other critics concerned with the emotional and intellectual impact of a text on READERS (1982, 12). An interest in the reader, then, is typical of what one can define as non-formalist literary semiotics. An interest in the AUTHOR is much less common among critics of this persuasion, many of them writing at a time when a belief in the death of the author was strongest.

Robert Scholes argues, thought-provokingly, that semiotics has become not so much the study of signs as the study of CODES, 'the systems that enable human beings to perceive certain events or entities *as* signs, bearing meaning' (1982, ix). For Derrida's critique of Saussure's use of the term semiology, see the entry for GRAMMATOLOGY.

Sender See SHANNON & WEAVER MODEL OF COMMUNICATION

Sense and reference The usual way in which a distinction made by the German philosopher Gottlob Frege between *Sinn* and *Bedeutung* is rendered in English, although sometimes *meaning and reference* has been preferred.

In the course of a complex discussion of the issue of what language can be said to refer to, Frege noted that phrases such as 'The Morning Star' and 'The Evening Star' can be said to share the same reference (that is, the planet Venus) but to be possessed of a different sense (or meaning). It is not just that the one phrase refers to the planet as seen in the morning, and the other to the planet as seen in the evening, but that each phrase has accrued a complex set of CULTURAL and literary associations of its own. Language, in other words, does not just divide the natural world up into segments which can then be referred to; it also encompasses human relations to that natural world along with a set of cultural and human MEANINGS which are in part created and in part reflected in language.

The distinction has appealed to aestheticians and literary theorists concerned to avoid two polarized responses to the question as to whether WORKS of literature or art can be said to refer to the real world (however defined). Such theorists reject the views that (i) the literary work makes no reference to the real world, but rather creates its own reality, and (ii) the literary work has no meaning independent of its reference to the real world. Instead, they argue that the literary work does have a reference to the real world, but that it also has a sense which is not wholly dependent upon or restricted to its reference. The argument is important, because if accepted it suggests that the literary reader or critic should neither be totally ignorant of nor oblivious to that extra-textual world to which the work in question refers or points, nor should he or she feel that the artistic or aesthetic quality of the work can be reduced to (and thus explained by) that same extra-textual reality.

Another term often used to describe words with the same reference but a different sense is *partial synonymy* (see the discussion in Scott 1990, 108–14).

Sequence See FUNCTION

Shannon & Weaver model of communication In 1948 the American electronic engineer Claude Shannon published two influential essays concerned to propose statistical ways of measuring the information-value of a message. Part of his argument included a diagrammatic model of the communication process, which has been extremely influential. As these essays were republished in book-form in 1949 with an additional essay by Warren Weaver, the model in question has become known as the Shannon and Weaver model. It has been adapted by many who have used it, but generally looks something like the following:

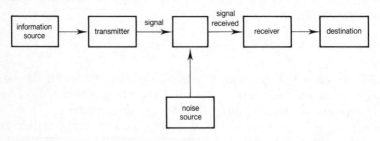

Shannon and Weaver model of communication, 1949

The model clearly aims at a high level of generality and abstraction, but it is important to remember that its creators were electronic engineers, used to working with information in a technical sense, information that could be *quantified* unproblematically. However it seized the imagination of many working in very different fields, and the development of SEMIOTICS gave it a wider circulation than its creators had probably intended or anticipated.

The influence of the model can almost certainly be detected in the influential passage in Roman Jakobson's 'Linguistics and Poetics' in which Jakobson attempts to break linguistic communication into its component parts: *addresser*, *message*, *addressee*, *context*, *code*, and *contact*. Jakobson's suggestion is discussed in the section on FUNCTIONS OF LANGUAGE, in which the case against using such terms in the study of art or poetry is considered. It certainly seems possible to claim that the rôle of interpretation in the understanding of art makes this process rather different from the transmission of quantifiable information undertaken by the electronic engineer. The electronic engineer wants his or her 'message' to reach its 'destination' in unchanged form: the poet or novelist – even according to the most pro-intentionalist of theorists – does not want merely to recreate in the mind of the READER exactly what occurred in his or her mind during the composition of the work. It is probably not irrelevant to note that the word *message* has generally been used in a somewhat pejorative sense in discussions of art.

Perhaps a more successful adaptation of terms which probably originate with Shannon and Weaver can be found in recent NARRATIVE theory. Here a more schematic analysis of what in traditional terminology used to be called *point of view* (discussed in the entry for PERSPECTIVE AND VOICE) has proved to be genuinely illuminating, and in this context terms such as *addresser* and *addressee* serve a useful and generally non-reductive function.

See also ACT/ACTOR.

Shifter In Linguistics: a linguistic unit which shifts reference according to the context in which it appears. Thus 'I', or 'the Pope' can both refer to a range of different historical or fictional individuals depending upon who utters them, to whom, and in what situation. The term has sometimes been used in discussions of literature, although not widely.

See also DEIXIS.

Sign Much modern literary and critical theory has been dominated by or founded on a version of SEMIOTICS – that is, upon a general theory (or 'science') of the nature of the sign and of its life in CULTURE and history. Semiotics is not the child of literary criticism or theory, however, and no theory of the sign can be said to be literature-specific, or directed primarily or exclusively towards literature. Thus a concern with semiotic theories on the part of literary critics and theorists is both the result of a lessening belief in the specificity of literature and what can be clumsily called literary communication, and also the basis for a further search for what literary works and their reading have in common with what one must then refer to as 'non-literary communication'.

A useful starting point is to distinguish between *sign* and *symptom*. The key difference would appear to be that of the *conventional* nature of the sign: a symptom is fixed by and interpreted in the light of nature, a sign by and in the light of CONVENTION. Some theorists would be prepared to see a symptom as a sub-set of sign, while others would distinguish sharply between the two. It will be clear that the issue of INTENTION, or MOTIVATION can be brought in here. (See the entry for SYMPTOMATIC READING in this context.)

Probably the theory of the sign which has been most influential so far as literature is concerned is that of the Swiss linguistician Ferdinand de Saussure. It is worth remembering that Saussure's definition is not of the sign as such, but of the *linguistic* sign, although many of his followers have generalized his definition to include non-linguistic signs as well. It should be remembered, however, that when one reads a statement along the lines of, 'Saussure defined the sign as . . .', one should bear in mind that this broadening of reference is neither unproblematic nor uncontroversial. (Saussure did, it is true, talk of the as then yet unborn science of semiology, which would study signs in general and their rôle in social life, but even here he closely associates the laws of semiology with laws applicable in Linguistics.)

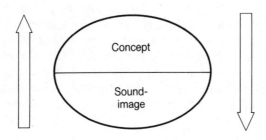

Saussure denied the common-sense view that the linguistic sign was a name that could be attached to an object, arguing instead that the linguistic sign was a 'two-sided psychological entity' that could be represented by the above diagram (1974, 66; sometimes translated as 'sound pattern' rather than 'sound image').

Saussure admits that this goes against then current usage (according to him the term *sign* was normally taken to designate only a sound-image), but argues that to avoid ambiguity three related terms were needed:

> I propose to retain the word *sign* [*signe*] to designate the whole and to replace *concept* and *sound-image* respectively by *signified* [*signifié*] and *signifier* [*signifiant*]. (1974, 67)

The English translations of *signifié* and *signifiant* given here have been questioned, and in one suggestion *significance* and *signal* have been proposed as alternatives.

It should be noted that subsequent theorists, Jacques Lacan included, have seen the link between signifier and signified to be far more problematic:

shifting, multiple and context-dependent. And Jacques Derrida has seen Saussure's writing about the sign to double back on its own revolutionary insights; according to him, by equating the *signatum* (that which is signified) with the concept, Saussure leaves open the possibility 'of thinking a *concept signified in and of itself*, a concept simply present for thought, independent of a relationship to language, that is of a relationship to a system of signifiers' (1981b, 19). This, Derrida claims, allows Saussure to fall back into the 'classical exigency' of the TRANSCENDENTAL SIGNIFIED (1981b, 19). In other words, the concept is seen to be possessed of an identity separate from the defining system of differences between signifiers: it is seen as extra-systemic and complete in itself.

It will be noted that what drops out in the movement from what I called the common-sense view to Saussure's definition is the object, or that which represents extra-linguistic reality. This has led many Saussureans to claim that language has no connection with extra-linguistic reality, an assertion that has been advanced especially forcefully by some *literary* critics and theorists concerned to adapt Saussure's theory of the sign to literature. Such assertions have very often brought in Saussure's argument concerning the ARBITRARINESS of the sign in support of this thesis, as well as the claim that Saussure's Linguistics is purely SYNCHRONIC and that it rejects the validity of any DIACHRONIC or historical, study of language. I have argued elsewhere (Hawthorn 1987, 52–7) that all of these assertions are incorrect, and that Saussure specifically rejects the basis for all of them in his *Course in General Linguistics*. The acceptance of all or some of these assertions as correct, however, has often provided a theoretical basis for a new formalism since the 1960s, a formalism that involves the isolation of literature from life, and art from society, culture and history. One quotation will perhaps suffice to confirm this; writing about Saussure's theory of the sign in his book *Semiotics and Interpretation* Robert Scholes states confidently that

> Saussure, as amplified by Roland Barthes and others, has taught us to recognize an unbridgeable gap between words and things, signs and referents. The whole notion of 'sign and referent' has been rejected by the French structuralists and their followers as too materialistic and simpleminded. Signs do not refer to things, they signify concepts, and concepts are aspects of thought, not of reality.
>
> (1982, 24)

To do Scholes justice it should be said that he goes on to challenge this 'recognition', although he does not challenge the justice of blaming it on Saussure. His summary is otherwise a fair account of an orthodoxy which flourished in the 1970s and 1980s.

A good summary of other important theories of the sign is given by Edmund Leach in the second chapter of his book *Culture and Communication* (1976, 9–16). Leach cites not just Saussure, but also C.S. Peirce, Ernst Cassirer, L. Hjelmslev, Charles Morris, Roman Jakobson and Roland Barthes as influential theorists in this context, but allots the word 'sign' only a limited function in his own terminology, which he represents by means of a complicated grid diagram. (Roland Barthes is driven to the same resort, which I have myself deliberately avoided, in his early work *Elements of Semiology*.) Discussing the work of Peirce, Jonathan Culler has pointed out (1981, 23) that his influential tripartite distinction between icon, index and symbol is only one of the many semiotic taxonomies he proposed, and that he finally committed himself to a core 66 classes of sign – a figure which has not been found worthy of adoption by subsequent theorists.

Gérard Genette has suggested an adaptation of Saussure's definition of the sign to the needs of the theory of NARRATIVE; he proposes 'to use the word *story* for the signified or narrative content . . . to use the word *narrative* for the signifier, statement, discourse or narrative text itself, and to use the word *narrating* for the producing narrative action (1980, 27). The vocabulary proposed is useful, but whether it depends upon the analogy with Saussure's definition of the linguistic sign is debatable.

Jacques Derrida has argued that not a single signified escapes 'the play of signifying references that constitute language'.

> The advent of writing is the advent of this play; today such a play is coming into its own, effacing the limit starting from which one had thought to regulate the circulation of signs, drawing along with it all the reassuring signifieds, reducing all the strongholds, all the out-of-bounds shelters that watched over the field of language. This, strictly speaking, amounts to destroying the concept of 'sign' and its entire logic. (1976, 7)

Others, however, have felt that this obituary is premature.
See also SEMEME.

Signifiance See SIGN

Signifiant See SIGN

Significance/Signification/*Signifié*/Signified/Signifier See SIGN; MEANING AND SIGNIFICANCE

Signifying practice In his Introduction to Julia Kristeva's *Desire in Language* Leon S. Roudiez quotes Kristeva's definition of this term from her *La Traversée des Signes*:

> I shall call signifying practice the establishment and the countervailing of a sign system. Establishing a sign system calls for the identity of a speaking subject within a social framework, which he recognizes as a basis for that identity. Countervailing the sign system is done by having the subject undergo an unsettling, questionable process; this indirectly challenges the social framework

with which he had previously identified, and it thus coincides with times of abrupt changes, renewal, or revolution in society. (Kristeva 1980, 18)

For Roland Barthes, a signifying practice is 'first of all a differentiated signifying system, dependent on a typology of significations (and not on a universal matrix of the sign)'. This means, he continues, that signification is not produced at the abstract level of LANGUE, but through 'a labour in which both the debate of the subject and the Other, and the social context, are invested in the same movement' (1981b, 36). According to Barthes, this notion restores its active energy to language.

A signifying practice thus involves a struggle for MEANINGS within a social context and against other interests, a struggle which is inseparable from the identity granted or claimed for him- or herself by the individual and by others.

See also DISCOURSE; UTTERANCE.

Singulative See FREQUENCY

Site A word that has accrued a particular polemical force in recent years, although a force that, paradoxically, is linked to a claimed neutrality, ideological innocence, and lack of proper energy or initiatory force. To describe something as a site has become a favoured way of giving (sometimes exclusive) precedence to external determining forces while playing down or denying the self-initiation of movement or development.

Thus when the SUBJECT is described as site, an attack is being made on views of the subject as in control – or even aware – of its own destiny; a subject is, according to such a view, more or merely a site on which extra-subjective forces clash and resolve their differences. These extra-subjective forces which are given priority can be either language, or history, or ideology, or the class struggle, or whatever. Put simply, the argument thus invoked by the use of *site* denies that the individual is in charge of his or her life, or consciousness, and asserts rather that the subject is constituted by other forces which then proceed either to nest or to fight in it.

Those fond of the term have sometimes come dangerously near to a sort of infinite regress: the subject is a site upon which different ideological forces battle, but then ideology is itself a site on which different class interests war with one another, while class is, in its turn, a site on which different relationships to the forces of production meet in conflict, and so on.

The term is sometimes invoked by those DECONSTRUCTIONISTS arguing for a rejection of any TRANSCENDENTAL SUBJECT or PRESENCE.

In literary criticism the term is often associated with attempts to downgrade the extent to which the AUTHOR is seen to be in control (conscious or otherwise) of his or her creation.

Situate See READING POSITION

Skaz

Sjužet See STORY AND PLOT

Skaz A mode or technique of narration that mirrors oral NARRATIVE. A useful alternative definition of the term is given by Ann Banfield, who points out that apart from the epistolary form, *skaz* 'is the only type of literary first person narrative which clearly has a second person' (1982, 172). The term comes from the Russian, as Russian Formalist theorists were the first to tackle the issues raised by *skaz*, but there are many non-Russian examples. For example, from a technical point of view much of Joseph Conrad's *Heart of Darkness* can be described as *skaz*, as much of what we read represents the character Marlow's oral address to listeners.

For the Russian Formalist Boris Eichenbaum, *skaz* allots – or can allot – a special rôle to aspects of a NARRATOR's verbal delivery such as articulation, miming, and sound gestures. Eichenbaum also distinguishes between the concept of PLOT and the concept of STORY-stuff, or, alternatively, between construction and material. *Skaz* for Eichenbaum is important because it is 'the constructional principle of the plotless story' (Èjxenbaum 1971a, 21). (See the entry for STORY AND PLOT.)

Mikhail Bakhtin takes issue with Eichenbaum, claiming that the most important thing about *skaz* is not '*orientation toward the oral form of narration*', but 'orientation toward *someone else's speech*' (1984, 191). Bakhtin's argument seems to be that crucial to *skaz* is not the oral mode of delivery (or its imitation or representation), but the AUTHOR's recruitment of an alternative voice (with all the significance that this last word has in Bakhtin's work). Thus Bakhtin would, presumably, argue that Conrad's use of Marlow in *Heart of Darkness* is important not so much because of Marlow's oral delivery, but because of Conrad's use of Marlow's voice, a voice that is 'socially distinct, carrying with it precisely those points of view and evaluations necessary to the author' (1984, 192).

Bakhtin's points are important, but they are probably overstated. Marlow (to continue with this example) is probably important to Conrad because of the voice (in a Bakhtinian sense) which he provides, but the oral manner of delivery is also very important, and carries with it certain possibilities and restrictions which conventional first-person narrative (as, for example, in Charles Dickens's *David Copperfield*) does not, even though such first-person narrative provides an author with the same voice.

Ann Banfield adds a number of other, more complex points. She claims that *skaz* is not actually a form of narration, but 'the imitation of a discourse'. For her, DISCOURSE is characterized by the inseparability of telling from expression, whereas the function of a sentence in narration is 'solely to tell' (1982, 178). Her claim is by no means uncontroversial, and relies upon definitions of *discourse* and *narration* that would not find universal acceptance. She makes one additional, important technical point: represented speech and thought (see the entry for FREE INDIRECT DISCOURSE) are not found in oral literature, or literature derived from the oral – and this includes *skaz* (1982, 239–40).

Slippage The (normally unconscious) redefinition of terms or commitments in the course of an argument, often as a result of ideological pressure. The term appears to be an anglicizing of the French *glissade*.

Slow-down The narrative equivalent to that slow-motion experience which frequently accompanies moments of great danger or tension. A narrative may suddenly provide what seems (in contrast to that which has gone before or that which comes after) a disproportionate number of pages to what takes place in a (relatively) very short span of time. Precisely because the technique does resemble 'slow-motion experience' it suggests by analogy that what is narrated is of great subjective importance either to narrator or character, or both.

Compare the (now clichéd) use of filmic slow-motion at moments of high tension in motion pictures: a famous example is the final machine-gunning in *Bonnie and Clyde*.

The obvious justification for slow-down is that its use in the appropriate context creates an impression of psychological REALISM, as at moments of high tension – especially those involving physical danger – human beings do experience events as if they were happening in slow motion. Beyond this, slow-down allows a writer to go more into detail at times when detail is more interesting and of greater significance.

Sociolect Formed by analogy with *dialect* (compare IDIOLECT and GENDERLECT), and used to denote language (PAROLE rather than LANGUE) which is specific to a particular social group, and which thus carries with it the values and status of the same group. The social group in question can be defined in terms of class (various understood), age, or GENDER – or a permutation of all three. Sociolects are normally associated with speech, although as lexical, grammatical and syntactical elements can serve to isolate a sociolect it is possible to trace sociolects in written TEXTS. Other defining elements involve aspects of pronunciation: certain sounds are indicative of certain sociolects in British English; (the glottal stop, for example).

Many writers have attempted to convey sociolects by means of idiosyncratic spelling, but this is problematic in English as the sounds of spoken English are not rendered into writing in a consistent manner (as those learning English as a second language soon discover). Thus use of a spelling such as *wimmin* (for *women*) in the speech of a cockney character probably works more by the association 'can't spell – therefore uneducated' than by suggesting cockney pronunciation (*wimmin* is, after all, a spelling that reflects educated pronunciation pretty accurately).

Socio-linguistic horizon See HORIZON

Solution from above/below Also known as 'hypothesis driven' (above) and 'data driven' (below) solutions. From the psychology of visual perception: a solution from above is a perceptual interpretation which has been arrived at as a result of a hypothesis which predates the input of sensory data; a solution from below is a perceptual interpretation which has been prompted by the actual input of sensory data which is itself then interpreted.

By extension, a literary interpretation which is 'from above' or hypothesis driven is one prompted by a hypothesis which the WORK itself, or the readings of 'Common readers', do not overtly suggest; a literary interpretation which is 'from below' or data driven is one which is prompted by the work itself.

The distinction seems more straightforward than it is, as what a work 'overtly suggests' is arguably dependent upon the READER's expectations, critical awareness, social and CULTURAL background, and so on. (See, for example, the discussion in the entry for TRANSACTIONAL THEORY OF THE LITERARY WORK on this point.) Nevertheless, the distinction has its merits, especially during the present time when many critical theories propose the need for the critic to step outside a *naturalized* understanding of, or RESPONSE to, the work of literature, and to give it instead an OPPOSITIONAL READING.

As a crude generalization, then, we can say that whereas the period dominated by the ideas and approaches of the New Critics privileged 'solution from below' readings and interpretations, the past two or three decades have seen the rise of theories and movements committed to arguing for 'solution from above' readings and interpretations, often on the grounds that these offer an escape from the ideological thrall of particular literary works or of particular INTERPRET[AT]IVE COMMUNITIES.

In this context it is worth noting that recent literary theory has often obscured the distinction between *empiricism* (the belief that direct experience or observation is the only source of knowledge), and *empirical* research (which relies upon such direct experience or observation but does not necessarily rest upon the view that such experience or observation is the *only* source of knowledge, or that its significance is self-evident without the application of non-empirical ideas or theories.

Sous rature See ERASURE

Spacing See PUNCTUATION

Speech Attempts to render Ferdinand de Saussure's distinction between LANGUE AND PAROLE into English frequently use *speech* as the preferred term for *parole*. However, it is increasingly common to use the original terms in untranslated form, in part because *speech* is a rather unsatisfactory translation of *parole* – something like *the sum of all actual or possible UTTERANCES* would probably come nearer to what Saussure seems to have had in mind. An utterance, like *parole*, does not need to be actually spoken: it can be written or expressed to oneself in silent thought.

We can compare the problems associated with translating ÉCRITURE as *writing*, discussed in the entry for this term.

As a general principle, then, it is worth exercising care when one encounters words such as *speech* and *writing* in English translations of French theoretical writing. Jacques Derrida's commitment to the primacy of Writing over Speech, for example (reiterated in a number of his texts) seems less bizarre when his original terms are borne in mind: he is certainly not saying that human speech is historically subsequent to writing in the everyday meanings of these words.

See also SPEECH ACT THEORY; voice (in PERSPECTIVE AND VOICE).

Speech act theory As its name suggests, speech act theory is a theory which attempts to explain exactly what happens when human beings speak to one another. The theory has been influential not just within Linguistics and PRAGMATICS, but also within Literary Criticism – as a result of books such as Mary Louise Pratt's *Toward a Speech Act Theory of Literary Discourse* (1977). Speech act theory originated with the philosopher John Austin's book *How to do Things with Words* (1962), in which Austin argues against the philosophical assumptions that verbal statements can be analysed in isolation and in terms only of their truth or falsity.

A number of other philosophers – most notably John Searle but also H. P. Grice and P. F. Strawson – have developed and extended Austin's arguments. They have drawn attention to the manner in which the public uttering of statements is governed by rules and CONVENTIONS which have to be understood and abided by on the part of utterers and listeners if effective communication is to take place, and also to the fact that statements not only *are* things, but they typically also *do* things. In Searle (1969) we find a useful distinction between a number of different sorts of verbal act:

(a) Uttering words (morphemes, sentences) = performing *utterance acts*.
(b) Referring and predicating = performing *propositional acts*.
(c) Stating, questioning, commanding, promising, etc. = performing *illocutionary acts*. (1969, 24)

Searle's usage is not identical to Austin's: for Austin an illocutionary act could be either what Searle calls a propositional act or what he calls an illocutionary act. And what Searle calls an illocutionary act, Austin refers to as a *performative*. Austin distinguishes between *constatives* – utterances which can either be true or false because they claim to report that certain things are the case in certain worlds – and performatives, which are utterances used to do something rather than to say that something is the case (e.g. 'I promise to marry you') and of which it makes no sense to claim that they are either true or false. One should add that a constative can also have a performative aspect – by pragmatic implication, for example.

Utterance acts are also referred to as *locutionary acts* if they involve the production of a recognizably grammatical utterance within a language community. *Illocutionary acts* include such things as asserting, warning, promising and so on, and Austin claimed that over a thousand different possible such acts can be performed in English. Searle has suggested that illocutionary acts can be classified into five basic categories: *representatives*, which undertake to represent a state of affairs; *directives*, which have the aim of getting the person addressed to do something; *commissives*, which commit the speaker to doing something; *expressives*, which provide information about the speaker's psychological state, and *declarations*, which bring about the state of affairs they themselves refer to (e.g. 'I now declare you man and wife') (1976, 10–14).

Searle has also pointed out that a person who performs an illocutionary act may also be performing what he has dubbed a *perlocutionary act*, in other words, achieving certain intended results in his or her listener. He gives as examples, *get him to do something, convince him (enlighten, edify, inspire him, get him to realize)* (1969, 25).

The conventions underlying successful conversation are known as *appropriateness conditions* or *felicity conditions* by speech act philosophers, and together are taken to constitute the *co-operative principle* (a term suggested by H. P. Grice) that governs conversation in ideal situations. They include (1) *maxim of quantity*: (Make your contribution no more or less informative than is required); (2) *maxim of quality*: (Make your contribution one that is true, and that does not include either false or inadequately substantiated material); (3) *maxim of relation*: (Be relevant); (4) *maxim of manner*: (Be perspicuous, avoiding obscurity, ambiguity, unnecessary prolixity). (Based on Pratt 1977, 130, following Grice.)

On the basis of such maxims, and on their assumed observance by participants in a conversation, statements not immediately interpretable as relevant can be seen to have a particular *implicature* or implication. Thus in the following exchange between husband and wife: 'Do you want to go home?' 'It's getting rather late'. The second statement may seem to be changing the subject, but its pragmatic meaning or implicature is clearly 'Yes'.

A theory of utterances which reduced the importance of truth reference and emphasized instead the compact formed between utterer and listener by the mutual adoption of a set of conventions, made literary critics sit up and take notice, for it seemed of far greater potential use in literary criticism than more traditional philosophical approaches to verbal statements had been. An obvious application of such a theory was to the conversations between characters in plays and literary NARRATIVES, but there were more interesting and sophisticated ones. In his essay 'The Death of the Author' Roland Barthes suggested that the word writing (see ÉCRITURE) no longer designated 'an operation of recording, notation, representation, "depiction"', but rather 'a performative . . . in which the enunciation has no other content . . . than the act by which it is uttered' (1977, 145–6; see also the entry for AUTHOR). Clearly such an approach could be used as support for the argument that the literary work did not say anything about the extra-literary world, but rather performed itself, repeated in endlessly different ways the statement 'I express myself'.

In a very different way the theory of implicature seemed especially promising for literary-critical application. When a writer wrote something that seemed to be irrelevant to what the READER had been led to be interested in, was this not because the writer could rely upon the reader's *searching* for relevance in the TEXT? Do not readers assume that everything that is there in a literary text is there for some purpose, has in other words some implicature? The problem with this use of speech act theory would seem to be that all it did was to give a new name to something about which literary critics and readers had known for a very long time anyway.

Moreover, were not author and writer, and their intercourse, comparable to the participants in a conversation governed by the co-operative principle? Was it not the case that just as a conversation which did not abide by the different Gricean maxims would necessarily be ill-fated and unproductive, so too that any reading of a literary work which did not respect the conventions of literary communication would become pointless and unproductive?

There are a number of possible objections to such an argument. The first is actually a criticism of speech act theory itself, that speech act theory tends to stress co-operation at the expense of struggle and disagreement. Most conversations are not conducted between equals whose interests are identical; they are conducted between individuals who have divergent interests and who either possess, or are subject to the exercise of, social power and authority. Most participants in conversations thus, the argument continues, typically break many of the maxims quoted above to further their own interests, and they expect their fellow conversationalists to do the same. Much the same is true of literary reading: the author and the reader have different interests and are as much trying to outwit as to co-operate with one another. In her poem 'Murder in the Dark' Margaret Atwood compares the literary process to the party game referred to in her title, with the writer as murderer and the reader as detective, and the NEW HISTORICIST critic Stephen Greenblatt reminds us that Plato's rival Gorgias 'held that deception – *apate* – is the very essence of the creative imagination: the tragic artist's special power is the power to deceive' (1990, 52). (Greenblatt goes on to note that Gorgias did not thereby exclude the power of art to strip away fraud, as 'its successful practitioner is nearer to reality than the unsuccessful, and the man who lets himself be deceived is wiser than he who does not' [1990, 52, quoting from Gorgias].)

Even if one grants this sort of objection, it remains the case that both in conversations and in literary readings, manoeuverings, battles for position, attempts to further one's interests, take place according to mutually recognized conventions.

In Grice's defence it needs to be noted that he never intended the co-operative principle to have a normative force. His argument was, rather, that in the absence of evidence suggesting that a conversational partner was knowingly refusing to co-operate, individuals continued to assume that the partner was following the rules, and consequently continued to search for a meaning in what was said that was consistent with that assumption.

The second objection to a literary-critical appropriation of speech act theory is that literary works are not oriented to the achievement of specific goals in quite the way that the typical conversation is. Literary works are objects for APPRECIATION, interpretation, and (sometimes) performance. They thus have the potentiality to generate new experiences, new SIGNIFICANCE, in a manner quite different from that of a conversation. Moreover, although it is not meaningless to talk of interaction between author and reader, this interaction is nonetheless of a quite different sort from the mutually adjusting and instantaneous reaction involved in ordinary conversation. We can talk back to Emily Brontë as we read *Wuthering Heights*, but this will not change her text or whatever of herself is in that text.

Literary works have, too, an aesthetic dimension which conversations lack. This explains why it is that literary works seem actually to be prized to the extent that they break some of the Gricean maxims – that involving ambiguity, for example. Does it always make sense to talk about a writer of literature providing the reader, in an ideal situation, with no more or less information than is required?

Whether one grants such criticisms a certain truth or not, speech act theory has probably had a positive effect upon literary critics inasmuch as it has stressed the importance of mutually accepted conventions in the reading and writing of literature, and it has refocused attention on to the conventional elements implicit in LITERARINESS.

Speed See DURATION

Spots of indeterminacy See CONCRETIZATION

Stereotype Originally taken from a process in printing, the term has become a Standard English phrase for something that is fixed and unchanging – normally with a pejorative ring. It has played an important part in recent FEMINIST theory in connection with the description of fixed and, normally, PATRIARCHAL or sexist views of GENDER rôles and characteristics.

Thus the central third chapter in Mary Ellmann's very influential book *Thinking About Women* (first published 1968) is devoted to 'Feminine Stereotypes', and lists formlessness, passivity, instability, confinement, piety, materiality, spirituality, irrationality and compliancy – along with 'two incorrigible figures': the shrew and the witch. Ellmann's list has been discussed and amended by subsequent writers, and it is fair to say that an investigation into stereotyping plays a key rôle in the discussion of a range of ideological processes.

Stereotyping is not directed only at women, of course: we can isolate stereotypes based on race or CULTURE, on age, on profession, and so on. Moreover, a stereotype may present itself as positive: thus the view that women are naturally intuitive, or that Black people are always happy and have a wonderful sense of rhythm, are no less stereotypical than more overtly negative views. (It will be noticed that such 'positive' stereotypes typically serve to advance more concealed, negative portrayals.)

Stereotypes are, it has been argued, part of the means whereby SUBJECTS are INTERPELLATED by ideological forces.

Story and plot With this item we are concerned with an essentially very simple distinction surrounded by minefields of confusing vocabulary. The simple distinction is between, on the one hand, a *series of real or fictitious events, connected by a certain logic or chronology, and involving certain ACTORS*, and on the other hand, the *NARRATION of this series of events*. Thus were one to be asked to give the story of *Wuthering Heights* a suitable response would be to start with the first arrival of the child Heathcliff at Wuthering Heights and then proceed to recount the events of the novel in chronological order until the death of Heathcliff and the (possible) reuniting of him with Cathy. But the plot of *Wuthering Heights* is these events *as they are actually presented in Emily Brontë's novel*. Clearly the same story can give rise to many different plots, as FORMULAIC literature reveals very clearly.

The minefields of which I spoke arise from the fact that the same distinction is also referred to by means of the Russian words *fabula* (story) and *sjužet* (plot), and in some translations these are rendered in ways that conflict with the usage associated with story and plot. Mieke Bal, for example, renders our story and plot as *fabula* and *story* (1985, 5), which gives *story* the opposite meaning from that with which we started. Meanwhile other translators of Russian Formalist texts have suggested that fabula be rendered as *plot* – thus further giving also this term exactly the opposite meaning from the plot in our pair plot and story. (Other translators have suggested *fable and subject* for fabula and sjužet, which introduces yet further possibilities of confusion.)

Speaking as one who has himself trodden on some of these mines, my advice is as follows. When reading these terms always proceed with care and try to confirm what convention of usage the writer is following. When writing, explain your own convention of usage by making reference to what seems to be the one reliably unambiguous term: the paired *fabula and sjužet*. Do not use terms such as *story* or *plot* on their own without making it very clear to what you are referring.

I cannot resist closing this entry with a comment by the novelist Ivy Compton-Burnett, who I am glad to say follows the usage I recommend in the first paragraph above:

> As regards plots I find life no help at all. Real life seems to have no plots at all, and as I think a plot desirable and almost necessary, I have this extra grudge against life. (Quoted in Furbank 1970, 124)

String of pearls narrative A NARRATIVE that consists of a number of relatively or completely unrelated episodes strung together by a thin thread. The thread can consist of a causal sequence, or the person of an individual character, or whatever. Otherwise known as an *episodic* narrative.

Strong poet See REVISIONISM

Strong textualist See TEXTUALIST

Structuralism It is worth starting off by distinguishing between modern structuralism, which is essentially a post-Second World War development, and the structuralism of the Prague School theorists (for which see the entry for Prague School). Although these have something in common – notably a central and substantial debt to the work of Ferdinand de Saussure – their differences are such as to justify our treating them separately. The present entry will therefore concentrate upon what we can term modern structuralism, which in its initial phase in the 1950s and 1960s is a largely French phenomenon whose most important figures are probably the anthropologist Claude Lévi-Strauss, and the literary and cultural critic Roland Barthes. Following them, however, many other individuals produced work which has been labelled structuralist. These include a group of MARXIST theorists of differing persuasions within Marxism such as Louis Althusser and Lucien Goldmann (originally Romanian and known as a 'genetic structuralist'); NARRATOLOGISTS such as Gérard Genette, and Michel Foucault who, for want of a better classification, we can call a historian. We can add that in his insistence that the UNCONSCIOUS is structured like a language, Jacques Lacan also advances a classic structuralist position.

   Common to all of these is an interest in structures or SYSTEMS which can be studied SYNCHRONICALLY rather than in terms of their emergence and development through traceable processes of historical causation (this applies even to Foucault, but only with qualifications to Goldmann), and a debt to the theories of Saussure – often involving a commitment to the implications of the LINGUISTIC PARADIGM. Put crudely, structuralism is (at least in its early or 'pure' form) interested rather in that which makes MEANING possible than in meaning itself: even more crudely – in form rather than content.

   Not surprisingly, then, many structuralist ideas can be traced back to the Russian Formalists, either directly or as mediated through the Prague School. A classic early example of a structuralist involvement with literature (or at least with NARRATIVE, depending upon how one defines literature) is to be found in Vladimir Propp's *Morphology of the Folktale*, first published in Russian in 1928. Typical features of Propp's study are its concern to generalize features (or FUNCTIONS) across TEXTS, and thus to concentrate upon a system capable of generating meanings which goes beyond the confines of the individual WORK, and its concomitant lack of interest in the interpretation of individual works or, even, in their individual specificity. (Roland Barthes's proposed CODES OF READING can be seen to be the direct descendants of Propp's functions.) From this perspective it is as if the work is written not by its AUTHOR (collective or individual), but by the 'grammar' or system of transformations that pre-exists its creation. A fundamental distinctive feature of structuralism can perhaps be indicated by comparing this to the way in which Lévi-Strauss can treat the system of gift-giving in a CULTURE, or Roland Barthes can treat 'Steak and Chips' or 'Striptease' in his *Mythologies*. What all of these studies have in common is a concern with the pre-existing system which allows individual UTTERANCES to be made. Indeed, use of the linguistic paradigm means that for the structuralist a particular meal, or giving of a gift, can be treated as a sort of utterance, an example of PAROLE behind which lies a complete LANGUE. When we give a visitor a meal of steak and chips, the meaning which this has for him or her is determined not just by (or not perhaps even primarily by) the actual taste and appearance of the meal, but the grammatical function which 'steak and chips' is allowed to play in the *langue* of meals. How and why this *langue* has developed into the system that exists is a matter of less (or no) interest to structuralism.

Clearly, this downplays the importance of 'the meal itself' and of the individual cook's skill, and thus it is not surprising that when structuralism is applied to literary works, it downgrades or rejects ideas that either the 'work itself' or the author determines how the work is to be read. As Genette puts it,

> The project [of Structuralism], as described in Barthes's *Critique et verité* and Todorov's 'Poétique' (in *Qu'est-ce que le structuralism?*), was to develop a poetics which would stand to literature as linguistics stands to language and which therefore would not seek to explain what individual works mean but would attempt to make explicit the system of figures and conventions that enable works to have the forms and meanings they do. (1980, 8)

Many structuralists have used Saussurean linguistics as a basis to argue that such structures, like language, are self-enclosed and are neither affected (or caused) by extra-structural pressures (the 'real world'), nor can they change or even refer to an extra-structural reality. My own opinion is that Saussure provides a dubious basis for such an assertion, which seems to me to be as false as the argument that Saussure rejects the historical approach in favour of the synchronic one (in actual fact he argues that both are necessary). Be this as it may, structuralist literary theory and criticism often tend to be characterized by solipsistic and idealistic positions, although in the work of, for example, Roland Barthes, structuralist analyses can also be directed outwards towards social, ideological and political realities.

Although structuralism has been (and remains) a controversial movement, it has undoubted successes to its credit across a range of disciplines and subject matters. Within literary criticism its most unqualified successes have probably been within the field of NARRATOLOGY. Genette – one of its leading practitioners within this field – has argued that structuralism is more than just a method and needs to be seen as a general tendency of thought or an ideology

(1982, 11). Interestingly, Genette sees the concern of structuralism with form at the expense of content as a *corrective* one, as can be seen from his (much-quoted) comment that 'Literature had long enough been regarded as a message without a code for it to become necessary to regard it for a time as a code without a message' (1982, 7). He explains the need for such a corrective shift of focus by characterizing structuralism as a reaction to 'positivism, "historicizing history" and the "biographical illusion"', and sees structuralism as

> a movement represented in various ways by the critical writings of a Proust, an Eliot, a Valéry, Russian Formalism, French 'thematic criticism' or Anglo-American 'New Criticism.' In a way, the notion of structural analysis can be regarded as a simple equivalent of what Americans call 'close reading' and which would be called in Europe, following Spitzer, the 'immanent study' of works.
>
> (1982, 11–12)

This broadens structuralism very considerably, as does Genette's claim that 'any analysis that confines itself to a work without considering its sources or motives would, therefore, be implicitly structuralist' (1982, 12).

Structure The concept of structure is not limited to STRUCTURALIST theory. The term is in common use in literary-critical discussion, and as one might expect, it is used in a number of relatively loose senses. It is usual to make a distinction between a literary work's structure and its plot (see STORY AND PLOT): whereas a work's plot can be seen as the NARRATIVE arrangement of its story, *structure* refers to its total (or total aesthetic) organization.

The term tends to be given a SYNCHRONIC, non-historical force, mainly as a result of the influence of Structuralist theories which see historical change in terms of the successive replacement of structures (rather than of the modification or development of a structure).

A more technical definition developed both from Structuralism and Systems Theory is given by Anthony Wilden: 'Structure is the ensemble of laws which govern the behavior of the system' (1972, 242). Moreover, these laws control elements or components which are interchangeable – thus an economic system stays the same even though the economic acts which it enables and controls are all unique. This takes us to the Structuralist commitment to a set of enabling rules ('LITERARINESS') which remain the same even though the literary works or acts of reading enabled or controlled by the rules change.

The paired terms *deep structure* and *surface structure*, originated by the Linguistician Noam Chomsky, denote elements in his Standard Theory. According to this theory, the following sentences would be seen to have the same deep structure, but different surface structures:

> The ploughman homeward plods his weary way
> Weary, the ploughman plods his way homeward
> The ploughman plods his weary way homeward

Surface structure is derived from deep structure by means of transformations: hence transformational grammar. Chomsky's theory is controversial amongst Linguisticians, and amongst non-Linguisticians (literary critics, for example) it seems fair to say that the terms *deep structure* and *surface structure* are used only metaphorically. Thus to argue that two of Dickens's novels have the same deep structure is to say only that they share a common theme, or a common concern with certain linked issues, or a common PLOT. (The fact that one comes up with all these different possible meanings testifies to the fundamentally metaphorical usage to which the Chomskyan distinction is here being put.) After all, from a literary-critical point of view, the example given above would suggest that to concentrate on deep structure in Chomsky's sense would be to cut out a good deal of what literary critics find of value in Thomas Gray's line of poetry.

Structure in dominance A term popularized in English by the writings of Louis Althusser, especially his essay 'On the Materialist Dialectic', which is to be found in *For Marx* (1969). Althusser uses the term to introduce a hierarchical element into the set of contradictions which, according to him, constitute a structured unity. This can be seen as a way of escaping one of the problematic elements inherent in the limitation to the SYNCHRONIC which characterizes STRUCTURALISM and neo-structuralism. Because the synchronic by definition excludes development, and because developmental change is the classic way of distinguishing determining from non-determining (or dominant from subservient) influences and forces, structuralism faces the problem that although it can trace relationships it lacks the ability to rank these relationships according to their importance (varyingly defined). The concept of structure in dominance can thus be seen as a reintroduction of the historical to an essentially synchronic schema by Althusser: dominance can only be asserted or revealed on a temporal continuum.

The term has been used on occasions by those advancing a structuralist literary criticism who wish to escape from the wilderness of unhierarchized relationships with which their approach might otherwise leave them.

Structures of feeling The term is the coinage of the Welsh CULTURAL theorist and novelist Raymond Williams, who devotes a single chapter of his book *Marxism and Literature* to it. Williams introduces his discussion by arguing against a reduction of the social to 'fixed forms' and against its separation from the personal (1977, 128, 129). Thus Williams distances himself from what he sees as a tendency in more traditional Marxism to take 'terms of analysis as terms of substance' (1977, 129), and thus to deal with lived experience at at least one remove.

According to Williams, the term is deliberately chosen to emphasize a distinction from more formal concepts such as *world-view* or ideology; the reason for this, he states, is that we are 'concerned with meanings and values as they are actively lived and felt', and with 'characteristic elements of impulse,

restraint, and tone; specifically affective elements of consciousness and relationships: not feeling as against thought, but thought as felt and feeling as thought:
practical consciousness of a present kind, in a living and interrelating
continuity' (1977, 132).

The term, Williams adds, represents a cultural hypothesis (1977, 132), and
it can be seen as one of a number of attempts to retain Marxism's analytical
socio-historical approach while taking it closer to the ways in which people
actually experience their lives.

So far as its relation to literature is concerned, Williams gives a relevant
example. He argues that whereas early Victorian ideology specified the
exposure caused by poverty, debt or illegitimacy as social failure or deviation,
the structure of feeling represented in the works of Dickens, Emily Brontë and
others specified exposure and isolation as a general condition, and poverty,
debt, or illegitimacy as its connecting instances – a view represented at the
ideological level only later (1977, 134). In this view structures of feeling are
pre-ideological formations developed almost unconsciously, antagonistic to
existing ideological formations, and expressed through (among other things) art
and literature. What is important about such a view is that it challenges a belief
(very popular at the time Williams was writing) that literature expresses and is
in thrall to the dominant ideology.

Style and stylistics The noun *style* has a long history and wide set of meanings:
the OED devotes over six page-columns to its various definitions. It derives
from a Latin term meaning stake, or pointed instrument for writing (it shares
a broad etymology with *stylus*), and modern meanings involve metaphorical and
metonymic extensions of this meaning. It is the thirteenth of the OED's
definitions that is most relevant to our present concerns: 'The manner of
expression characteristic of a particular writer (hence of an orator) or of a
literary group or period; a writer's mode of expression considered in regard to
clearness, effectiveness, beauty, and the like.'

In the course of the present century Stylistics has grown up as a recognized
academic discipline, situated on the borderline between the study of language
and the study of literature (although stylistic analysis can be and is applied to
non-literary TEXTS), and concerned to engage in technical study and analysis
of what the OED calls 'manners of expression'. It is important for students of
literature because – as a result of its close relation to and impingement on
Literary Studies – it has brought a number of more specifically linguistic terms
and methods of analysis into literary criticism and theory.

Styles can be categorized according to a number of principles: deliverer's
intention (a humorous style); receiver's evaluation (an imprecise style); context
(an inappropriate style or REGISTER); aesthetic (an ornate style); level of
formality (a colloquial style); social class (an urbane style) – and so on. For a
Linguistician these are relatively imprecise categories, of course, and the
academic study of style typically involves an attempt to analyse what are
perceived impressionistically to be distinctive styles in more formal and

objective ways, often through the use of statistical analysis directed at syntax, vocabulary, grammar, and so on. At this level Stylistics involves an attempt to back up the hunches of common READERS ('Hemingway has a distinctive, plain style') with statistical evidence. At another level, Stylistics can involve an attempt to go beyond the hunches of the common reader, detailing significant stylistic differences which may be functional but which are not necessarily noticed by the reader or listener.

At this point the question of purpose must be confronted. According to Geoffrey Leech and Michael Short's *Style in Fiction*, we normally study style, 'because we want to explain something, and in general, literary stylistics has, implicitly or explicitly, the goal of explaining the relation between language and artistic function' (1981, 13). This of course is a central concern of the traditional discipline of *Rhetoric*, and in many ways Stylistics inherits and develops fundamental concerns of rhetoricians throughout the ages.

Stylisticians have often gone outside the Anglo-American literary-critical tradition for theoretical ideas and approaches. The Russian Formalists, the Prague School, the circle around the Russian Mikhail Bakhtin, the Swiss Linguistician Ferdinand de Saussure, the German-American Leo Spitzer – the ideas of these have perhaps been of more interest to stylisticians than has the work of most Anglo-American literary critics: possibly because of the different trajectories taken by the academic study of literature in Britain and the USA on the one hand, and Continental Europe on the other. What is more, Anglo-American literary critics have frequently expressed reserve or scepticism about the possibility of the 'objective' analysis of literary texts producing results relevant to literary criticism: a good example is the chapter entitled 'Jakobson's Poetic Analyses' in Jonathan Culler's *Structuralist Poetics* (1975).

It is an interesting fact that the contribution of Stylistics to the literary-critical study of prose has been far less controversial, and more influential among literary critics, than has its contribution to the analysis of poetry. Even the most traditionalist of literary critics could hardly fail to find much of value and little to take objection to in Leech and Short's *Style in Fiction* (1981); in contrast, Roman Jakobson's analyses of poetry have generally been taken by literary critics much as Culler takes them: as valuable demonstrations of what stylistic analysis cannot do. It seems that formal and statistical approaches are more suited to the analysis of NARRATIVE technique than they are to poetic expression – perhaps because many decisions that the writer of narrative has to make involve, at one level, choice from a relatively finite set of alternatives.

Style indirecte libre See FREE INDIRECT DISCOURSE

Styleme See SEMEME

Subaltern See MARGINALITY

Subject and subjectivity The traditional sense of *subject* as an abbreviation of *the conscious or thinking subject*, meaning the self or ego (OED), or individual *cogito*, has been pressed into service in a largely pejorative sense in recent theoretical writing. The main targets for attack in this process have been (i) the view that the human subject is somehow a point of origin for larger historical, social or even personal movements and events, and (ii) the belief that the individual human being is possessed of valid self-knowledge and is self-actuating – in a phrase, in charge and control of him/herself.

A more detailed account of one particular example of this use of *subject* can be found in the entry for INTERPELLATION, in which the position of the French MARXIST philosopher Louis Althusser is outlined. According to Althusser, all ideology '*hails or interpellates concrete individuals as concrete subjects*, by the functioning of the category of the subject' (1971, 162). Thus *subject* represents the individual's self-consciousness and consciousness of self after having been 'body-snatched' by ideology. Althusser's position here forms the theoretical basis for a discussion by Etienne Balibar and Pierre Macherey of the specific rôle played by literature in this process. According to them, through the endless functioning of its TEXTS,

> literature unceasingly 'produces' *subjects*, on display for everyone. So paradoxically using the same schema we can say: literature endlessly transforms (concrete) individuals into subjects and endows them with a quasi-real hallucinatory individuality. (1973, 10)

These subjects are not just the Readers of literature, but also the Author and his Characters (Balibar and Macherey's capitals). The argument appears in part to be that as subjects are always opposed and seen in relation to objects and things, the impression is given that the motor or guiding element in history is the individual self or consciousness, rather than extra- or supra-individual forces. (The subject is active and living: external forces are dead and passive.)

It can be seen that this to a certain extent reflects a traditional Marxist subordination of the rôle of the individual to extra-individualistic forces. This same form of subordination can also be seen in obituaries for the death of the AUTHOR, except that in the case of Barthes's argument in 'The Death of the Author' it is language rather than the class struggle or the forces of production which is the extra-individual element involved. The individual reappears in this essay in the guise of the READER, however; the dissolution of the subject is perhaps more complete and more consistent in Michel Foucault's 'What is an Author?', and in this essay Foucault stresses that 'it is a matter of depriving the subject (or its substitute) of its role as originator, and of analyzing the subject as a variable and complex function of discourse' (1980b, 158).

Another way to express this position is to claim that the subject is SITE rather than CENTRE or PRESENCE, in other words that the subject is where things happen, or that to which things happen, rather than that which makes things happen: extra-individual forces use the subject to exert their sway, the subject does not use them (although it thinks that it does, and this is part of the cunning of the system). Compare, for example, Jonathan Culler's suggestion that as the self is broken down into component systems and is deprived of its status as source and master of meaning, it comes to seem more and more like a construct: 'a result of systems of convention', such that 'even the idea of personal identity emerges through the discourse of a culture: the "I" is not something given but comes to exist as that which is addressed by and relates to others' (1981, 33).

This is the stance generally adopted by POST-STRUCTURALISM, for which a major target is the view of the subject as primary, unified, self-present, self-determining, autonomous, and homogeneous. For post-structuralism the subject is, rather, secondary, constructed (by language, or ideology, for instance), volatile, standing in its own shadow, and self-divided. An important influential theorist here is the French psychoanalyst Jacques Lacan, whose writing on the mirror-stage is much quoted by subsequent theorists concerned to explore the creation of the subject from a rather different angle from that adopted by Althusser.

If we turn to recent FEMINIST theory we find a rather more nuanced attitude to the subject and to subjectivity. During the earlier years of the rebirth of the Women's Movement in the 1960s and 1970s one finds evidence of a far less antagonistic view of the subject – a belief that the subjective might actually provide a rallying point *against* sexist ideas, and against the ideology of PATRIARCHY. In June 1971, for example, Doris Lessing wrote a new *Preface* to her novel *The Golden Notebook* – a novel which from its first publication in 1962 had been extremely influential in what became known as the Women's Liberation Movement. It is noteworthy that Lessing devotes a lot of attention to the issue of subjectivity in her comments on the novel.

> When I began writing there was pressure on writers not to be 'subjective'. This pressure began inside communist movements, as a development of the social literary criticism developed in Russia in the nineteenth century, by a group of remarkable talents, of whom Belinsky was the best known . . . (1973, 12)

Lessing notes, however, that alongside this pressure on the writer to ignore 'stupid personal concerns when Rome is burning', novels, stories, art of every sort, became more and more personal (1973, 13). And finally, she reports, she became aware that the way out of the dilemma with which this confronted the writer was to recognize that 'nothing is personal, in the sense that it is uniquely one's own', and that the way to deal with the problem of subjectivity was to make the personal general by seeing the individual as a microcosm (1973, 13).

Lessing's position here is representative of a widespread tendency in the women's movement in the 1960s and 1970s, a tendency to consider (especially a woman's) subjective feelings, responses, beliefs as true and worthy of being encouraged and nurtured as a force oppositional to patriarchy. It is true that this went alongside a concern to cleanse sexist ideas out of the subject – through, among other means, consciousness-raising sessions. But this meant that the view of the subject's relationship to what one can refer to as the ideas and beliefs of the dominant ideology was rather different from that of later theorists influenced by Althusser and Lacan.

We can compare the Romantic reaction to the dominant ideas of their Augustan predecessors in Britain. Whereas subjectivity was treated with great suspicion by Augustan writers such as Alexander Pope and Samuel Johnson, for the great Romantics such as Wordsworth and Keats the essential purity of the pre-social self – 'the holiness of the heart's affections' – served as a rallying point against what was seen as an artificial order.

Changing attitudes towards the subject inevitably affect both the writer and the critic. If Doris Lessing helped as it were to legitimize the personal and the subjective, the theories of Althusser, Lacan and others have placed pressure on the writer and critic to DECONSTRUCT the subject, to take it not as starting-point and reliable measure, but as a lumber-room of (mainly or wholly) false ideas stacked there by a range of external forces.

See also INTERSUBJECTIVITY.

Sub-text That which is implied but not directly or overtly stated. The term originates in theatrical usage, and is associated with the so-called *Theatre of Silence* – the normal English translation of the *Théâtre de l'Inexprimé* founded by Jean-Jacques Bernard in the 1920s. The modern dramatist most associated with the term is Harold Pinter, whose plays typically have, critics agree, sub-texts of a violent or sexual nature which is unstated on the surface. The term typically also implies a certain consistency in implied MEANING: thus the sub-text of a given work is unlikely to consist of a sequence of meanings which have nothing in common with one another.

The term has achieved wide usage in recent years, partly because of its points of contact with the influential theory of conversational implicature contained in SPEECH ACT THEORY, and partly because it chimes in with a range of critical theories which, in various ways, argue that literature in particular and language in general often function by means of indirect, hidden, or implied meanings as much as by overt and direct ones.

A related but somewhat different theoretical term that has achieved a much more restricted circulation is that of the *suggestiveness* of literary works. Krishna Rayan's book *Text and Sub-text: Suggestion in Literature* (1987) attempts to establish a link between the two terms, and the attempt is thought-provoking. In general usage, however, *suggestion* and cognate terms, when applied to literary works, normally imply a less consistent or structured series of implications. Rayan does however make a useful distinction between two usages: discussing Douglas Bush's and Christopher Ricks's use of the term 'suggestion' in criticism of Milton's *Paradise Lost*, he notes that whereas for Bush the term denotes 'suggestive vagueness', for Ricks it involves 'a notion of suggestiveness as delicate and subtle verbal life, consisting in niceties and nuances of meaning, those more or less specific semantic extensions achieved through word-order, metaphor, word-play, anticipation, echo – even alliteration and punctuation' (1987, 18–20).

It should be pointed out that there is a further important distinction between *sub-text* and *suggestiveness* on the theoretical plane. A sub-text is the creation (conscious or unconscious) of the AUTHOR; it can be discovered by READER or audience, but not created by them. But at the heart of the theory of suggestiveness is the idea that the writer encourages the reader to bring his or her creativity into play, and by textual means indicates a direction in which the reader or audience may proceed to explore unstated possibilities. Suggestion, in brief, offers a possible way whereby reader- or audience-creativity may be theoretically justified and legitimized.

Suggestiveness See SUB-TEXT

Summary See DURATION

Supplement See MARGIN

Surface structure See STRUCTURE

Surfiction See MODERNISM AND POSTMODERNISM

Suspense The everyday meaning of this word has long been applied to the reading of literature, especially FICTION, and to the experience of the spectator of drama. Being in a state of heightened excitement as a result of wanting to know what happens next and what will happen ultimately is one of the forces that keeps the READER turning the pages (or which glues the audience to its seats). Suspense is in part the product of identification and involvement: where we do not care for any of the characters or what they represent, we feel little interest in the outcome of the STORY in which they are involved. Suspense is an interesting example of a particular sort of experience which we normally do not like to have in real life, but which we find pleasurable when modelled in our responses to art. It is, therefore, sometimes cited by those arguing that one of the functions of art is to allow us to 'play through' and thereby learn to control, emotions and behaviour-patterns which we need to master in everyday life (just as children ask to have frightening stories read to them). The same evidence is, however, used by those wishing to argue against theories which grant literature the ability to reflect or to influence the extra-literary world.

Clemens Lugowski has suggested a useful distinction between 'result-oriented suspense' and 'process-oriented suspense' (1990, 37). The former is where the reader/audience is anxious about *what* will happen; the latter where the anxiety is directed towards *how* it will happen. The reader of a Mills and Boon romance knows that the heroine will be happy in the arms of the hero on the last page of the work, but will experience process-oriented suspense as to how this happy ending will be reached. (A similar point could be made about each of Jane Austen's novels.) The reader of *Great Expectations* will experience result-oriented suspense, wondering whether Pip will marry Estella, who Pip's benefactor is, and so on.

The concept and the experience have often been considered rather unsophisticated or crude, and unworthy of the producers or consumers of high art or literature. The creation of suspense is, however, a crucial element in much major literature, and not just in popular or 'classic REALIST' writers such as Dickens has been alleged to be – it is an important part in much of Kafka's work, for example – although the reaction against suspense is more a feature of MODERNIST literature than of its predecessors.

Suture The technical term for the stitching up or joining-together of the lips of a wound has been applied by Steven Cohan and Linda M. Shires to the production of the SUBJECT. According to them the subject is as it were 'stitched' to DISCOURSE by the SIGNIFIER (1988, 162). They base their argument on the expansion of a comment of Jacques Lacan's by Jacques-Alain Miller. Lacan had referred to suture as the conjunction of the imaginary and the symbolic; Miller develops this suggestion by arguing that suture names the relation of the subject to the chain of its discourse, in which it is said to figure as an element lacking, or stand-in. Cohan and Shires in turn consider the relevance of these ideas to NARRATIVE, and they suggest that reading or viewing narrative 'involves the continuous suturing of a narrated subject whose pleasure is secured, jeopardized, and rescued by a signifier' (1988, 162).

Switchback See ANALEPSIS

Syllepsis A cluster or gathering (of events, circumstances, experiences, etc.) ordered according to some principle other than temporal unity or sequence. 'John told her all the things that had happened in his mother's house, and she recounted all the times that she had visited a boy-friend's parents' contains two syllepses: one based on situational coherence, and the other on thematic coherence.

Symbolic code See CODE

Symptomatic reading See READERS AND READING

Synchronic See DIACHRONIC AND SYNCHRONIC

Synecdoche See SYNTAGMATIC AND PARADIGMATIC

Synonymous characters A concept suggested by Mieke Bal, and related to her proposal that one distinguish between a character's relevant characteristics and his or her secondary characteristics through a mapping of these characteristics on suitable SEMANTIC AXES. Those characters who end up with exactly the same positive, negative, and unmarked elements after such a mapping are deemed to be synonymous. The concept has much in common with the more traditional term *type*, except that synonymous characters share characteristics which may be specific to a particular WORK whereas types normally have a CONVENTIONAL significance which goes beyond the confines of an individual work. Thus to suggest that characters in different works are synonymous one needs to use a term such as type or FUNCTION, (function in the sense in which a writer such as Vladimir Propp uses it, although Propp focuses upon 'action-by-a-character' rather than upon character as such).

Syntagmatic and paradigmatic According to Saussure's account of language in the *Course in General Linguistics*, '[c]ombinations supported by linearity are *syntagms*', while those 'co-ordinations formed outside discourse' that are 'not supported by linearity' but are 'a part of the inner storehouse that makes up the language of each speaker', 'are *associative relations*' (1974, 123). Present-day usage tends to favour the term *paradigms* over *associative relations*. The distinction can perhaps best be explained by means of a particular example. To construct a grammatical sentence we have to select words according to one set of rules, and combine them according to another set. The first are *paradigmatic* (or *associative*) rules and the second are *syntagmatic* rules. Thus in the sentence

> The cat sat on the mat

The first word could be replaced by 'A' or 'No'; the second word could be replaced by 'dog' or 'boy'. The relations between these groups of interchangeable words (interchangeable according to the rules of grammar and syntax, but not, of course, *semantically* interchangeable) are *paradigmatic*; that is to say, they involve rules which govern the *selection* (not the combination) of words used in a sentence. But once one has chosen 'The' as the first word, one's selection of the second word is constrained: it cannot, for example, be 'a'. This is because there are rules governing the *combination* of words in a sentence: *syntagmatic* rules.

Another way of expressing the distinction is as Jonathan Culler puts it: syntagmatic relations bear on the possibility of combination; paradigmatic relations determine the possibility of substitution (1975, 13).

In 1956 Roman Jakobson published an article entitled 'Two Aspects of Language and Two Types of Aphasic Disturbances' which relied heavily upon a distinction between what Jakobson referred to as the metaphoric and the metonymic modes. In traditional usage *metonymy* is a figure of speech in which the name of one item is given to another item associated by *contiguity* to it. Thus 'The pen is mightier than the sword' works by means of metonymy: *pen* and *sword* stand for those activities with which they are closely associated. Under the heading of 'metonymy' Jakobson includes *synecdoche* – that is, the use of a part to represent a whole: 'bloodshed' for war, for example. *Metaphor*, in contrast, relies upon *similarity* rather than contiguity. Thus 'Eddie the eagle' was so-called not because he was often in the company of eagles, but because it was suggested (with a generous helping of irony) that a similarity could be observed between his ski-jumping and the flight of an eagle.

Through reference to the varying forms of aphasia experienced by patients with cerebral impairments, Jakobson was able to show that the metaphoric and metonymic processes were governed by localized brain functions. These different processes (or modes) Jakobson related, in turn, to what he described, following Saussure, as the selection and combination axes of language. Metaphor and metonymy were thus, according to Jakobson, governed by specific brain functions which also governed these two fundamental axes of language. According to Jakobson, all examples of aphasic disturbance consisted in some impairment of either the faculty for selection or of that for combination and contexture.

> The former affliction involves a deterioration of metalinguistic operations, while the latter damages the capacity for maintaining the hierarchy of linguistic units. The relation of similarity is suppressed in the former, the relation of contiguity in the latter type of aphasia. Metaphor is alien to the similarity disorder, and metonymy to the contiguity disorder. (Jakobson & Halle 1971, 90)

Jakobson did not stop here, but attempted to generalize his discoveries and to claim that although both processes were operative in normal verbal behaviour, the influence of cultural pattern, personality or verbal style could lead to preference being given to one of the two processes over the other. From here, Jakobson then moves to consider literature. He claims that whereas the metaphoric process is primary in Romanticism and Symbolism, metonymy is predominant in REALISM (Jakobson & Halle 1971, 91–2).

According to Anthony Wilden, because in Jakobson's theory the metonymic pole of language represents its syntagmatic, connectional or 'concatenated' aspect, 'Lacan states that metonymy *is* desire'. This, Wilden explains, is because for Lacan metaphor is related to being as metonymy is related to non-being, and as the phallus signifies the lack of object in the relation between mother and child, it becomes the representation of a lack or ABSENCE which circulates between human beings in the Symbolic order. 'Consequently, possibly the most fundamental question in the analytic relationship is that both "analyst" and "patient" must recognize . . . that one cannot *be* the phallus, for that is to be the desire of the Other' (1972, 29n; see also the entries for OTHER; PHALLOCENTRIC).

Jakobson's article has itself been very influential; Jacques Lacan refers to it in his essay 'The Agency of the Letter in the Unconscious or Reason Since Freud' (in Lacan, 1977, 146–78), and David Lodge structures his book *The Modes of Modern Writing* (1977) around an attempt to apply and extend what Jakobson says about metaphor and metonymy to the analysis and interpretation of literary TEXTS.

In an essay entitled 'The Semantics of Metaphor' Umberto Eco has suggested that metaphor and metonymy are linked at a deeper level, claiming that 'each metaphor can be traced back to a subjacent chain of metonymic connections which constitute the framework of the code and upon which is based the constitution of any semantic field, whether partial or (in theory) global' (1981, 68).

According to Robert Scholes, 'neo-Freudians' such as 'Jacques Lacan and his circle' have reminded us that Jakobson's metaphor and metonymy are very close in meaning to Freud's CONDENSATION AND DISPLACEMENT (1982, 75–6).

System Unlike the term STRUCTURE, *system* tends to be given a number of varied meanings in current theoretical discussion. Perhaps its most precise meaning is to be found in structural Linguistics: here language is seen as a system of relationships based on DIFFERENCE and capable of generating MEANINGS.

Apart from this relatively precise usage the term can be used more or less synonymously with the STRUCTURALIST term *structure* – somewhat confusingly, as a system is typically characterized by its dynamic, goal-seeking impetus, whereas a structure is more usually seen as a succession of over-arching, constant rules (see the separate entry for this term). As Josué Harari puts it, in a discussion of Lévi-Strauss's structural anthropology, 'history' tends to be replaced by 'diachrony', with the former falling under the tutelage of the '*System*' – rather than, we presume, *structure* (1980, 20).

Doubtless it is for this reason that Robert Young insists that for Roland Barthes, *codes of reading* (see CODE) do not constitute 'a rigorous, unified system': they operate simply as 'associative fields', a supra-textual organisation of notations which impose a certain idea of structure' (1981, 134).

In Michel Foucault's writing a discipline (in the sense of an academic discipline) is seen as 'a sort of anonymous system at the disposal of anyone who wants to or is able to use it' (1981, 59).

For Michael Riffaterre, a literary work's system is 'a network of words related to one another around a central concept embodied in a kernel word' (1981, 114).

T

Telos See CENTRE

Tempo See DURATION

Tense See LINGUISTIC PARADIGM

Terrorism A term coined by the French writer Jean Paulhan, and made use of by Gérard Genette, to describe a type of writing which refuses to make use of the 'flowers of rhetoric' and which entails a refusal of any of the traditional supports and devices of literature or *belles lettres* (Genette 1982, 60 n5). Also used more pejoratively to suggest a method of argumentation that is unprincipled and aggressive (and often sexist).

Tessera See REVISIONISM

Text and work In his essay 'Theory of the Text' Roland Barthes suggests that whereas the work is 'a finished object, something computable, which can occupy a physical space', 'the text is a methodological field', and that 'The work is held in the hand, the text in language'. Barthes continues, suggesting that one can put the matter in another way:

> [I]f the work can be defined in terms that are heterogeneous to language (everything from the format of the book to the socio-historical determinations which produced that book), the text, for its part, remains homogeneous to language through and through: it is nothing other than language and can exist only through a language other than itself. In other words, 'the text can be felt only in a work, a production': that of 'signifiance'. (1981b, 39–40; Barthes's quotation is from his own *Image-Music-Text*. For *signifiance*, see the entry for SIGN)

This suggests a different definition of *work*, at any rate, from that current in most contemporary literary-critical usage, in which the term applies to the literary composition seen independently of its particular physical manifestations (*Hamlet* the work would still exist even if there were no physical copies of it so long as there were anyone who could recall the words that comprise it and pass these on to others). Following Barthes's definition it is doubtful whether *Hamlet* could be said to have existed as work during that period of its early stage production before one authoritative and unified 'finished object' with the title *Hamlet* on it could be held in the hand. It is clear that Barthes's view of text and work is related to his belief in the death of the AUTHOR and in the need to grant the READER greater power, status and freedom. If the work is attached to the author by an uncut umbilical cord, the text in contrast assumes a sort of parthenogenic status, quite free of parental control.

In practice, these two terms have come to enjoy a rather different usage in recent years: *text* has become the preferred term for referring to a literary or other work (not necessarily linguistic or verbal) stripped of traditional preconceptions about autonomy, authorial control, artistic or aesthetic force, and so on. Thus use of the term text and its cognates in contemporary literary-critical circles is often associated with an attempt to argue that the traditional distinction between literary and non-literary texts should be either made less absolute, or scrapped altogether. Mieke Bal, for example, defines a text for her purposes as 'a finite, structured whole composed of language signs' (1985, 5)

– which could of course apply equally well to both a novel and, for example, a political speech. *Work*, in contrast, has an undeniably more traditional ring to it, and carries with it more traditional implications, and it is revealing that Bal does not bother to define this term in her *Introduction to the Theory of Narrative*. Thus one might attempt to summarize by saying that in current literary-critical usage a work stripped of many of its traditional entailments is a text – but then, so are many non-literary (even, in some usages, non linguistic) productions.

Text Linguistics forms a sub-section of the discipline of Linguistics, and is very close to discourse analysis (which, as the entry for DISCOURSE argues, is itself a term with no clear single meaning). Michael Stubbs (1983) treats text and discourse as more or less synonymous, but notes that in other usages a text may be written while a discourse is spoken, a text may be non-interactive whereas a discourse is interactive (see the quotation from Leech and Short below), a text may be short or long whereas a discourse implies a certain length, and a text must be possessed of surface cohesion whereas a discourse must be possessed of a deeper coherence. Finally, Stubbs notes that other theorists distinguish between abstract theoretical construct and PRAGMATIC realization, although, confusingly, such theorists are not agreed upon which of these is represented by the term *text*. Text Linguistics is generally taken to be broader than discourse analysis, however, and is normally taken to include, among other things, elements from STYLISTICS and NARRATOLOGY. Geoffrey Leech and Michael Short argue for one way of distinguishing between text and discourse that has already been mentioned:

> Discourse is linguistic communication seen as a transaction between speaker and hearer, as an interpersonal activity whose form is determined by its social purpose. Text is linguistic communication (either spoken or written) seen simply as a message coded in its auditory or visual medium. (1981, 209)

The key phrase here is clearly 'seen simply as a message', an emphasis which is contrasted with 'a transaction between speaker and hearer'. This suggests that the identical words can both constitute a text, if seen simply as a message, but can also be seen as an element in a discourse is seen in terms of their mediating a transaction between speaker and hearer. As we have already noted, this implies that to talk of a text is to concentrate on the language used and to ignore or play down the context in which it is used. The problem comes when one tries to define what is meant by 'seen simply as a message', for some theorists would argue, not illogically, that to see something as a message (even 'simply') one has to posit some sort of a context, for a message is defined as a message not just by its linguistic characteristics, but by the message *function*. 'Get lost' is a message only when used to convey information from a source to a destination: when used to illustrate English spelling it is not a message. (The OED starts its definition of *message* as follows: 'A communication transmitted through a messenger or other agency; an oral or written communication sent from one person to another.' This sounds very like 'a transaction between speaker and hearer'.)

Katie Wales quotes the seven criteria for textuality given by de Beaugrande and Dressler in their *Introduction to Text Linguistics* (1981): cohesion and co-herence, intentionality, acceptability, situationality, informativity, and intertextuality (1989, 459). These certainly offer a relatively workable definition, but one which is different from the definition implied by most current usages of (literary) work. (Some – but not all – might claim that all of these were necessary preconditions for determining that a set of words con-stituted a literary text or work, but many would wish to add extra requirements: artistic or aesthetic quality, conformity to certain generic requirements, FICTIONALITY or some form of modified reference, and so on.)

Determining where one text (or work) ends and another begins is an issue that is much less discussed than one might expect. In practice, even those convinced of the death of the author have frequently been prepared to allow the author to decide this. Critics have generally assumed that textual variants produce different texts, but merely modify the same work, although again there is no clear agreement on this, and less theoretical energy has been expended on the issue than one might have expected. (An exception can be found in various interesting discussions of this and related problems in several of Jerome McGann's works.)

Textualist According to Richard Rorty,

> In the last century there were philosophers who argued that nothing exists but ideas. In our century there are people who write as if there were nothing but texts. (1982, 139)

These last Rorty dubs 'textualists'. In his list of textualists Rorty includes the 'so-called "Yale School" of literary criticism', which he claims centres around Harold Bloom, Geoffrey Hartmann, J. Hillis Miller, and Paul de Man; POST-STRUCTURALIST French thinkers such as Jacques Derrida and Michel Foucault, historians such as Hayden White, and social scientists such as Paul Rabinow.

What all of these individuals have in common, according to Rorty, is (i) an antagonistic position to natural science and (ii) the belief that we can never compare human thought or language with 'bare, unmediated reality' (1982, 139). Rorty sees these positions as constituting a textualism which is the contemporary counterpart of idealism, and its practitioners as the spiritual descendants of the idealists (1982, 140).

He goes on to distinguish between what (drawing on Harold Bloom) he terms *weak textualists* and *strong textualists*. He argues that the weak textualist 'thinks that each work has its own vocabulary, its own secret code, which may not be commensurable with that of any other'. The strong textualist, in contrast, 'has his own vocabulary and doesn't worry about whether anybody shares it' (1982, 150).

Rorty's argument clearly uses simplification for ironic and polemical effect, but at the time it appeared it served to rally a number of rather different forces against the growing influence of the individuals described by him as textualists, and it can be seen in retrospect to have constituted an important moment in the development of a counter-movement directed against post-structuralism.

Topic Usefully defined by Umberto Eco as the textual operator which is needed to realize all of the relevant semantic disclosures in a DISCURSIVE structure (1981, 23).

Eco contrasts this term with Greimas's term *isotopy*, quoting Greimas's definition of this as 'a redundant set of semantic categories which make possible the uniform reading of the story' (1981, 26). The distinction, for Eco, is that whereas the topic governs the semantic properties that can or must be taken into account during the reading of a given TEXT, an isotopy is the actual textual verification of that hypothesis which the topic produces. Put another way: a topic leads the READER to have certain expectations, whereas an isotopy is a READING based upon these expectations. (Whether Eco interprets Greimas correctly here is, however, open to question.)

Totalizing discourse Any DISCOURSE which seeks to occupy all the available ground and thus deny any oppositional SITE to those whom it excludes.

Trace See ARCHE-WRITING

Transactional theory of the literary work A theory associated with Louise M. Rosenblatt, who outlines it in her book *The Reader, The Text, The Poem* (1978). Rosenblatt takes as her starting point the inadequacy of theories which base themselves on an exclusively active and an exclusively passive component: the READER actively interpreting the literary TEXT, or the text acting upon the reader and producing a response in him or her. According to her, the relation between reader and text is not linear but is a situation, 'an event at a particular time and place in which each element conditions the other' (1978, 16). Rosenblatt adopts the 'transactional' terminology developed by John Dewey and Arthur F. Bentley, a terminology which arises from a philosophical approach with its roots in the thinking of William James and C. S. Peirce. For Dewey and Bentley 'transaction' had certain important advantages over 'interaction'; for them the latter term implied the acting upon each other of 'separate, self-contained, and already defined entities', whereas the former term designated 'an ongoing process in which the elements or factors are . . . aspects of a total situation, each conditioned by and conditioning the other' (1978, 17), and she sees her proposed revision of previous views of the READING process to be analogous to the revolution in Linguistics brought about by the shift from UTTERANCE to SPEECH ACT (1978, 19).

Such an approach has, oddly enough, something in common with DECONS-TRUCTIVE criticism, for although it uses a different set of terms it does seem to posit a ceaseless play between the different elements involved in the reading process, none of which is fixed in the manner of a TRANSCENDENTAL SIGNIFIED and therefore capable of determining the course taken by any particular reading. In Deconstructive criticism, of course, the play is between SIGNIFIERS and is of a rather different nature, but the two approaches share a common view of successive reading acts as the ceaseless generation of something new. For Rosenblatt, this is because all perception is conditioned by interest, expectations, anxieties, and other factors based on past experience (1978, 19), and these must clearly vary not just from reader to reader but also from reading to reading. (My second reading of *Mrs Dalloway* will necessarily be different from my first – and my third – because I will take to it a new set of past experiences, expectations, and so on; the text remains the same only in as much as it remains the same collection of signifiers; to the extent that the text's aesthetic significance is constituted by interaction between it and a reader, it is in constant process of renewal.)

This takes us to the second important element in Rosenblatt's theory: the distinction between aesthetic and non-aesthetic reading, one which bears resemblances to a number of traditional distinctions (including Roman Jakobson's CODES OF READING). She argues that whereas during a non-aesthetic reading the reader is chiefly concerned with what he or she will carry away from the reading, in aesthetic reading 'the reader's primary concern is with what happens *during* the actual reading event' (1978, 24).

The theory can be seen as one of a number of attempts to move away from one particular element in the practice of the New Criticism: the treatment of the literary WORK as if it were fixed, solid object – W. K. Wimsatt's 'verbal icon' or Cleanth Brooks's 'well-wrought urn'. As Rosenblatt puts it,

> Instead of thinking of the structure of the work of art as something statically inherent in the text, we need to recognize the dynamic situation in which the reader, in the give-and-take with the text, senses or organizes a relationship among the various parts of his lived-through experience. (1978, 90)

Transcendental pretence/signified/subject The influence of Jacques Derrida has radically changed the connotations of the word *transcendental* and its cognates for many. Whereas at one time its associations were mainly positive – 'that which is above all other categories of thing' – since Derrida the word is associated with a belief in fixed, extra-linguistic points of meaning-determination, a view which he characterizes as LOGOCENTRIC and representative of the METAPHYSICS OF PRESENCE.

According to Derrida himself, from his very first published work he sought to 'systematize a deconstructive critique precisely against the authority of meaning, as the *transcendental signified* or as *telos*, in other words history determined in the last analysis as the history of meaning, history in its logocentric, metaphysical, idealist . . . representation' (1981b, 49–50). According to Alex Callinicos, Derrida believes that any attempt to halt the endless play of signifiers, above all by appealing to the concept of reference, must . . . involve postulating a 'transcendental signified' which is somehow present to the consciousness without any discursive mediation. (1989, 74)

The implications of such a position for literary criticism are not far to seek: the TEXT is also subject to a totalizing play of linguistic DIFFERENCE which cannot be fixed or organized by any extra-systemic reference-point – AUTHOR, authorial intention, 'common reader's' interpretation, or whatever.

Analogous objections are raised against the transcendental SUBJECT – that is, against the belief that the *ego* is undetermined by and independent of social and CULTURAL forces, and that it constitutes a unity rather than a SITE for the play of contradictions. The transcendental pretence, according to Robert C. Solomon, rests on an ideological belief that the 'white middle classes of European descent were the representatives of all humanity, and that as human nature is one, then so too must its history be one as well' (1980, xii).

Finally, in *Positions* Derrida points out that it is also possible to believe in a transcendental signif*ier*, and he gives as example the *phallus*, when seen 'as the correlate of a primary signified, castration and the mother's desire' (1981b, 86). (See the entry for PHALLOCENTRISM.)

Transcoding See MEDIATION

Transgredient According to Tzvetan Todorov's *Mikhail Bakhtin: The Dialogical Principle* (1984), a term which Bakhtin borrowed from Jonas Cohen, *Allgemeine Ästhetik* (Leipzig, 1901). Todorov sees this as a term complementary to *ingredient*, 'to designate elements of consciousness that are external to but nonetheless absolutely necessary for its completion, for its achievement of totalization' (1984, 95).

See also EXOTOPY.

Transgressive strategy A term sometimes used by POST-STRUCTURALISTS to indicate any way of dealing with a TEXT which attempts to go beyond the assumptions upon which it is based and which (if not challenged) it will reproduce. Transgressive strategies are *denaturalizing* – that is, they prevent us from seeing the text *as* natural or *in* a 'natural' way (a way that does not go against the grain of CONVENTION).

See also OPPOSITIONAL READING.

Transparent criticism See OPAQUE AND TRANSPARENT CRITICISM

Transtextuality See INTERTEXTUALITY

Transworld identity See HOMONYMY

U

Uncanny See FANTASTIC

Unconscious In an article on rhythm and imagery in English poetry published in 1962, William Empson remarks that four major thinkers – Darwin, Marx, Frazer and Freud – 'gave grounds for the belief that the artist often does not know what he is doing' (1962, 36). The comment is a useful reminder that it is not just Sigmund Freud who has helped to ensure that in comparison to other periods of history the modern age is one in which we are relatively unconvinced of our having conscious access to all that our minds contain, and it also reminds us that literary critics have been interested in such ideas because they seem to be confirmed by study of the process of literary composition or creation, in which things happen that are apparently not under the writer's conscious control.

Freud's theory of the Unconscious can be seen emerging in *Studies in Hysteria* – both in the parts of this work written by him and in those written by Joseph Breuer. Both writers were able to draw on a number of important traditions in Psychology in forming a coherent theory, but their actual case-histories also played an important rôle in this. Much could be written about the Freudian Unconscious, but for our present purposes it is probably most important to indicate the connection between the concept and the idea of *repression*. This has proved very convenient again to literary critics interested in explaining why a given literary work may have a tendency seemingly much at odds with the author's expressed or consciously held beliefs and opinions.

Since Freud, various theorists have developed or challenged his theory of the Unconscious. Most influential in literary-critical circles is probably Jacques Lacan, who makes his position clear when he talks of Freud's *discovery* of the Unconscious. Lacan defines the unconscious (he does not grant the term a capital letter) as 'that part of the concrete discourse, in so far as it is trans-individual, that is not at the disposal of the subject in re-establishing the continuity of his conscious discourse' (1977, 49), and as 'that chapter of my history that is marked by a blank or occupied by a falsehood: it is the censored chapter' (1977, 50). Even so, it can be rediscovered – in monuments, in archival documents such as childhood memories, in semantic evolution, in traditions, and in surviving (conscious) traces (1977, 50).

Anthony Wilden has drawn attention to Lacan's debt to the work of Lévi-Strauss in arriving at a linguistic model of the Unconscious (in which the Unconscious is seen to be structured like a language). Wilden further draws attention to the fact that Lévi-Strauss has said that his own development of a theory of the Unconscious was influenced both by Freud and Marx – and also by geology! Wilden argues that Lévi-Strauss reformulates the concept of the

Unconscious as a locus 'not of instincts, not of phantasies, not of energy or entities, but as a locus of a *symbolic function* – a set of rules governing the possible messages in the system, a sort of syntax or code' (1977, 15). It was this formulation, Wilden argues, that allowed Lacan to declare first that 'The Freudian Unconscious is the discourse of the other' (1953), and shortly afterwards that 'The unconscious is structured like a language'.

Fredric Jameson's *The Political Unconscious* attempts to rehistoricize Freud's concept of the Unconscious and to reassign the CENTRE of the Freudian interpretive system (which Jameson sees as wish-fulfilment) to history and society rather than to the individual SUBJECT and individual psychobiology. Thus a number of associated Freudian concepts – repression, censorship, and so on – are resituated in a socio-historical context by Jameson, and thence applied to the reading of literary works. Jameson's historicizing of the concept of the Unconscious can be compared with the earlier use made of Freud by Gilles Deleuze and Félix Guattari in their *Anti-Oedipus: Capitalism and Schizophrenia*. They remark, for example, that 'Women's Liberation movements contain, in a more or less ambiguous state, what belongs to all requirements of liberation: the force of the unconscious itself, the investment by desire of the social field, the disinvestment of repressive structures' (1983, 61). (For a critical FEMINIST view of Deleuze and Guattari, see the entry for DESIRE.)

See also ARCHE-WRITING; CONDENSATION AND DISPLACEMENT.

Unfolding A term used in the English translation of Roland Barthes's *S/Z*. As example Barthes suggests that 'to enter' can be unfolded into 'to appear' and 'to penetrate' (1990, 82). In other words, unfolding involves the semantic, CONNOTATIVE or ideological unpacking of a term or word.

Unmotivated See ARBITRARY

Utterance An utterance is generally regarded as a natural unit of linguistic *communication*. In her editorial Preface to her translation of M. M. Bakhtin's *Problems of Dostoevsky's Poetics*, Caryl Emerson claims that the distinction between utterance and sentence

> is [Bakhtin's] own: a sentence is a unit of language, while an utterance is a unit of communication. Sentences are relatively complete thoughts existing within a single speaker's speech, and the pauses between them are 'grammatical,' matters of punctuation. Utterances, on the other hand, are impulses, and cannot be so normatively transcribed; their boundaries are marked only by a change of speech subject. (Bakhtin 1984, xxxiv)

In like manner, Jan Mukařovský attributes 'uniqueness and nonrepeatability' to the utterance in his essay 'The Esthetics of Language' (1964, 63).

It should be noted that an utterance can be either spoken or written (or, presumably, expressed in silent thought to oneself).

See also DISCOURSE; ÉCRITURE; ENUNCIATION; LANGUE AND PAROLE; and SPEECH.

Virtuality See PHENOMENOLOGY

Vision See PERSPECTIVE AND VOICE

Voice See PERSPECTIVE AND VOICE; POLYPHONY

Vraisemblance A French loan-word meaning 'appearing real', close to the English *verisimilitude*, and used in discussions of REALISM. The term is not new (its use in discussion of art dates from the seventeenth century), but what is new is that it is used in an increasingly pejorative or dismissive sense the more the status of realism has been brought into question.

Weak textualist See TEXTUALIST

Work See TEXT AND WORK

Writerly See READERLY AND WRITERLY

Writing See ÉCRITURE

Z

Zero (degree writing) See ÉCRITURE

Bibliography

This bibliography lists all works from which extracts are quoted, along with some other important works mentioned in entries. Where works are not listed in the bibliography, the date given in the text is that of the first edition.

Abrams, M. H. (1977). The limits of pluralism: the deconstructive angel. *Critical Inquiry*, 3, 425–438.

Abrams, M. H. (1988). *A Glossary of Literary Terms.* (5th edn). London: Holt, Rinehart & Winston.

Althusser, Louis (1969). *For Marx.* Brewster, Ben (trans.). London: Allen Lane.

Althusser, Louis (1971). *Lenin and Philosophy and Other Essays.* Brewster, Ben (trans.). London: New Left Books.

Anderson, Perry (1969). Components of the national culture. In Cockburn, Alexander & Blackburn, Robin (eds), *Student Power: Problems, Diagnosis, Action.* Harmondsworth: Penguin.

Austin, John (1962). *How to do Things with Words.* Oxford: Oxford University Press.

Bakhtin, M. M. (1968). *Rabelais and his World.* Iswolsky, Helene (trans.). London: MIT Press.

Bakhtin, M. M. (1981). *The Dialogic Imagination. Four Essays.* Holquist, Michael (ed.), Emerson, Caryl & Holquist, Michael (trans). Austin: University of Texas Press.

Bakhtin, M. M. (1984). *Problems of Dostoevsky's Poetics.* Manchester: Manchester University Press.

Bal, Mieke (1985). *Narratology: Introduction to the Theory of Narrative.* Van Boheemen, Christine, (trans.). London: University of Toronto Press.

Balibar, Etienne & Macherey, Pierre (1973). Literature as an ideological form. *Oxford Literary Review* 3(1), 4–12.

Banfield, Ann (1982). *Unspeakable Sentences: Narration and Representation in the Language of Fiction.* London: Routledge.

Banfield, Ann (1985). Écriture, narration and the grammar of French. In Hawthorn, Jeremy (ed.), *Narrative: from Malory to Motion Pictures.* London: Arnold.

Barrett, Michèle (1989). Some different meanings of the concept of 'difference': feminist theory and the concept of ideology. In Meese, Elizabeth &

Parker, Alice (eds), *The Difference Within: Feminism and Critical Theory*. Amsterdam: John Benjamins.

Barthes, Roland (1967a). *Elements of Semiology*. Lavers, Annette & Smith, Colin (trans). (First published in French, 1964.) London: Cape.

Barthes, Roland (1967b). *Writing Degree Zero*. Lavers, Annette & Smith, Colin (trans). (First published in French, 1953.) London: Cape.

Barthes, Roland (1973). *Mythologies*. Lavers, Annette (ed. & trans.). (First published in French, 1972.) Frogmore: Granada.

Barthes, Roland (1975). An introduction to the structural analysis of narrative. *New Literary History*, 6(2), 137–72.

Barthes, Roland (1976). *The Pleasure of the Text*. Miller, Richard (trans.). (First published in French, 1975.) London: Cape.

Barthes, Roland (1977). The death of the author. In Heath, Stephen (ed. & trans.), *Image-Music-Text*. London: Fontana.

Barthes, Roland (1981a). Textual analysis of Poe's 'Valdemar'. Bennington, Geoff (trans.). In Young, Robert (ed.), *Untying the Text: a Post-structuralist Reader*. London: Routledge.

Barthes, Roland (1981b). Theory of the text. In Young, Robert (ed.), McLeod, Ian (trans.), *Untying the Text: a Post-structuralist Reader*. London: Routledge.

Barthes, Roland (1990). *S/Z*. Miller, Richard (trans.). (First published in French, 1973.) Oxford: Blackwell.

Belsey, Catherine (1980). *Critical Practice*. London: Methuen.

Blanchot, Maurice (1981). The narrative voice (the 'he', the neuter). In Davis, Lydia (trans.), *The Gaze of Orpheus and Other Literary Essays*. New York: Station Hill Press.

Bloch, Ernst, Lukács, Georg, Brecht, Bertolt, Benjamin, Walter & Adorno, Theodor (1977). *Aesthetics and Politics*. London: New Left Books.

Bloom, Harold (1973). *The Anxiety of Influence: A Theory of Poetry*. New York: Oxford University Press.

Bloom, Harold (1982). *Agon: Towards a Theory of Revisionism*. Oxford: Oxford University Press.

Booth, Wayne C. (1961). *Rhetoric of Fiction*. London: University of Chicago Press.

Booth, Wayne C. (1988). *The Company We Keep: An Ethics of Fiction*. London: University of California Press.

Bowlt, John (1972). Introduction to special issue on *Russian Formalism*. *20th Century Studies*, 7/8, December 1972.

Bremond, Claude (1966). La logique des possibles narratifs. *Communications*, 8, 60–76.

Bremond, Claude (1973). *Logique du Récit*. Paris: Seuil.

Brooke-Rose, Christine (1981). *A Rhetoric of the Unreal: Studies in Narrative and Structure, Especially of the Fantastic*. Cambridge: Cambridge University Press.

Brooks, Cleanth (1946). Empson's criticism. In Quinn, Kerker & Shattuck, Charles (eds), *Accent Anthology*. (First published 1944.) New York: Harcourt Brace.

Brooks, Cleanth (1983). In search of the New Criticism. *The American Scholar*, 53(1), Winter 1983/4, 41–53.

Brown, Pamela & Levinson, Stephen (1978). Universals in language usage: politeness phenomena. In Goody, Esther N., (ed.), *Questions of Politeness: Strategies in Social Interaction*. London, Cambridge University Press.

Brown, Pamela & Levinson, Stephen (1987). *Politeness: Some Universals in Language Usage*. London: Cambridge University Press.

Burden, Robert (1991). *Heart of Darkness*. London: Macmillan.

Bürger, Peter (1984). *Theory of the Avant-garde*. Shaw, Michael (trans.). Minneapolis: University of Minnesota Press.

Butor, Michael (1964). L'usage des pronoms personnels dans le roman. In *Répertoire II*. Paris: Les Editions de Minuit.

Callinicos, Alex (1989). *Against Postmodernism*. London: Polity Press.

Cameron, Deborah (1985). *Feminism and Linguistic Theory*. London: Macmillan.

Cawelti, John 1977: Literary formulas and cultural significance. In Luedke, Luther (ed.), *The Story of . . . American Culture/Contemporary Conflicts*. Deland, Fla.: Everett/Edwards.

Caws, Mary Ann (1985). *Reading Frames in Modern Fiction*. Princeton: Princeton University Press.

Cioffi, Frank (1976). Intention and interpretation in criticism. (First published 1964.) In Newton-De Molina, David (ed.), *On Literary Intention*. Edinburgh: Edinburgh University Press.

Cohan, Steven & Shires, Linda M. (1988). *Telling Stories: A Theoretical Analysis of Narrative Fiction*. London: Routledge.

Cohn, Dorrit (1978). *Transparent Minds: Narrating Modes for Presenting Consciousness in Fiction*. Princeton: Princeton University Press.

Conrad, Joseph (1986). *Lord Jim*. Hampson, Robert (ed.). Watts, Cedric (introduction and notes). Harmondsworth: Penguin.

Cranny-Francis, Anne (1990). *Feminist Fiction: Feminist Uses of Generic Fiction*. Oxford: Polity Press.

Culler, Jonathan (1975). *Structuralist Poetics. Structuralism, Linguistics and the Study of Literature*. London: Routledge.

Culler, Jonathan (1980). Prolegomena to a theory of reading. In Suleiman, Susan R. & Crosman, Inge (eds), *The Reader in the Text*. Guildford: Princeton University Press.

Culler, Jonathan (1981). *The Pursuit of Signs: Semiotics, Literature, Deconstruction*. London: Routledge.

Culler, Jonathan (1988). *Framing the Sign: Criticism and its Institutions*. Oxford: Blackwell.

Curle, Richard (ed.) (1928). *Conrad to a Friend: 150 Selected Letters from Joseph Conrad to Richard Curle.* Curle, Richard (introduction & notes). London: Sampson Low, Marston.

Dallenbach, Lucien (1989). *The Mirror in the Text.* Whiteley, Jeremy & Hughes, Emma (trans). Oxford: Polity Press.

Daly, Mary (1979). *Gyn/ecology: The Metaethics of Radical Feminism.* London: The Women's Press.

Daly, Mary (1984). *Pure Lust: Elemental Feminist Philosophy.* London: The Women's Press.

Deleuze, Gilles & Guattari, Felix (1983). *Anti-Oedipus: Capitalism and Schizophrenia.* (First published 1977.) Minneapolis: University of Minnesota Press.

Derrida, Jacques (1973). Differance. In Allison, David B. (trans.). *Speech and Phenomena, and other Essays on Husserl's Theory of Signs.* Evanston, Il: Northwestern University Press.

Derrida, Jacques (1975). The purveyor of truth. *Yale French Studies*, 52, 31–113.

Derrida, Jacques (1976). *Of Grammatology.* Spivak, Gayatri Chakravorty (trans.). (First published in French, 1967.) London: Johns Hopkins University Press.

Derrida, Jacques (1978). *Writing and Difference.* Bass, Alan, (trans.). London: Routledge.

Derrida, Jacques (1981a). *Dissemination.* Johnson, Barbara (trans.). London: Athlone Press.

Derrida, Jacques (1981b). *Positions.* Bass, Alan (trans.). London: Athlone Press.

Doubrovsky, Serge (1973). *The New Criticism in France.* Coltman, Derek (trans.). London: University of Chicago Press.

Draper, Hal (1978). *Karl Marx's Theory of Revolution: The Politics of Social Class.* New York: Monthly Review Press.

Eagleton, Terry (1976). *Marxism and Literary Criticism.* London: Methuen.

Eagleton, Terry (1983). *Literary Theory: An Introduction.* Oxford: Blackwell.

Eagleton, Terry (1991). *Ideology: An Introduction.* London: Verso.

Eco, Umberto (1972). Towards a semiotic inquiry into the television message. Splendore, Paola (trans.). (First read as a paper in Italian in 1965.) *Working Papers in Cultural Studies* 3, 103–21.

Eco, Umberto (1981). *The Role of the Reader: Explorations in the Semiotics of Texts.* London: Hutchinson.

Eichenbaum, Boris (1965). The theory of the 'formal method'. (First published in Ukrainian, 1926; this translation from the Russian version 1927.) In Lemon, Lee T. & Reis, Marion J. (eds & trans), *Russian Formalist Criticism: Four Essays.* Lincoln: University of Nebraska Press.

Èjxenbaum, Boris M. (1971a). The theory of the formal method. (First published 1927, but see previous entry.) In Matejka, Ladislav & Pomorska,

Krystyna (eds), Titunik, I. R (trans.), *Readings in Russian Poetics: Formalist and Structuralist Views*. London: MIT Press.

Èjxenbaum, Boris M. (1971b). Literary environment. (First published 1929.) In Matejka, Ladislav & Pomorska, Krystyna (eds), Titunik, I. R. (trans.), *Readings in Russian Poetics: Formalist and Structuralist Views*. London: MIT Press.

Eliot, T. S. (1961). *On Poetry and Poets*. New York: Noonday Press.

Ellmann, Mary (1979). *Thinking about Women*. (First published 1968.) London: Virago.

Ellmann, Maud (1981). Disremembering Dedalus: *A Portrait of the Artist as a Young Man*. In Young, Robert (ed.), *Untying the Text*. London: Routledge.

Empson, William (1961). *Seven Types of Ambiguity*. (First published 1930.) 3rd edn. Harmondsworth: Peregrine.

Empson, William (1962). Rhythm and imagery in English poetry. *British Journal of Aesthetics*, 2(1), 36–54.

Engels, Frederick (1964). *Dialectics of Nature*. 3rd rev. edn. Dutt, Clemens (trans.). London: Lawrence & Wishart.

Fish, Stanley (1980). *Is There a Text in this Class? The Authority of Interpretive Communities*. London: Harvard University Press.

Forgacs, David (1982). Marxist literary theories. (First published, 1982.) In Jefferson, Ann & Robey, David (eds), *Modern Literary Theory: A Comparative Introduction*. 2nd expanded edn. London: Batsford.

Foucault, Michel (1972). *The Archaeology of Knowledge*. Sheridan Smith, A. M. (trans.). London: Tavistock.

Foucault, Michel (1980a). *Power/Knowledge*. Brighton: Harvester.

Foucault, Michel (1980b). What is an author? (First published in English, 1977, in Bouchard, Donald F. [ed.], *Language, Counter-memory, Practice: Selected Essays and Interviews*. New York: Cornell University Press.) In Harari, J. V. (ed.), *Textual Strategies: Perspectives in Post-structuralist Criticism*. London: Methuen.

Foucault, Michel (1981). The order of discourse. Originally Foucault's inaugural lecture, delivered at the Collège de France 2 December 1970. In Young, Robert (ed.), McLeod, Ian (trans.), *Untying the Text*. London: Routledge.

Fowler, Roger (1990). *The Lost Girl*: discourse and focalization. In Brown, Keith (ed.), *Rethinking Lawrence*. Milton Keynes: Open University Press.

Fox, Ralph (1979). *The Novel and the People*. (First published 1937.) London: Lawrence & Wishart.

Freud, Sigmund (1976). *The Interpretation of Dreams*. Strachey, James (ed., assisted by Alan Tyson), Strachey, James (trans.). Harmondsworth: The Pelican Freud Library, Vol. 4.

Freud, Sigmund, & Breuer, Joseph (1974). *Studies on Hysteria*. Strachey, James & Alex (eds, assisted by Angela Richards), Strachey, James & Alex (trans). Harmondsworth: The Pelican Freud Library, Vol. 3.

Furbank, P. N. 1970: *Reflections on the Word 'Image'*. London: Secker & Warburg.

Gagnon, Madeleine (1980). Body I. An excerpt from 'Corps I'. (First published in French, 1977.) In Marks, Elaine & de Courtivron, Isabelle (eds), Courtivron, Isabelle de (trans.), *New French Feminisms: An Anthology*. Amherst: University of Massachusetts Press.

Garvin, Paul (ed. and trans.) (1964). *A Prague School Reader on Esthetics, Literary Structure, and Style*. Washington, D.C.: Georgetown University Press.

Genette, Gérard (1980). *Narrative Discourse*. Lewin, Jane E. (trans.). Oxford: Blackwell.

Genette, Gérard (1982). *Figures of Literary Discourse*. Sheridan, Alan (trans.). Oxford: Blackwell.

Goffman, Erving (1974). *Frame Analysis: An Essay on the Organization of Experience*. Cambridge: Harvard University Press.

Goldmann, Lucien (1969). *The Human Sciences and Philosophy*. White, Hayden V. & Anchor, Robert (trans). London: Cape.

Graff, Gerald (1979). *Literature against Itself: Literary Ideas in Modern Society*. London: University of Chicago Press.

Gramsci, Antonio (1971). *Selections from the Prison Notebooks of Antonio Gramsci*. Hoare, Quintin & Nowell Smith, Geoffrey (eds & trans). London: Lawrence & Wishart.

Green, Michael (1976). Cultural Studies at Birmingham University. In Craig, David & Heinemann, Margot (eds), *Experiments in English Teaching: New Work in Higher and Further Education*. London: Arnold.

Greenblatt, Stephen J. (1990). *Learning to Curse: Essays in Early Modern Culture*. London: Routledge.

Gregor, Ian (1970). Criticism as an individual activity: the approach through reading. In Bradbury, Malcolm & Palmer, David (eds), *Contemporary Criticism*, Stratford-upon-Avon Studies 12. London: Arnold.

Gregory, R. L. (1970). *The Intelligent Eye*. London: Weidenfeld & Nicolson.

Hallberg, Robert von (1985). *Canons*. London: University of Chicago Press.

Hampton, Christopher (1990). *The Ideology of the Text*. Milton Keynes: Open University Press.

Harari, Josué V. (ed.) (1980). *Textual Strategies: Perspectives in Post-structuralist Criticism*. London: Methuen.

Harland, Richard (1987). *Superstructuralism: the Philosophy of Structuralism and Post-structuralism*. London: Methuen.

Hartman, Geoffrey (1970). *Beyond Formalism*. New Haven: Yale University Press.

Harvey, David (1989). *The Condition of Postmodernity*. Oxford: Blackwell.

Hassan, Ihab (1985). The culture of postmodernism. *Theory Culture and Society*, 2(3), 119–131.

Havránek, Bohuslav (1964). The functional differentiation of the standard language. (First published in Czech, 1932.) In Garvin, Paul L. (ed. & trans.), *A Prague School Reader on Esthetics, Literary Structure, and Style.* Washington: Georgetown University Press.

Hawthorn, Jeremy (1987). *Unlocking the Text: Fundamental Issues in Literary Theory.* London: Arnold.

Hazlitt, William (n.d.). *Table Talk or Original Essays.* London: Everyman Library/J. M. Dent.

Hewitt, Douglas (1972). *The Approach to Fiction: Good and Bad Readings of Novels.* London: Longman.

Hirsch, E. D. 1967: *Validity in Interpretation.* London: Yale University Press.

Hoggart, Richard (1970). Contemporary cultural studies: an approach to the study of literature and society. In Bradbury, Malcolm & Palmer, David (eds), *Contemporary Criticism*, Stratford-upon-Avon Studies 12. London: Arnold.

Holderness, Graham (1982). *D. H. Lawrence: History, Ideology and Fiction.* Dublin and London: Gill & Macmillan.

Holland, Norman N. (1975). *5 Readers Reading.* London: Yale University Press.

Hume, Kathryn (1984). *Fantasy and Mimesis: Responses to Reality in Western Literature.* London: Methuen.

Humm, Maggie (1989). *The Dictionary of Feminist Theory.* London: Harvester Wheatsheaf.

Hunt, Alan (1977). Theory and politics in the identification of the working class. In Hunt, Alan (ed.), *Class and Class Structure.* London: Lawrence & Wishart.

Huyssen, Andreas (1988). *After the Great Divide: Modernism, Mass Culture and Postmodernism.* London: Macmillan.

Ingarden, Roman (1973). *The Literary Work of Art: An Investigation on the Borders of Ontology, Logic, and Theory of Literature.* (First published 1931.) Grabowicz, George G. (trans.). Evanston, Ill.: Northwestern University Press.

Iser, Wolfgang (1974). *The Implied Reader: Patterns of Communication in Prose Fiction from Bunyan to Beckett.* London: Johns Hopkins University Press.

Jakobson, Roman 1960: Closing statement: linguistics and poetics. In Sebeok, Thomas A. (ed.), *Style in Language.* Cambridge, Mass.: The Technology Press/MIT & New York: John Wiley.

Jakobson, Roman (1971). On realism in art. (First published in Czech, 1921.) In Matejka, Ladislav & Pomorska, Krystyna (eds), Magassy, Karol (trans.), *Readings in Russian Poetics: Formalist and Structuralist Views.* London: MIT Press.

Jakobson, Roman (1971). The dominant. (Delivered as a lecture in 1935.) In Matejka, Ladislav & Pomorska, Krystyna (eds.), Eagle, H. (trans.),

Readings in Russian Poetics: Formalist and Structuralist Views. London: MIT Press.

Jakobson, Roman & Halle, Morris (1971). *Fundamentals of Language.* 2nd rev. edn. The Hague: Mouton.

Jameson, Fredric (1981). *The Political Unconscious: Narrative as a Socially Symbolic Act.* London: Methuen.

Jauss, Hans Robert (1974). Literary history as a challenge to literary theory. In Cohen, Ralph (ed.), *New Directions in Literary History.* London: Routledge.

Kermode, Frank (1989). *An Appetite for Poetry: Essays in Literary Interpretation.* London: Collins.

Kesteloot, Lilyan (ed.) (1968). *Anthologie Négro-africaine.* Collection Marabout Université. Verviers: Gérard.

Kettle, Arnold (1975). Literature and ideology. *Red Letters,* 1, 3–5.

Knapp, Steven & Michaels, Walter Benn (1985). Against theory. In Mitchell, W. J. T. (ed.), *Against Theory: Literary Studies and the New Pragmatism.* London: University of Chicago Press.

Konstatinov, F. V. *et al.* (1974). *The Fundamentals of Marxist-Leninist Philosophy.* Daglish, Robert (trans.). Moscow: Progress Publishers.

Kress, Gunther & Hodge, Robert (1979). *Language as Ideology.* London: Routledge.

Kristeva, Julia (1980). *Desire in Language: A Semiotic Approach to Literature and Art.* Roudiez, Leon S. (ed.), Gora, Thomas, Jardine, Alice & Roudiez, Leon S. (trans). Oxford: Blackwell.

Kuhn, Thomas S. (1970). *The Structure of Scientific Revolutions.* 2nd edn. London: University of Chicago Press.

Lacan, Jacques (1976). Seminar on 'The Purloined Letter'. *Yale French Studies,* 48, 38–72.

Lacan, Jacques (1977). *Écrits. A Selection.* Sheridan, Alan (trans.). London: Tavistock.

Larrain, Jorge (1986). *A Reconstruction of Historical Materialism.* London: Allen & Unwin.

Leach, Edmund (1976). *Culture and Communication: The Logic by which Symbols are Connected.* Cambridge: Cambridge University Press.

Leavis, F. R. (1962a). *The Common Pursuit.* (First published 1952.) Harmondsworth: Peregrine.

Leavis, F. R. (1962b). *The Great Tradition.* (First published 1948.) Harmondsworth: Peregrine.

Leavis, F. R. (1964). *Revaluation: Tradition and Development in English Poetry.* (First published 1936.) Harmondsworth: Peregrine.

Leech, Geoffrey N., & Short, Michael H. (1981). *Style in Fiction: A Linguistic Introduction to English Fictional Prose.* Harlow: Longman.

Lehman, David (1990). Derridadaism. *Times Literary Supplement,* 18–24 May.

Lentricchia, Frank & McLaughlin, Thomas (eds) (1990). *Critical Terms for Literary Study*. London: University of Chicago Press.

Lessing, Doris (1973). *The Golden Notebook*. (First published 1962.) Frogmore: Granada.

Levinson, Stephen C. (1983). *Pragmatics*. Cambridge: Cambridge University Press.

Lévi-Strauss, Claude (1972). *The Savage Mind*. London: Weidenfeld & Nicolson.

Lodge, David (1977). *The Modes of Modern Writing: Metaphor, Metonymy, and the Typology of Modern Literature*. London: Arnold.

Lodge, David (ed.) (1988). *Modern Criticism and Theory*. London: Longman.

Lovell, Terry (1980). *Pictures of Reality: Aesthetics, Politics and Pleasure*. London: British Film Institute.

Lugowski, Clemens (1990). *Form, Individuality and the Novel: An Analysis of Narrative Structure in Early German Prose*. (First published in German 1932.) Halliday, John Dixon (trans.). Oxford: Polity Press.

Lukács, Georg (1969). *The Historical Novel*. (First published in German 1937.) Mitchell, Hannah & Stanley (trans). Harmondsworth: Peregrine.

Lüthli, Max (1984). *The Fairytale as Art Form and Portrait of Man*. (First published in German, 1975.) Erickson, Jon (trans.). Bloomington: Indiana University Press.

Lyotard, Jean-François (1984). *The Postmodern Condition: a Report on Knowledge*. Minneapolis: University of Minnesota Press.

MacKinnon, Catharine A. (1982). Feminism, Marxism, method, and the state: an agenda for theory. In Keohane, Nannerl O., Rosaldo, Michelle Z., & Gelpi, Barbara C. (eds), *Feminist Theory: A Critique of Ideology*. Brighton: Harvester.

McGann, Jerome J. (1983). *A Critique of Modern Textual Criticism*. London: University of Chicago Press.

McHale, Brian (1987). *Postmodernist Fiction*. London: Methuen.

Macherey, Pierre (1978). *A Theory of Literary Production*. (First published in French 1974.) Wall, Geoffrey (trans.). London: Routledge.

Machin, Richard & Norris, Christopher (eds) (1987). *Post-structuralist Readings of English Poetry*. Cambridge: Cambridge University Press.

McLuhan, Marshall (1964). *Understanding Media: The Extensions of Man*. London: Routledge.

McQuail, Denis, Blumler, Jay G., & Brown, J. R. (1972). The television audience: a revised perspective. In McQuail, Denis (ed.), *Sociology of Mass Communications*. Harmondsworth: Penguin.

Manocchio, Tony & Petitt, William (1975). *Families under Stress: A Psychological Interpretation*. London: Routledge.

Marx, Karl (1970a). *Capital. A Critique of Political Economy*. Vol. 1: *The Process of Production*. London: Lawrence & Wishart.

Marx, Karl (1970b). *Economic and Philosophical Manuscripts of 1844*. Struik, Dirk J. (ed.), Milligan, Martin (trans.). London: Lawrence & Wishart.

Marx, Karl (1971). *A Contribution to the Critique of Political Economy*. Ryazanskaya, S. W. (trans.). London: Lawrence & Wishart.

Marx, Karl & Engels, Frederick (1962). *Selected Works*. 2 vols. London: Lawrence & Wishart.

Marx, Karl & Engels, Frederick (1970). *The German Ideology*. Part 1, with selections from parts 2 & 3. Arthur, C. J. (ed.). London: Lawrence & Wishart.

Medvedev, P. N./Bakhtin M. M. (1978). *The Formal Method in Literary Scholarship*. (First published in Russian in 1928.) Wehrle, Albert J. (trans.). London: Johns Hopkins University Press.

Millard, Elaine (1989). French feminisms. In Mills, Sara, Pearce, Lynne, Spaull, Sue, & Millard, Elaine, *Feminist Reading*. Hemel Hempstead: Harvester.

Miller, J. Hillis (1982). *Fiction and Repetition: Seven English Novels*. Oxford: Blackwell.

Mistacco, Vicki (1980). The theory and practice of reading nouveaux romans: Robbe-Grillet's *Topologie d'une Cité Fantôme*. In Suleiman, Susan R. & Crosman, Inge (eds), *The Reader in the Text*. Guildford: Princeton University Press.

Mitchell, Juliet (1974). *Psychoanalysis and Feminism*. London: Allen Lane.

Moi, Toril (1986). Feminist literary criticism. In Jefferson, Ann & Robey, David (eds), *Modern Literary Theory: a Comparative Introduction*. 2nd edn. London: Batsford.

Mukařovský, Jan (1964). Standard language and poetic language *and* The esthetics of language. (First published in Czech 1932.) In Garvin, Paul L. (ed. & trans.), *A Prague School Reader on Esthetics, Literary Structure, and Style*. Washington: Georgetown University Press.

Nadelson, Regina (1987). Eating Out with Atwood. Interview with Margaret Atwood. *The Guardian*, 18 May.

Nead, Lynda (1988). *Myths of Sexuality: Representations of Women in Victorian Britain*. Oxford: Blackwell.

Norrman, Ralf (1982). *The Insecure World of Henry James's Fiction: Intensity and Ambiguity*. London: Macmillan.

Norrman, Ralf (1985). *Samuel Butler and the Meaning of Chiasmus*. London: Macmillan.

Nuttall, A. D. (1983). *A New Mimesis: Shakespeare and the Representation of Reality*. London: Methuen.

Olsen, Stein Haugom (1978). *The Structure of Literary Understanding*. Cambridge: Cambridge University Press.

Olsen, Stein Haugom, (1987). *The End of Literary Theory*. Cambridge: Cambridge University Press.

Ong, Walter J. (1982). *Orality and Literacy: The Technologizing of the Word*. London: Methuen.

O'Toole, L. M. & Shukman, Ann (1977). A contextual glossary of formalist terminology. *Russian Poetics in Translation*, 4, 13–48.

Palmer, Paulina 1987: From 'coded mannequin' to bird woman: Angela Carter's magic flight. In Roe, Sue (ed.), *Women Reading Women's Writing*. Brighton: Harvester.

Pascal, Roy (1977). *The Dual Voice: Free Indirect Speech and its Functioning in the Nineteenth-century European Novel*. Manchester: Manchester University Press.

Pavel, Thomas G. (1986). *Fictional Worlds*. London: Harvard University Press.

Pettersson, Anders (1990). *A Theory of Literary Discourse*. Lund: Lund University Press.

Plimpton, George (ed.) (1989). *Women Writers at Work: The 'Paris Review' Interviews*. Harmondsworth: Penguin.

Poggioli, Renato (1971). *The Theory of the Avant-Garde*. Fitzgerald, Gerald (trans.). New York: Harper & Row.

Pratt, Annis (1982). *Archetypal Patterns in Women's Fiction*. Brighton: Harvester.

Pratt, Mary Louise (1977). *Toward a Speech Act Theory of Literary Discourse*. Bloomington: Indiana University Press.

Prince, Gerald (1988). *A Dictionary of Narratology*. Aldershot: Scolar Press.

Propp, Vladimir (1968). *Morphology of the Folktale*. Wagner, Louis A. (ed.), Scott, Laurence (trans.). Austin: University of Texas Press.

Rayan, Krishna (1987). *Text and Sub-text: Suggestion in Literature*. London: Arnold.

Register, Cheri (1975). American feminist literary criticism: a bibliographical introduction. In Donovan, Josephine (ed.), *Feminist Literary Criticism: Explorations in Theory*. Lexington: University Press of Kentucky.

Rich, Adrienne (1976). The Kingdom of the Fathers. *Partisan Review* 43(1), 17–37.

Richards, I. A. (1964). *Practical Criticism: A Study of Literary Judgment*. (First published 1929.) London: Routledge.

Rickword, Edgell (1978). *Literature in Society: Essays and Opinions (II), 1931–1978*. Manchester: Carcanet.

Riffaterre, Michael (1978). *Semiotics of Poetry*. London: Methuen.

Riffaterre, Michael (1981). Interpretation and descriptive poetry: a reading of Wordsworth's 'Yew Trees'. In Young, Robert (ed.), *Untying the Text*. London: Routledge.

Rimmon-Kenan, Shlomith (1983). *Narrative Fiction: Contemporary Poetics*. London: Methuen.

Rock, Irvin (1983). *The Logic of Perception*. London: MIT Press.

Rorty, Richard (1982). *Consequences of Pragmatism: Essays 1972–1980*. Brighton: Harvester.

Rosenblatt, Louise M. (1978). *The Reader, The Text, The Poem: The Transactional Theory of the Literary Work.* London: Southern Illinois University Press.

Ruthven, K. K. (1984). *Feminist Literary Studies: an Introduction.* Cambridge: Cambridge University Press.

Salusinszky, Imre (1987). *Criticism in Society.* London: Methuen

Sartre, Jean-Paul (1973). *Existential Psychoanalysis.* Barnes, Hazel E. (trans.). Chicago: Henry Regnery.

Saussure, Ferdinand de (1974). *Course in General Linguistics.* Bally, Charles & Sechehaye, Albert (eds). Buskin, Wade (trans.). Revised edn. London: Peter Owen.

Scholes, Robert (1982). *Semiotics and Interpretation.* London: Yale University Press.

Scholes, Robert (1985). *Textual Power: Theory and the Teaching of English.* New Haven: Yale University Press.

Scholes, Robert & Kellogg, Robert (1966). *The Nature of Narrative.* London: Oxford University Press.

Scott, William T. (1990). *The Possibility of Communication.* Berlin: Mouton de Gruyter.

Searle, John R. (1969). *Speech Acts: An Essay in the Philosophy of Language.* London: Cambridge University Press.

Searle, John R., (1976). A classification of illocutionary acts. *Language in Society*, 5, 1-23. (First presented as a lecture 1971.)

Segal, Lynne (1987). *Is the Future Female? Troubled Thoughts on Contemporary Feminism.* London: Virago.

Sell, Roger (ed.) (1991). *Literary Pragmatics.* London: Routledge. (Contains Sell's own essay, 'The Politeness of Literary Texts', pp. 208–224.)

Sharpe, R. A. (1984). The private reader and the listening public. In Hawthorn, Jeremy (ed.), *Criticism and Critical Theory.* London: Arnold.

Showalter, Elaine (1986). Feminist criticism in the wilderness. (First published 1981 in *Critical Inquiry* 8, 179–205.) In Showalter, Elaine (ed.), *The New Feminist Criticism: Essays on Women, Literature and Theory.* London: Virago.

Showalter, Elaine (1982). *A Literature of Their Own.* London: Virago.

Shklovsky, Victor (1965). Art as technique. (First published 1917.) In Lemon, Lee T. & Reis, Marion J. (eds & trans), *Russian Formalist Criticism: Four Essays.* Lincoln: University of Nebraska Press.

Šklovskij, Viktor (1971). *The Mystery Novel: Dickens's 'Little Dorrit'.* (First published in Russian 1925.) Carter, Guy (trans.). In Matejka, Ladislav & Pomorska, Krystyna (eds), *Readings in Russian Poetics: Formalist and Structuralist Views.* London: MIT Press.

Smith, Barbara Herrnstein (1968). *Poetic Closure: a Study of How Poems End.* London: University of Chicago Press.

Smith, Barbara Herrnstein (1978). *On the Margins of Discourse: The Relation of Literature to Language*. London: University of Chicago Press.

Solomon, Robert C. (1980). *History and Human Nature: A Philosophical Review of European Philosophy and Culture, 1750–1850*. Brighton: Harvester.

Soyinka, Wole (1984). The critic and society: Barthes, leftocracy and other mythologies. In Gates, Henry Louis Jr. (ed.), *Black Literature and Literary Theory*. London: Methuen.

Stierle, Karlheinz (1980). The reading of fictional texts. In Suleiman, Susan R. & Crosman, Inge (eds.), Crosman, Inge & Zachrau, Thekla (trans), *The Reader in the Text*. Guildford: Princeton University Press.

Stubbs, Michael (1983). *Discourse Analysis: the Sociolinguistic Analysis of Natural Language*. Oxford: Blackwell.

Todorov, Tzvetan (1969). *Grammaire du Décaméron*. Mouton: The Hague.

Todorov, Tzvetan (1981). *Introduction to Poetics*. Howard, Richard (trans.). Brighton: Harvester.

Todorov, Tzvetan (1984). *Mikhail Bakhtin: the Dialogical Principle*. Minneapolis: University of Minnesota Press.

Tomashevsky, Boris (1965). Thematics. (First published in Russian 1925.) In Lemon, Lee T. & Reis, Marion J. (eds & trans), *Russian Formalist Criticism: Four Essays*. Lincoln: University of Nebraska Press.

Toolan, Michael J. (1988). *Narrative: A Critical Linguistic Introduction*. London: Routledge.

Tynjanov, J. (1971). Rhythm as the constructive factor of verse. (First published in Russian 1924.) In Matejka, Ladislav & Pomorska, Krystyna (eds), Suino, M. E. (trans.), *Readings in Russian Poetics: Formalist and Structuralist Views*. London: MIT Press.

Tynyanov, Yu. *et al.* (1977). Formalist theory. O'Toole, L. M. & Shukman, Ann (trans). In *Russian Poetics in Translation*, 4.

Vodička, Felix (1964). The history of the echo of literary works. (First published in Czech, 1942.) In Garvin, Paul L. (ed. & trans.), *A Prague School Reader on Esthetics, Literary Structure, and Style*. Washington: Georgetown University Press.

Vološinov, V. N. (1986). *Marxism and the Philosophy of Language*. Matejka, Ladislav & Titunik, I. R. (trans.). London: Harvard University Press.

Wain, John (ed.) (1961). *Interpretations: Essays on Twelve English Poems*. (First published 1955.) London: Routledge.

Wales, Katie (1989). *A Dictionary of Stylistics*. Harlow: Longman.

Watson, George (1962). *The Literary Critics: A Study of English Descriptive Criticism*. Harmondsworth: Penguin.

Watt, Ian (1980). *Conrad in the Nineteenth Century*. London: Chatto.

Watzlawick, Paul, Beavin, Janet Helmick, & Jackson, Don D. (1968). *Pragmatics of Human Communication: a Study of Interactional Patterns, Pathologies, and Paradoxes*. London: Faber.

Webster, Roger (1990). *Studying Literary Theory*. London: Arnold.

Wilden, Anthony (1972). *System and Structure: Essays in Communication and Exchange*. London: Tavistock.

Willett, John (ed. & trans.) (1964). *Brecht on Theatre: The Development of an Aesthetic*. London: Eyre Methuen.

Williams, Raymond (1976). *Keywords*. Glasgow: Fontana.

Williams, Raymond (1977). *Marxism and Literature*. Oxford: Oxford University Press.

Wimsatt, W. K. (1970). *The Verbal Icon: Studies in the Meaning of Poetry*. (First published, 1954.) London: Methuen.

Wood, James (1990). Bardbiz. Letter in *London Review of Books*, 12(10), 24 May.

Woolf, Virginia 1929: *A Room of One's Own*. London: The Hogarth Press.

Woolf, Virginia (1966a). Professions for women. In *Collected Essays*, Vol. 2. London: Hogarth.

Woolf, Virginia (1966b). Women and Fiction. In *Collected Essays*, Vol. 2. London: Hogarth.

Woolf, Virginia (1967). De Quincey's autobiography. In *Collected Essays*, Vol. 4. London: Hogarth.

Woolf, Virginia (1977). *Three Guineas*. (First published 1938.) Harmondsworth: Penguin.

Yanarella, Ernest J. & Sigelman, Lee (eds) (1988). *Political Mythology and Popular Fiction*. Westport, Conn: Greenwood.

Young, Robert (ed.) (1981). *Untying the Text*. London: Routledge.